Education in Edge City

CASES FOR REFLECTION AND ACTION

Education in Edge City

CASES FOR REFLECTION AND ACTION

Reg Hinely

University of North Texas

Karen Ford

Ball State University

ST. MARTIN'S PRESS
NEW YORK

THIS BOOK IS DEDICATED TO THE HUNDREDS AND THOUSANDS

OF ELEMENTARY, MIDDLE, AND SECONDARY SCHOOL TEACHERS

ACROSS THE NATION WHOSE STORIES GO UNTOLD—

TEACHERS WHO, EACH DAY, MAKE VITAL DECISIONS THAT HAVE

A MAJOR IMPACT ON THE LIVES OF OUR CHILDREN.

Editor: Naomi Silverman
Managing editor: Patricia Mansfield-Phelan
Project editor: Erica Appel
Production supervisor: Alan Fischer
Art director: Sheree Goodman
Text design: Silvers Design
Cover design: Hothouse Design Inc.
Cover photo: Michael Zide Photography

Library of Congress Catalog Card Number: 92-62797
Copyright © 1994 by St. Martin's Press, Inc.

Manufactured in the United States of America.
8 7 6 5 4
f e d c b a

For information, write:
St. Martin's Press, Inc.
175 Fifth Avenue
New York, NY 10010

ISBN: 0-312-09074-9

Foreword

The idea of using cases to educate teachers has gained enormous popularity in just a few years. Although this idea is not new—law and medicine have educated their students by means of cases since before the turn of the century—it has only now achieved momentum within professional education.

This emphasis on cases in teacher education reflects a larger movement toward the centrality of story in our understanding of human cognition and the demands of professional practice. It is now widely accepted in the social sciences that people lead storied lives. In contrast to the formal propositions of the scholarly report or textbook, everyday knowledge and feelings are organized around concrete stories with characters, events, durations, and sequences. We understand who we are, what we care about, how we fit into the world, and what things mean by the stories we construct.

A narrative structure is especially characteristic of professional knowledge because it captures the particularities and action requirements of practice. The deliberate use of stories to educate professionals is based on the realization that the central task of any practice is to bring general knowledge to specific contexts and then to act in helping ways. Although the public often wants simple and universal answers to questions of health, law, or education, professionals know that every decision with a particular patient, client, or class of students is contingent upon a profusion of immediate circumstances and feelings and thus is fraught with uncertainty. Learning to practice a profession requires, therefore, a form of knowledge that captures this sense of contingency and uncertainty without losing sight of the more general accumulation of knowledge from both experience and systematic research. Cases as stories of practice are especially suited to this requirement.

Education in Edge City is a superb exemplar of the case movement. By bringing us stories of the teachers, students, parents, and administrators of Edge City, Hinely and Ford give us a rich picture of life in schools and enrich our conceptions of instruction, management, assessment, culture, exceptionality, school organization, religious principles, legal rights, and other complex issues that educators regularly face. And by insisting that these stories be seen as occasions for reflection, decision making, and action, they remain true to the modern conception of the fundamental nature of teaching practice.

This is more than an ordinary casebook, however. Its special power rests in its sense of the whole. In a standard collection, the cases have an ad hoc quality, each with new characters participating in events that represent only a thin slice of their lives. In contrast to such an anthology of short stories, this book is more like a novel with its larger and more fully developed plot and cast of personalities. We come to know and care about Derrick, Raphael, Nanci, Clarise, Clifford, Sarah, Ms. Mason, Coach Pratt, Mrs. Kessler, and others as individuals. As in real schools, we hear their voices in class, see the work they do, and watch them interact in a variety of situations. The potential for learning the full scope and feel of the complexities of schooling is clearly heightened within such an integrated portrait of educational activity in a particular locale.

In addition to taking on the formidable task of depicting an entire setting, the authors have carefully framed questions, activities, and assignments to help us think about the cases, connect them more broadly to knowledge in the field, and formulate plans for action. They are clearly aware that cases do not necessarily "speak for themselves" but need to be interpreted by experienced practitioners to achieve maximum utility as educative tools. It is important to know, in other words, what a case is a case of, and this determination is not always readily apparent. At the same time, the authors avoid simplifications by remaining sensitive to the multiplicity of interpretations and reactions that any case can provoke. Indeed, a wealth of meaning is precisely the advantage of a case literature. This is not an easy path to navigate— to classify for instructional clarity and yet keep the windows open to alternative sights and sounds.

As I read the stories of Edge City, I was impressed with how well the authors met and overcame the inherent difficulties of writing an integrated casebook such as this one. Hinely and Ford, as teachers and writers, are expert storytellers. We, as readers of this adventure and teachers in our own right, would do well to emulate them.

Kathy Carter
The University of Arizona
Tucson, Arizona

Preface

The premise of this book is that the decision-making process used by professional educators is always context-based: each teacher makes decisions in a particular classroom with a particular group of students who live in a specific community and come from a given range of family and cultural backgrounds.

Education in Edge City presents a complete educational context. A town, residential communities, a school district, and school buildings are described; within this setting, students, teachers, administrators, parents, and board members are all introduced and portrayed in varying detail.

A series of cases, all dealing with characters and situations in the Edge City context, provide students with experience in making professional decisions and in dealing with the consequences of those decisions. Although they are not a substitute for actual experience, the hands-on exercises in this casebook will give students a realistic picture of what the practice of teaching is all about and will increase their awareness of the professional aspects of teaching.

Each chapter in the book includes a short introduction to a case, the case itself, questions for reflection and discussion about the issues raised, class and individual projects related to the case, questions based on those activities, a section on additional teaching and learning skills, and suggestions for further reading. Detailed information on the elements in this book and how they are organized is contained in the Introduction.

The topics and organization of the book parallel those found in many introduction to education and foundations of education courses—Instruction and Classroom Management (Part I), Issues in Education (Part II), and Foundations: Teaching as a Profession (Part III)—and therefore the activities provide a natural supplement to the information provided in those courses. The cases can be used in conjunction with a class text, in a seminar accompanying student teaching, or in in-service programs.

We want to stress that this book is intended to be used as a stimulus *for reflection and for action*. The activities approximate those that real teachers engage in, and are intended to facilitate thoughtful discussions of those activities and of their possible consequences. What we have provided for you is a framework—a basic cast of characters and glimpses of the environment in which they operate—within which you and your students can exercise your creativity in elaborating on and supplementing the suggestions we have made.

Each case has one or more specific foci, but just as in real life, the issues raised and the possibilities for reflective thinking and action are not limited to these categories. Since each chapter is self-contained, there is no necessity to work through the book from beginning to end. You should feel free to vary the order of presentation, to pick and choose from among the questions and activities, and, with your students, to create additional learning opportunities related to your unique purposes, using the Edge City characters and setting.

For example, term papers, debates, and class presentations may be assigned, giving students an opportunity to gather research and other kinds of current data to build their knowledge base, to enrich their in-class discussions of the cases, and to inform their decisions.

Or the cast of characters may be expanded and the context enriched. Suppose, for instance, that you are concerned with the problem of the role of school in teenage pregnancy. There is nothing in this book specifically dealing with this topic, but **Clarise Gerrard** is described as a sexually promiscuous girl. You could create a scenario in which she becomes pregnant, and role-play **Clarise** with **Mr. Kelly**, the counselor, or with one of the teachers, or with some of **Clarise**'s peers, or with her parents. Or it could be one of the more advantaged girls such as **Nanci Drake** who becomes pregnant. How would the situation differ as far as the school is concerned? This same procedure may be used with other topics and issues, such as instructional strategies, homework, standardized testing, drugs, gangs, or just about any issue related to public school education.

Because we are both associated with departments of secondary education and have primarily secondary public school backgrounds, we decided to limit the cases to a middle school and a senior high school; but nearly all of the issues are generic and could be used equally well in elementary-level courses and with elementary school teachers.

The people, places, and incidents in the book are fictitious, but represent real classrooms, teachers, students, and events. Most of the cases are based on actual incidents from our own teaching experience; one was supplied by a student teacher; three are derived from incidents reported in the professional literature. In each case, we have adapted the circumstances and characters to fit the context of Edge City and its school district.

We encourage you to use the materials in this book in creative ways, and hope that you and your students get the same kind of pleasure and satisfaction from using these materials that we have in our graduate and undergraduate classes at the University of North Texas and Ball State University.

Acknowledgments

We would like to thank our reviewers for their many helpful comments: John Barrell, Montclair State University; Mary Daly Lewis, Roosevelt University; Barbara Barry Levin, University of California, Berkeley; and Selma Wasserman, Simon Fraser University.

Special thanks go to our editor Naomi Silverman, whose ongoing support and encouragement helped this project become a reality. Thanks also to all of our teachers and students. You are what this book is all about.

Reg Hinely
Karen Ford

Contents

Introduction

■

What This Book Is About and How It Is Organized

■ Two teachers are walking down the hall in a modern suburban middle school. One teacher is saying,

I just don't know what I'm going to do with my fourth period class. It's a split period, and just about the time I get them started it's time to go to lunch, and when we get back they're all ready to go to sleep. Part of the problem may be that I'm sleepy too. It doesn't help that my room is right next to the lunchroom and people keep going by the door and distracting them when I do get them to do something. It's about to drive me crazy.

■ A young man is sitting with his father and mother at the dinner table. He is obviously upset.

I really am scared. I want to teach, I really do—but the idea of getting up in front of a class terrifies me. What if they act up? What am I going to do?

■ The woman in her third week of student teaching is talking to her college supervisor after school.

My student teaching is going a lot better than I thought it would. I think that the kids really like me. If it weren't for the Hispanic students in my regular English classes I could look forward to going to school each day. They barely speak English. When I lecture to the class they just sit there and I know that they are not understanding. I don't speak Spanish and I don't have the time to work with them one on one. My cooperating teacher really hasn't helped me much with this problem. I've got to do something but I don't know what.

■ Rationale

These statements by teachers, both in-service and preservice, point up one of the most important features of the teaching profession. Teachers are like other professionals, doctors and lawyers, in that they are constantly being forced to make context-based decisions, often without adequate data. Teachers make literally hundreds of professional decisions each day, and each of these decisions has important implications for the educative processes in their classes.

Which student should I call on next? Why?

I know that Chris isn't really listening to me. Should I stop and call him down or will that interrupt the flow of the lesson for the other students?

I don't have time to teach all of the Sandburg poems in the anthology, so which ones will I teach?

What is the best way for me to get the students interested in *The Road Not Taken*?

The answer that Miguel wrote on this test is probably wrong, but from what he said in class yesterday and his answer to question number 6, I really believe he understands the concept. Should I give him partial credit? How much credit?

The local professional association is organizing a protest to the school board about the condition of the elementary school in the black area of town. Should I participate? Will it jeopardize the excellent relations I have with the parents in the white community?

I would really like to take my students to the museum to see the King Tut exhibit, but some of them can't afford to buy a ticket and the principal says that the school doesn't have any money. Is there anyplace else I could look for financial help?

Unfortunately, the vast majority of the questions that teachers have do not have "right answers." The answer that most often fits is "it depends." It depends on the time of day, the particular mix of students, what happened yesterday, or what is going to happen tomorrow. It depends on the philosophy of the teacher, the policy of the district, the teacher's best guess as to the consequences of alternative courses of action, and a host of other variables. It depends on the breadth and depth of the teacher's subject matter knowledge, and on her ability to translate that knowledge into a form that will enable her students to understand the concepts being taught.

Hopefully the answer given or the actions taken will also be informed by the teacher's wealth of knowledge of research findings, of practices that have been successful for other teachers, of practical knowledge gained in the act of teaching and dependable professional knowledge gained from a variety of other sources.

What is frequently missing in teacher preparation programs is experience in making professional decisions and in dealing with the consequences of those decisions. Lawyers-in-training spend hours preparing briefs and looking up precedents, and then they must defend their conclusions in intensive in-class questioning. They must participate in "mock" trials at which they fill the role of prosecutor or defense attorney. Even then, most lawyers are quick to say that they really learned their professions when they began to practice law. After completing a bachelor's degree, doctors-to-be spend three or more years learning the practice of medicine, first in simulated situations, then on cadavers, and finally on live patients under close supervision. Once again, doctors are quick to say that they learned to "doctor" by doctoring.

In a more perfect world, preservice teachers would learn to teach by teaching real students. They would spend two or three years beyond the bachelor's degree learning and practicing the skills of the expert teacher. They would learn in "clinic" schools that are analogous to the teaching hospitals of the medical profession. They would come to realize that the successful practice of teaching requires a broad and a deep knowledge of the subject to be taught; an extensive catalog of examples, non-examples, analogies, and other ways of presenting the material; and a wealth of information about children, pedagogy, school structure, and all of the other data that are necessary to make informed professional decisions.

It is a less than perfect world. The amount of time spent in most in-service and preservice programs of teacher education is severely limited. The most common objective is to provide the teaching student with the information that is needed in order to make the decisions. As a result, with the exception of student teaching, little or no time is spent in actually doing the things that teachers do. Teacher educators recognize the limitations of this approach, and students often decry the perceived lack of relevance of the presented information.

It is the purpose of this text to provide you with the opportunity to make the kinds of decisions that "real" teachers make. You will be able to discuss your decision with your peers and with your professor or mentor.

If you are an undergraduate or graduate student seeking initial certification, it is hoped that the experience of interacting with others concerning the problem situations and the hands-on exercises in this casebook will

1. help you to see the relevance of the content being presented in your pedagogy courses and in the courses in your discipline,

2. encourage you to do additional reading to increase your knowledge of research information and of effective teaching practices, and

3. give you a more realistic picture of what the practice of teaching is really about.

If you are a practicing teacher engaged in an in-service program or if you are taking a graduate class, this casebook provides a vehicle for you to do something that you can seldom do with your own classes. You can make a decision or complete an exercise in a leisurely and nonthreatening environment. Unlike most of the decisions you make in your class, with these cases you have the time to reflect on what you would do and to articulate a rationale for your decision. You can discuss your actions with peers, mentors, professors, or other professionals with whom you are associating. You may use the incidents depicted in *Edge City* as stimuli for sharing experiences from your career with the other members of your group.

■ *Organization*

The decision-making process used by educational professionals is always context-based. Decisions are made in a classroom with a particular group of students who live in a specific community and who come from differing family and cultural backgrounds. Teachers, administrators, board members, and other professionals almost never have all of the information they need, but as a general rule, the more good data that are available the better is the decision.

This book describes an educational context, and participants in that context, in considerable detail. A town, a school district, a school building, residential communities, students, teachers, administrators, parents, and board members are all introduced and described in varying detail. When a student teacher goes out to a school, or when a new teacher is hired in a community, they are *gradually* inducted into the life of that community. That is to say, they do not learn everything about the politics of the area, the life-styles of the inhabitants, the characteristics of all of the students, and other valuable information all at once. They learn about the students in their class, the teacher in the room across the hall, the assistant principal who evaluates them, the secretary in the main office, and others with whom they have daily contact.

They also learn which of these individuals is most useful in providing reliable information to help them make decisions. Almost invariably, there are one or two students in the class who serve as barometers for deciding whether the class is understanding the content, whether the pace is too fast or too slow, and other information to help make instructional decisions.

The longer they remain on the job, the more extensive their knowledge of the entire educational context becomes. They learn who is on the school board and the position each member takes on certain issues. They learn which sections of town are "good" and which ones are "bad." They learn the power structure within their school and also within the school district.

In this book, you will be introduced to the town and the school district in the same way. In Chapter One you will be given a cursory introduction to the physical and demographic setting of the cases that are to follow. In Chapter Two you will meet **Ms.**

Mason and her third-period political science class. As you become familiar with this teacher and with these students, you will gradually learn things about the school and the community. In Chapter Twelve you will see the town through the eyes of **Cassie Hudgins**, a young woman who is considering accepting a position in the district. In other chapters you will get to know the administrators, counselors, parents of honors and at-risk students, school board members, businesspeople, and others. You will also get better acquainted with **Ms. Mason** and some of her students in other contexts, such as planning a protest rally, in a committee meeting, or in other classes.

■ *How to Use the Book*

One purpose of this book is to sensitize you to some of the realities of teaching. In order to do this, it is important that you use each chapter in a variety of ways. As you are working through the chapter on grading and evaluation, for example, you should not only view the presented problems from the point of view of the teacher, but also think about how the student will react to the grade you have given. If you know something about the home environment of the student, how might the grade affect the interrelationships in the family? What do your decisions about grading have to say about your "philosophy" of education?

In addition to the questions asked and the activities described, there are an almost infinite number of questions and decisions that may arise as you and your professor and/or colleagues work through this casebook. To help you derive maximum benefit, we have provided some ways in which you can use this book to concentrate on the particular issue you are addressing.

> *Names in bold type.* Every time a person's name is used, it is presented in **bold**. This should help you quickly locate persons in the text.
>
> *Index of names.* An index of names is provided at the end of the text, so that if you are trying to decide what to do about **Clarise Gerrard**, you can quickly find other cases in which she is a character.
>
> *Biographical sketches of students.* Appendix I contains brief biographical sketches of each student, in alphabetical order.
>
> *Cumulative student folders.* Following each biographical sketch in Appendix I is that student's cumulative folder, which contains test scores, family information, discipline records, and comments by teachers.

Each chapter has a focus, or maybe two or three foci. For example, Chapter Two, *Hey, Teach! Are You Rocking the Boat?* presents a picture of a teacher changing methodologies, but it also gives you practice in making grouping decisions and decisions about how to most effectively implement cooperative learning strategies. Chapter Three, on grading and evaluation, requires you to evaluate a test, to construct test items, and to actually grade a set of papers, assigning weight to individual items, a number grade and a letter grade. You then explain and justify your decisions to your colleagues in the class. You also, of course, get to see what grades they assigned and how they rationalize their decisions.

The cases are grouped under the three major headings that are usually found in a foundations of education text. It must be stressed, however, that just as in real life, the issues raised and the possibilities for reflective thinking and action are not limited to these rubrics. For example, the central focus in Chapter Five is classroom management, but the incident could be used for a thoughtful consideration of teacher–pupil relationships, of the impact of the physical environment on instruction, or of differences in teaching math and English. Chapter Seven is primarily about the differing family backgrounds of the students, but issues such as affirmative action, individualized instruction, motivation, and many others could be addressed in a concrete way using these individuals and the community in which they live and the schools that they attend.

Since each chapter is self-contained, there is no reason to work your way through the casebook from front to back. You may use the cases in conjunction with a class text, in a seminar accompanying student teaching, in an in-service activity identified by the teaching staff of a school or any other organization that is useful to you.

The authors believe that using the materials in this casebook has the potential for increasing individuals' awareness of the professional aspects of teaching. We know that it is not a substitute for actual experience, but it is almost certainly more relevant to a career in teaching than is a class or workshop that concentrates solely on information about teaching, with no attempt to have students apply that information in the solution of contextual problems.

Nature of the Cases

The people, places, and incidents in this book are fictitious, but they are based on, and representative of, real classrooms, teachers, students, and events. Most of the cases are based on actual incidents from the teaching experience of the two authors; one of the cases was supplied by a student teacher; three were derived from incidents reported in the professional literature. In every instance the authors took the liberty of adapting the circumstances and characters to fit the context provided in Edge City and the Edge City school district.

Teaching in a rural area is different from teaching in a suburb, which is different from teaching in an inner city. Teaching the first grade presents different problems from teaching high school physics. Teaching math is not the same as teaching English literature. It is also true, of course, that all of these teaching situations contain much in common. The decision was made to make this book representative, at least to some extent, of these differing contexts. Our mythical Edge City is located within easy driving range of two metropolitan areas, but many of its students come from farms and ranches. Various racial and ethnic groups are represented in the professional personnel and in the student body. Examples come from differing subject areas. Because both of the authors are associated with a department of secondary education, and because their public school background is primarily secondary, it was decided to limit the context to a senior high school and a middle school, but nearly all of the issues are generic and could be used in elementary-level courses and with elementary school teachers.

You are encouraged to use the materials in this book in creative ways. Additional cases using these same characters could be written and discussed. What would happen if **Clarise** became pregnant? What might occur in a conference between **Ms. Mason** and **Derrick**'s parents about his grades? Describe a scenario in which **Cassie** asks for help in teaching a particular concept.

Good luck as you explore the world of teaching.

FOR FURTHER READING

Adler, S. (1991). "The reflective practitioner and the curriculum of teacher education." *Journal of Education for Teaching* 17: 139–150.

Barnett, C. (1991). "Building a case-based curriculum to enhance the pedagogical content knowledge of mathematics teachers." *Journal of Teacher Education* 42: 263–272.

Boehrer, J., and Linsky, M. (1990). "Teaching with cases: Learning to question." *New Directions for Teaching and Learning* 42: 41–57.

Ditchburn, S., et al. (1990). "The emerging voice: Toward reflective practice." *Teaching and Learning* 4: 20–29.

Gore, J. M., and Zeichner, K. M. (1991). "Action research and reflective teaching in preservice teacher education: A case study from the United States." *Teaching and Teacher Education* 7: 119-136.

Kagan, D. M., and Tippins, D. J. (1991). "How teachers' classroom cases express their pedagogical beliefs." *Journal of Teacher Education* 42: 281–291.

McNamara, D. (1990). "Research on teachers' thinking: Its contribution to educating student teachers to think critically." *Journal of Education for Teaching* 16: 147–160.

Merseth, K.K. (1991). "The early history of case-based instruction: Insights for teacher education today." *Journal of Teacher Education* 42: 243–249.

Shulman, J. H. (1991). "Classroom casebooks." *Educational Leadership* 49: 28–31.

Shulman, J. H. (1991). "Revealing the mysteries of teacher-written cases: Opening the black box." *Journal of Teacher Education* 42: 250–262.

Zeichner, K. (1990). "Changing directions in the practicum: Looking ahead to the 1990's." *Journal of Education for Teaching* 16: 105–132.

Part I

Instruction
and
Classroom
Management

■

Chapter 1

But Where Am I?

■

EDGE CITY AND ITS SCHOOLS

Teachers do not just teach. They teach something to someone. They also teach somewhere. All through this book you will be meeting and getting to know the someones who are teaching and the someones who are being taught. In addition, Appendix I describes the major characters in this book in detail. There you will find brief biographies of students and portfolio data containing test scores, discipline records, and descriptions of extracurricular activities.

This chapter introduces you to the places where these characters interact, where this teaching and learning is going on. In contrast to all of the other chapters in this casebook, there are no questions or activities at the end. After reading this chapter you should at least have a feel for the setting in which all these activities are taking place.

The state of Westland and the cities of Bowie, Crockett, and Edge City are all fictitious, but they are similar to real states, cities, and towns throughout the United States. Edge City is typical of the hundreds of medium-sized cities and towns within commuting distance of metropolitan areas. It is a cross between a suburb and a small rural town. While it has some racial and ethnic diversity, it is primarily Anglo-American. It has all of the problems and all of the promise of other areas of the country.

The Edge City School District also is designed to be comparable to thousands of such districts throughout the nation. It has physical facilities, teaching materials, rules and regulations. It also has teachers, principals, custodians, counselors, and, most important, it has students. As you use this casebook it is hoped that you will form mental images of this place and of these people, so that the decisions you are asked to make and the tasks you are asked to complete will be meaningful and will be grounded in a real context. You may want to refer back to this account as you are interacting with the materials in other chapters in this book.

■ Edge City

The state of Westland is located in the south-central part of the United States. The northeastern section of the state is hilly and heavily forested, with pine and hard-woods predominating. Further south and west are areas of open space and grasslands; here the land is rolling in some places and relatively flat in others. The northwestern portion of the state is in the foothills of the Rocky Mountains.

Edge City is near the center of the state, and to a certain extent the vegetation and topography of the town mirror that of the state. Two larger metropolitan areas, Bowie and Crockett, are to the north of Edge City. Crockett, Bowie, and Edge City form an inverted triangle, with Edge City southeast of Bowie and southwest of Crockett. (See Figure 1-1).

Edge City started out as a trading post and pioneer settlement on the banks of the Apache River years before the Westland war of independence. It continued to grow, and became the seat of Edge County in 1877. An impressive native stone courthouse, built in 1898, stands in the middle of the square. Lining the streets that front each side of the courthouse are buildings in a variety of architectural styles. They vary greatly

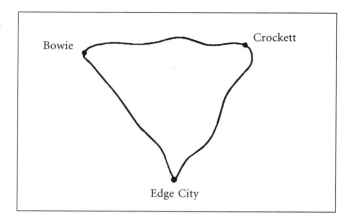

Fig. 1-1. Location of Edge City

in age. On one corner stands a building made of massive stones, with the message EDGE CITY STATE BANK AND TITLE COMPANY—FOUNDED 1897 emblazoned across the entrance. A movie theater with a blank marquee, a drugstore out of the twenties, a shoe store, and a pawn shop fill one street. The remainder of the square around the courthouse is occupied by various businesses, restaurants, a video store, and specialty shops. A few buildings are vacant and none of the shops appears to be doing a thriving business.

Up until ten or fifteen years ago this was the real center of town, not just the geographical center. Now everything is moving out to the malls. The city council is trying to save downtown, and is offering all sorts of inducements for businesses to stay, but so far it has been a losing battle.

Edge City serves as the distribution center for a large and fairly prosperous agricultural area that surrounds the city but is especially extensive to the south and west. The agricultural basis for the economy is seen in the rows of grain elevators and the large packing plant, all in the southeastern part of the city. There is some nonagricultural industry as well—a relatively new tractor assembly plant, several small electronics companies, a brick manufacturing plant, and a chemical manufacturing complex. The headquarters for one of the largest health maintenance organizations in the nation is here, as well as a regional office of the Mayflower Insurance Company. Retail outlets in the city include two shopping malls. One was built in 1975; another, newer mall, north of the city, is one of the largest in the southwest. A large farmers' market draws retailers from Crockett, Bowie, and the rest of the metropolitan area. Small strip shopping centers are found in various parts of the city.

An important stabilizing factor in the city's economy is Westland State University. Although Edge City has an official population of about 50,000, another 25,000 are added during the fall and spring semesters and about half of that number in the summer. WSU started out as Westland Normal School in 1896. It has also been known, at different times, as Westland Teacher's College and Westland State College; it got its present name in 1971. WSU is an excellent school. The campus contains a mixture of old, vine-covered buildings and modern structures of glass and stone. The medical school is nationally recognized, and the music school is outstanding. The College of Education has the reputation of being the finest in the state and probably in the Southwest. A heavily funded research program supports an outstanding graduate school of education.

As with most cities, Edge City has clearly definable residential and industrial areas. The south-central area is heavily wooded, with native oak predominating. Large homes are set far back from the street, with spacious lawns and attractive landscaping.

In spring and summer the green lawns contrast sharply with the color from the many flower beds and planters. Known as Sans Souci, this is the city's most exclusive living area. The homes are in the $250,000- to- $500,000 range. Most of the people living in Sans Souci are professionals, airline pilots, and businesspeople. Many of them commute to Bowie or Crockett. This entire area has been developed only within the last ten years.

Adjoining Sans Souci on the north and west is the area known as Idiot's Hill. Most of the houses in Idiot's Hill were built thirty-five or forty years ago. The average price back then was $25,000 to $30,000, but today most homes are worth well over $100,000. The unusual name of the area refers to the large number of university professors living there. Before being developed this was an area of eroded, worthless, mesquite-covered hills. When the developer opened up the first lots and put them up for sale at $2,500, the townspeople said that only the idiots from the university would pay that much for a quarter-acre lot. The name just stuck. The area now contains over 300 homes.

The far southeastern part of the city is an industrial area filled with warehouses, wholesale outlets, and small manufacturing plants. It also contains a large public housing project with nine separate brick apartment buildings. Many of the windows of these apartments have been boarded up. Clotheslines, huge trash containers, abandoned cars, and assorted junk give the place a hopeless feeling. Small children play in the dirt yards. The residents of this area are all African-American. Just north of here is an area of small houses. Most are of wood siding with an occasional brick veneer. Much cleaner, this area is also inhabited primarily by African-Americans, with an occasional Hispanic family in the northern section. Northeast Edge City is largely Hispanic. The houses are modest. In some sections they are well-kept and clean; in others it is evident that extreme poverty prevails.

Outside the city limits to the east but still in the Edge City school district is a transition area between the city and the farms. Here the residents are a mixture of African-Americans, Hispanics, and Anglo-Americans. Most of them, regardless of color, are poor. The surrounding farms are nearly all owned by Anglos, but they hire quite a few Hispanics.

Approximately two miles beyond the city limits, a large, faded sign informs visitors that they are approaching Acorn Acres Mobile Home Community. A narrow blacktop road, full of potholes and lined with litter, is the only access to Acorn Acres. The park itself is a sea of mobile homes stretching across the prairie, with little distance between the trailers and only an occasional clump of grass in the tiny yards. This is an all-white neighborhood, and it has the highest crime rate in Edge City. A good number of children of all ages live in Acorn Acres. Most of those of high school age have dropped out of school, but most of the middle school kids attend Hooker Middle School.

There are two other mobile home parks on this side of town. One of them has quite a few Hispanics, but the other one is also primarily Anglo. Students from these three parks make up a very small percentage of the total student body, but a much larger percentage of the discipline problems, in the Edge City schools.

The town had maintained a slow but steady growth in population until the 1970s, when the actions of an aggressive city council, coupled with the rapid economic growth of Crockett and Bowie to the north, caused the population to mushroom to its present size of approximately 50,000. Seventy percent of the population is Anglo-American, 12 percent African-American, and 16 percent Hispanic. The remaining 2 percent is primarily Asian and Native-American.

The government is run by a city manager under the direction of a seven-member city council elected at large. The minority community has been rather inactive in politics, but there is an African-American city council member. There is a small, but increasingly vocal, group in the black and Hispanic communities pushing for single-member districts for both city council and school board membership.

■ *Edge City School District*

Prior to 1963 there were two high schools in Edge City. Carver High School was an all-black school that drew students from as far as twenty-five miles away. The school was in the middle of the black area of the city. Although at the time the building was more than thirty years old, it was well constructed and in good shape. The students, faculty, and community were particularly proud of their football team. Carver went to the state quarter-finals every year from 1959 to 1963, and won the championship in '62 and '63. In 1963 the school board integrated all of the schools in Edge City. Carver was closed down and became a storage facility for the district. The Carver students were all bused to the previously Anglo and Hispanic Edge City High School.

Edge City High was constructed in 1986. It is a modern, multibuilding campus located on prairie land on the western edge of the city. The majority of the students are eligible for busing, although a large percentage own their own cars and drive them to school each day. The four buildings consist of (1) a large classroom building that also houses the administrative offices and science labs; (2) a sports facility with two basketball courts, an indoor swimming pool, offices for coaches and the PE faculty, and a band hall with practice rooms; (3) a fine arts building with a large auditorium, arts labs, and classrooms; and (4) a large industrial arts building with equipment for teaching electronics, auto repair, woodworking, welding, and agriculture. When it was built, the facility was expected to meet the needs of the district for at least fifteen years, but some parts of the school are already overcrowded, and steps are being taken to acquire land and begin planning for an additional high school.

Hooker Middle School is located within three blocks of the courthouse square. It is housed in the renovated former Edge City High School and was originally constructed in 1928. This building also contains the administrative offices for the school district. Hooker is a three-story building that, although structurally sound, shows the effects of the sixty-plus classes of students that have passed through its doors and hallways. A new middle school is located near Edge City High School. Seven elementary schools are located throughout the city.

While in facilities and in official philosophy Edge City High would certainly be classified as a comprehensive high school, there is a strong academic emphasis throughout the school system. Honors programs exist at all grade levels in the high school, and there is considerable community pressure to begin honors programs at the middle schools and in the elementary schools. The high school curriculum includes the state-required courses of study in English, math, biology, history, and political science. In addition, there are strong programs in foreign languages (Spanish, French, Latin, and Russian), physics, advanced math, and computer science. The community takes great pride in the quality of the art program and the drama productions. The vocational programs have excellent facilities, but enrollment is largely limited to students who are less able academically.

The program at the two middle schools was initially designed to be consistent with the middle school philosophy of exploration. With the advent of increased emphasis on testing and on state control, many of the exploratory courses have been dropped from the curriculum, and tracking is being used in the math, English, and science courses.

Chapter 2

Hey, Teach! Are You Rocking the Boat?

■

STUDENTS' RESISTANCE TO CHANGE

How teachers teach is determined in many different ways. Sometimes teachers teach the way they themselves were taught in high school or in college. Occasionally they may try to teach the way their education professors taught them to teach. Quite frequently, they teach much in the way their cooperating teacher taught during their student teaching days. Most often, of course, it is a combination of these influences and many other personal experiences that molds the major methodology used by a teacher. The method of choice is also greatly influenced by the personality of the teacher, and by the context in which the teaching occurs. What works well with academically able and highly motivated students might fail miserably with a class of at-risk students.

As a result, the methods used in public and private secondary schools vary greatly from teacher to teacher. Some teachers in a high school setting will "lecture" to their classes for as much as 80 percent of class time. Other teachers, in the same building, will use seat work as the predominant class activity, and students will spend a majority of their in-class time reading from the textbook or doing worksheets. Still other teachers will have the students involved in a variety of small-group and individual activities.

Secondary students, early in the school year, will learn what "kind of a teacher" you are. They will form judgments about how much noise you will tolerate, what your expectations are for the quality of written work, whether they are expected to participate in class activities, whether you are a "tough" grader, and what your major teaching method is.

Once they have learned what to expect from you and have become comfortable with the classroom routines that you have established, many will be resistant to any attempts to make drastic changes in these routines. This is the major problem faced by the teacher in this case study.

Ms. Mason has been assigned a class composed of high school sophomores, juniors, and seniors that is extremely heterogeneous in academic ability, social class, and ethnicity. She has been attempting to teach them as she usually teaches her classes, through a combination of lecture and discussion. Disenchanted with the results of this procedure, she has decided to use one version of cooperative learning to teach the unit on the Constitution of the United States.

There are many questions that you might ask as you read this account of her attempts to make the transition in teaching methods. Why did **Ms. Mason** choose the particular way she did to introduce the unit? What are other ways that she might have done this? What kinds of conclusions might you draw about her relationships with the students in her class? What do you think are the cognitive objectives that she is trying to achieve? The affective or social objectives? What rationale would she have for choosing these particular objectives? Are these the objectives you would have chosen? What do you believe is the philosophy that guides her decision making?

Please notice that these questions do not have "right" answers. These are the kinds of questions that teachers must answer daily. The answers that a teacher gives, or the actions that a teacher takes, are based, it is hoped, on the best data that the teacher has at her disposal at that moment. As you get to know **Ms. Mason** and the students in her class, attempt to put yourself in the shoes of the various participants—**Ms. Mason**, the students, parents, and others—and see how the situation looks from the different perspectives.

As you work your way through the various cases in this book you will meet many of these people again as they face other dilemmas. You will also be asked to make decisions about the situations that **Ms. Mason** faces as she goes through this process. **Ms. Mason** and her students are fictional characters, but the professional decisions she faces are real, and are the kind that are faced by teachers every day.

■ *Students' Resistance to Change*

"I am a policeman. **Gladys** told me that **Clarise** has been taking stuff from different stores in Northtown Mall. **Gladys** said she has been in **Clarise**'s room and that she literally has the stuff stacked to the ceiling. Being a conscientious cop, I grab **Clarise** by the arm, put her in my shiny black and white, drive her to her house, and force her to open the door. I go upstairs and sure enough, she's got a ton of stuff in there. I take her downtown, fingerprint her, and lock her up."

Ms. Mason has started talking before all the students are in their seats. Just over five feet two inches tall and weighing 196 pounds, **Ms. Mason** would have to be called obese. You would also have to say that she is attractive. With straight black hair, dark brown eyes, and a mouth that is almost constantly formed into an impish grin, she seems to radiate a joy in living. **Deborah** (her given name) is always immaculately groomed, and her clothes are always fashionable in an offbeat sort of way.

She is also well known in Edge City. For twenty-six of her fifty-one years she has been teaching school, and there are many people in Edge City who have had the pleasure of hearing her talk about American democracy and how it works. There is no question in anyone's mind that **Ms. Mason** is a "liberal," if liberal is defined as being concerned about the poor, minorities, and civil liberties. She is also an active member of the local Democratic party and the American Civil Liberties Union. Married, she has two grown children, one a lawyer and one a teacher like his mother.

Ms. Mason takes **Clarise** by the arm and pretends to be taking her to jail.

"You can't do that," **Wilma Booker** says.

"What do you mean I can't do it? You just saw me, didn't you? I told you I was a policeman, and policemen can arrest people."

"I still say you can't do it. At least not legitimately," **Wilma**, a quiet and highly intelligent senior, persists.

A buzz of conversation begins to swell in the classroom as the students begin to take sides.

"**Wilma**'s right and you know it," contends **Margie Laurence**. "Just because you are a policeman doesn't mean that you can do anything you want to. There are rules that apply to you too."

"OK, let's take a vote. I still say if I am a policeman I can arrest **Clarise**. **Wilma** and **Margie** say I can't. How many agree with **Wilma** and **Margie**?"

Ms. Mason's third-period political science class is a heterogeneous mixture of tenth-, eleventh-, and twelfth-grade students. The state of Westland requires that all students have one year of political science, but at Edge City High students may take it at any time in their four years of high school. This is a particularly diverse group of students, with four honors seniors who have put off taking the course, two seniors who are repeating the course, a mainstreamed multiply handicapped student, five "regular" sophomores, and three juniors—one "regular" and two Hispanic students with little command of the English language. The fact that there are only fifteen students in the class makes the task of planning for such a diverse group somewhat more manageable. The students' names, ethnic status, class standing, and academic classification are listed below.

STUDENT	ETHNICITY	CLASS	ACADEMICS
Abbott, Derrick	Anglo	Sr.	Remedial
Aquilar, Raphael	Hispanic	Jr.	Remedial (ESL)
Booker, Wilma	Anglo	Sr.	Honors
Drake, Nanci	Black	Soph.	Regular
Farrish, Gladys	Black	Soph.	Regular
Gerrard, Clarise	Anglo	Soph.	Regular
Handley, Clifford	Anglo	Sr.	Honors
Hinijosa, Eduardo	Hispanic	Jr.	Remedial (ESL)
Jackson, Mark	Anglo	Sr.	Remedial
Latham, Karl	Anglo	Soph.	Regular
Laurence, Margie	Black	Sr.	Honors
Scott, Art	Anglo	Jr.	Regular
Tompkins, Sarah	Anglo	Soph.	Special Ed.
Utter, Bobby	Anglo	Soph.	Regular
Zettler, Edwin	Anglo	Sr.	Honors

In response to **Ms. Mason**'s request for a vote, most of the students raise their hands. **Eduardo**, **Raphael**, **Sarah**, **Mark**, and **Derrick** keep their hands down.

"How many agree with me?" **Ms. Mason** asks.

Eduardo, **Derrick**, and **Sarah** raise their hands.

"Why do you think I am right, **Eduardo**?" she asks.

"You said you was a cop. Besides, you the teacher."

Ms. Mason is not surprised by **Eduardo**'s response. She is surprised that he raised his hand, since **Raphael** had not. A quiet, soft-spoken young man, **Eduardo** seldom speaks up in class. He is well behaved and never presents a discipline problem. **Raphael Aquilar** is his constant companion and model. Where ever **Raphael** goes, **Eduardo** goes; whatever **Raphael** does, **Eduardo** does. **Ms. Mason**'s limited knowledge of the Spanish language, and **Eduardo**'s limited facility in English, make it difficult for her to decide whether **Eduardo** is really limited in his academic ability or whether his lack of achievement can be attributed almost solely to his deficiency in English.

"What about you, **Mark**? You didn't vote either way. What do you think?"

Mark, 215 pounds and six feet tall, is slouched down at his desk. He shrugs his shoulders but doesn't answer.

Clifford Handley has been sitting with a bored look on his face while the interchange between **Ms. Mason** and **Mark** is taking place. One of the senior honors students, **Clifford** has already made up his mind that this class is a waste of his time, and he has little tolerance for the juniors and sophomores, particularly the academically less able, including the two Hispanic students.

"This is stupid," he explodes. "Anybody with one eye and half sense knows that law officers have to have a search warrant in order to go into somebody's house to look for evidence."

"Okay, smarty," says **Ms. Mason**. "So I have to have a search warrant. Who says so? Who says that I have to get permission? And who gives me permission? Are you trying to tell me, and the rest of the class, that there is someone higher than the policeman?"

"There's some kind of a law about reading your rights or somethin' that says you can't search somebody or somethin' like that," **Derrick** volunteers. **Ms. Mason** looks surprised. She can't remember the last time that **Derrick** has spoken in class, even when she has called on him. Before she can give him a positive response for his contribution, **Clifford** speaks.

"It's in the Constitution, stupid."

"Watch who you're callin' stupid or I'll be on you like black on white," **Derrick** says as he stands up at his desk.

Derrick is a real enigma to **Ms. Mason**. He has none of the obvious excuses for his nonachievement. He comes from an apparently stable, middle-class background. His father is a pharmacist and his mother an elementary teacher. He has two younger sisters, both of whom are excellent students. His IQ, according to a test taken in the eighth grade, is 109. He is almost totally withdrawn, not only from class activities but also from any kinds of social interactions with the other students in the class.

"Hold on! Sit down, **Derrick**. Knock it off. Knock it off. I didn't mean to start a riot." **Ms. Mason** walks back to **Derrick**'s desk and places her hand on his shoulder as she talks.

She stands quietly, looking from one student to another until the room is totally silent. Then she speaks in a low voice.

"Does anyone want to guess why I started the class off this way?" she asks.

"That's easy," **Edwin Zettler** says, smiling. "The next chapter in our textbook is on the Constitution so I 'spect you are trying to get us interested in that."

Edwin is an almost yellow-blond, slightly built seventeen-year-old. A deep scar from a childhood accident extends almost completely across his left cheek. The look on his face is the one he usually wears, and can best be described as a look of detachment. **Edwin** does not appear to be an unhappy young man, but neither does he appear to be happy. He reads widely and voraciously, and he enjoys thinking about and, if he could find someone to share them with, talking about the ideas contained in the books he reads.

Ms. Mason smiles at him and says, "Well you 'spect right. That's exactly what I am trying to do. We've got fifteen very different people in this class. There are nine boys and six girls; we have ten Caucasians, three African-Americans, and two Hispanics; we have six sophomores, three juniors, and six seniors; some of you have a lot of book sense and some of you a lot of common sense; some are good athletes, and **Mark** thinks he's a lover. We are different in many ways but we all have at least one thing in common. We are all governed by and protected by the provisions of the United States Constitution. Our lives are influenced in innumerable ways by this document, and it is absolutely essential that citizens know something about it. That's what we are going to be doing for the next few days.

"When we get through I expect each of you to know what the major provisions of the Constitution are, to be able to describe the major principles underlying the document, and to tell how our government is organized. In addition, you should understand how the Constitution is changed—that is what the process or processes of change are and what the major changes have been.

"This is a large order. To do it right is going to take a lot of hard work on all of our parts. I know that you can do it, though."

As she is talking, the members of the class are settling down to their "normal" ways of passing the fifty-five minutes devoted to the study of government. **Derrick**, after his rare comment and his confrontation with **Clifford**, appears to be ready to take his customary nap. Several of the students have opened their textbooks and their notebooks and are preparing to take notes. **Clifford** has his calculus textbook open and is busily trying to solve a problem for his next-period class. **Eduardo** and **Raphael** are sitting quietly with their hands folded on their desks. Like **Eduardo**, **Raphael** is usually quiet in class. Unlike **Eduardo**, **Raphael** is highly motivated to achieve and makes a conscientious effort to do whatever is necessary to make passing grades. His mother and older sister work to provide for him and his two younger sisters. They are never lacking food, but **Raphael** has begun feeling that he should drop out of school and get a job. Somehow he knows that is not what is best for him and he continues to resist the pressures from within, from his friends, and from his family.

The second six-week segment of the school year is just beginning, and the students have learned how **Ms. Mason** conducts her classes. The most common methodology is for her to talk to the class and intersperse her talking with questions. Occasionally, a full-blown discussion will break out for a few minutes. The better students have quickly learned to listen selectively and to take notes to help them on the weekly and six-weeks tests. Cues such as "This is important" or "You will need to know this" cause a flurry of writing. The most powerful cue of all is what she writes on the board.

Some of the students are able to participate in the class activity—that is, take useful notes—and also study for another class, read a book, or daydream and still make an A on the tests. One-third of the class—the two Hispanic students, **Eduardo** and **Raphael**; **Derrick** and **Mark**, the seniors who are repeating the course; and **Clarise**, one of the sophomore girls—either cannot or will not benefit from the class instruction. **Derrick** received an F and the others a D for their first six-weeks grade.

"OK, Listen up. You are not going to just sit here and listen to me. For the next couple of weeks we are going to try another way of learning. I have divided you into four groups. I am going to give each group a different part of the Constitution to learn and to present to the rest of the class. A large part of your grade for this six weeks is going to be based on how well your group does on its class presentations and also on its test grades."

·A murmur of apprehension sweeps across the classroom.

"Do you mean that how somebody else does is going to affect my grade?" **Clifford** asks.

"**Clifford**, for once in your life will you forget about what grade you are going to get and concentrate on what you might learn? You might even consider the fact that you could be helping someone else. But to answer your question, yes. Your individual grade on this unit will be affected by the group grade."

Several hands are up, and concern can be seen on several of the students' faces.

"Who am I going to be in a group with?" **Clarise** wants to know.

"Put your hands down. Shut up. Listen for a change. I am going to tell you who you are with. There is no appeal. Remember that everyone in here is a human being with worth and dignity. If I hear any one of you being cruel or even unkind to someone else in the group I'm going to come down on you—hard. Understood?"

Ms. Mason's eyes seek the eyes of each student in turn as they move around the room. It is quiet. She has everyone's attention. Even **Derrick** has lifted his head and has it propped on his hands as he stares at the teacher.

It is obvious that **Clarise** is not the only one concerned. **Sarah Tompkins** seems to be almost trying to' disappear in her wheelchair. Like **Clarise**, her concern is with whom she will be placed. Injured in a swimming accident that cost her the use of her legs, and with a learning disability, she has been in self-contained special education classes until this year. She is now mainstreamed in three of her classes. She is still not sure how students will react to her and how she should respond. The other sophomores in the class besides **Sarah** and **Clarise** are all in regular classes but there is a wide variation in their abilities and motivation.

Nanci Drake is the daughter of a sociology professor at the University. A reserved, fashionably dressed young lady, she takes the academic side of school seriously. She is well-liked by most of her peers. **Gladys Farrish**, the other African-American sophomore, is almost the exact opposite. From a family with very limited financial means, she is very insecure and often belligerent, particularly to **Nanci**. She sees little use for what goes on in school but her innate academic ability allows her to maintain passing grades.

The two sophomore boys, **Karl Latham** and **Bobby Utter**, are somewhat in awe of the juniors and seniors in the class. Although they seldom volunteer, they generally do their work and are cooperative with **Ms. Mason** and with the other students. **Art Scott** is new to Edge City. His father, a neurologist, has transferred from a district office of a health maintenance organization in Florida to the national office in Edge City. Although he has been in regular classes in Florida, **Ms. Mason** feels that **Art** probably would do well in the honors sections at Edge City High, particularly in English. **Art** sits across the aisle from **Margie Laurence**; they have gotten into the habit of talking before and after class and find that they have much in common. **Margie** and her family moved to Edge City from the same town in Florida two years ago and she and **Art** had attended the same junior high school in Florida. **Margie** is an extremely intelligent and creative student who also is actively involved in the Honor Society and in student government.

Sure that she has everyone's attention, **Ms. Mason** announces:

"All right, here it is. I will let you name your own groups so I will just give each group a number. Do not ask me how or why I assigned you to your particular group. Since there are fifteen members of the class, three of the groups have four members and one has three.

Group 1: **Karl Latham, Derrick Abbott, Sarah Tompkins,** and **Wilma Booker**.

Group 2: **Bobby Utter, Clifford Handley, Raphael Aquilar,** and **Gladys Farrish**.

Group 3: **Margie Laurence, Eduardo Hinijosa, Clarise Gerrard,** and **Art Scott**.

Group 4 is our small group, and the rest of you, **Edwin Zettler, Mark Jackson,** and **Nanci Drake** are in this group."

The silence continues. It is evident that **Ms. Mason** has created a different atmosphere in the class with this deviation from the usual *modus operandi*.

"Now, before you have a chance to get together in your groups, I want to tell you what your task is. I want you not only to listen carefully, but to take notes on what I am saying so that you will understand what it is that you are responsible for, both individually and as a group.

"As I have already indicated, we are going to be studying the Constitution of the United States of America. **Edwin** pointed out a while ago that this is the next chapter, chapter seven, in your textbook, and you will be able to use the material in your text to help you accomplish your task. Your primary source of information, however, is going to be the Constitution itself. Each group will be assigned one section of the main body of the Constitution. You are to find out everything you can about that section and to be prepared to teach it to the rest of the class. You not only have to tell what the purpose of each part is but also relate it back to the work we did during the last six weeks on the Constitutional Convention. That is, you should be able to tell, when appropriate, why the founding fathers put that particular sentence, phrase, or paragraph into the document. In addition to the Constitution and the textbook, you will of course have access to all of the reference materials here in the classroom, and we will spend one day in the library, where you can get additional material. Remember, what we are looking for is the *meaning* of the Constitution—what effect, if any, it has on our lives today."

Ms. Mason pauses and looks around the room. Everyone except **Derrick** seems to be almost in a state of shock. He has dropped his head once more to its accustomed place on his desk. Only the sophomores and **Wilma** appear to be taking notes.

"OK. Let's get acquainted with our group members. You all know each other, of course, but not in the sense of being team members. One way of breaking the ice and getting to know each other is to come up with a name for your team. I think that it would be nice if it had something to do with the Constitution, but I'm not going to require that. Just keep it clean. I am going to require that.

"So that **Sarah** won't have to move her wheelchair, why doesn't group 1 meet up here near her? Group 2 can meet around **Raphael**'s desk. Group 3, over by the back window, and group 4, up here with **Nanci**. OK, move!"

Chairs are scraped as the students begin to get out of their desks and move across the room. **Ms. Mason** starts back toward **Derrick**'s desk, but **Karl** slaps **Derrick** lightly on the back of his head and says, "Come on, sleepy. It looks like we're stuck with you."

Derrick raises his head quickly and gets out of his chair. It appears that he is about to take serious exception to **Karl**'s action, but, glancing up and seeing **Ms. Mason** staring steadily at him, thinks better of it and moves to a desk beside **Sarah** and slumps down into it, immediately laying his head on his arm.

"Come on. Hurry it up. We are going to run out of time and there's still a lot that I want to get done today. **Clarise**, you are in **Eduardo**'s group, not **Sarah**'s. You and **Derrick** can talk after class, not now. **Mark**, up here with **Nanci** and **Edwin**."

Gradually, they sort themselves out and find their seats. No one seems to be talking except **Clarise** who has started a conversation with **Art** that apparently has nothing to do with the assignment, and **Wilma** is taking the lead and trying to get her group started on its task.

"I think she wants us to pick a name for our group," **Wilma** says. The other three members of her group just stare at her and say nothing for a minute.

"What about the Aces?" **Karl** finally suggests.

"That would be OK," **Wilma** says, "except it doesn't have anything to do with the Constitution."

"OK, then. She said she was a cop when class started, so why don't we call ourselves the Fuzz?" **Karl** offers.

"That's better," agrees **Wilma**.

Ms. Mason is moving around the room trying to get the other groups started, and gradually a hum of conversation fills the room, punctuated with outbursts of laughter. After about ten minutes **Ms. Mason** walks back to the front of the room and begins to try to get the attention of the group.

"May I say something? Class. Hold it for a minute, will you."

Gradually the talking subsides and the class turns its attention to the teacher.

"Thank you for starting out so well," **Ms. Mason** says. "I really think that you will enjoy this assignment and get a great deal out of it if you will all take it seriously and work hard on it. The bell is going to be ringing in a few minutes, and I wanted to complete the assignment. If you haven't chosen the name for your group you will have time to finish that tomorrow. When you know which part of the Constitution you will be studying, that may influence what you want to call yourselves. Here are your assignments. Everybody get out your textbook and turn to the appendices in the back. The Constitution begins on page 588. Look at the Constitution as I am giving you your assignment.

"Group 1: Yours is a little longer than the other groups, but I'm sure you can handle it all right. I want you to take Article I. Not the preamble, just start at Article I and go down to the beginning of Article II.

"Group 2: You take all of Article II.

"Group 3: You take all of Article III.

"Group 4: You take the preamble and the other articles of the Constitution, Articles IV through VII. Do not include the amendments; we will study them later.

"If you have been looking at the notes in the margin of your book you will realize how I have divided the Constitution up for our study. The first three groups will be reporting, in order, on the legislative, executive, and judicial branches of the federal government. Group four has the preamble and the short articles that deal with such things as how the document is amended, the relationships among the states, and so on."

The class follows along in the textbook as she talks. The sense of uneasiness that has characterized the room while the assignment is being given has returned.

"I still don't understand what it is that you want us to do," says **Gladys**. "Are we supposed to read our part of the Constitution by tomorrow?"

"Yeah, this is stupid. I don't know what to do," agrees **Bobby**.

"OK, cool it. I know that this is a different procedure from what we usually do in this class, and maybe my directions weren't that clear. Just sit quietly. The bell will be ringing any time now. I will spend some more time tomorrow explaining what it is that I expect you to come out with."

The students begin closing their books, picking up their things, and getting ready to leave. Within a moment the bell rings and they file rather quietly from the room.

Deborah Mason has very mixed feelings as she stands and watches the students leave. She had been excited as she planned this unit. The idea had come from her reading of articles in *The Kappan* and in *Educational Leadership* on cooperative learning. She could also remember professors in some of her education courses, back in the Dark Ages, talking about the advantages of group work in the social sciences; and she had from time to time used student groups for debates, for short-term tasks, and as buzz groups prior to full class discussion. This time, though, she intends to let the groups be the primary focus for the entire two or three weeks of the unit on the Constitution.

During the first part of the period, while she had been doing her focus activity and getting the students involved in thinking about the Constitution, she had felt comfortable and at ease. She was good at this and she knew it. She had felt less at home when she was telling the class about the group work and making the group assignments, but she had gotten through that all right. She had been somewhat surprised and pleased about the extent of the involvement of most of the students in deciding on names for the groups.

Gladys's question at the end of the period, and the apparent agreement from most of the students that the assignment was not clear, caused her to be apprehensive about tomorrow's class. She would have to do some rethinking, and maybe revise some plans.

She had spent a long time and had given much thought to the makeup of the four groups. Ever since the beginning of the school year she had been concerned by the dynamics of this collection of students. In all of her years of teaching she has never seen such a diverse group, and in the month or so that school has been in session she has seen that diversity create small cliques and isolates. She can think of no other way to really meet the content-related needs of the students unless she goes to almost totally individualized instruction, and she does not have the experience or the materials to do this. Besides, she has the feeling that some of the social needs of these students might be as important as their academic needs.

For example, **Raphael** and **Eduardo** are almost totally ignored by the other students; **Clifford Handley** is brilliant but is an intellectual snob and probably a racist; **Edwin Zettler** was in her American History class last year and is the intellectual equal of **Clifford** but has become much more accepting of other people; she has heard rumors from other teachers of talk among the students that **Clarise Gerrard** was having sex with almost anyone who asked, and she has seen nothing in her behavior in class that would seem to give the lie to these rumors. **Sarah Tompkins** is a sweet girl, but **Deborah** feels that, so far, she is tolerated by the group but not really accepted. **Derrick** and **Mark** are in danger of failing the course for the second time and not being able to graduate. She is hoping that going to a form of cooperative learning might make it possible for the students to get to know and respect each other, and also for the more able students to help the ones who are having trouble.

It is the next day, and the class has filed in a little more quietly than usual. They are now looking toward **Deborah Mason** for direction. It is almost like the first day of class, when no one talks and everyone is trying to decide what kind of class and what kind of teacher this is going to be.

"OK, troops. We are going to begin our group work today. I know that this is threatening to some of you and that probably all of you are at least a little bit apprehensive. I have my reasons for changing the class procedure, and I am asking for your trust and for your cooperation to see how it works out. You all know that we have a very diverse group here. We each have our strengths and we each have our weaknesses. What I am hoping is that within your groups you will discover your strengths and utilize them for the benefit of the entire group. I will be moving around among you as you work and trying to help you get started.

"Remember what your assignment is. You are to learn everything that you can about the particular section of the Constitution for which you are responsible. You are then to decide how you are going to teach this information to the rest of the class. What I think that I would suggest is that you start off by having everyone in your group read the appropriate section in the textbook. Then you might read your section of the Constitution. After you have finished with the reading you might take turns telling each other what you think the most important ideas are. OK? Are there questions? No? All right, why don't the groups meet in the same place you were last time. Move it!"

Group 1 has arranged themselves around **Sarah**'s wheelchair, and **Sarah**, **Derrick**, and **Karl** automatically look toward **Wilma**.

"Why are you all looking at me?" **Wilma** asks.

"Well, you were the one that was running things yesterday," **Karl** replies. "If we're going to have to do this, somebody has to take charge, and you and **Derrick** are the only seniors and he won't stay awake long enough to do anything. Don't you all agree?"

Derrick shrugs his shoulders.

"I could care less," he says.

"I think **Karl**'s right," **Sarah** adds. "You go ahead and be the leader."

The look on **Wilma**'s face indicates that she realizes that if the job is going to get done she will have to do it.

"All right," she sighs. "I guess the first thing to do is settle on a name. A couple were mentioned yesterday. Do you remember what they were?"

"Yeah, I said the Aces and you didn't like that and so then I said the Fuzz," **Karl** answers. "You liked that better. I think I do too. I vote for the Fuzz."

"How about you **Derrick**?" **Wilma** asks.

"Sure, why not?" **Derrick** agrees.

"Sarah?"

Sarah nods her head.

"Then I guess we're the Fuzz," **Wilma** announces. "I guess we ought to start reading the material that **Ms. Mason** assigned."

Wilma picks up her book and begins thumbing through the chapter on the Constitution. **Karl** and **Sarah** follow her example, while **Derrick** turns his chair slightly so that he can stare out of the window.

"This stuff isn't organized by articles," **Karl** announces. "It talks about the Constitutional Convention, and the purposes of the Constitution, and checks and balances and how it's amended. I don't see any place where it says 'legislative branch.'"

Ms. Mason walks up while Karl is talking.

"You're right, Karl. You're just going to have to dig it out. I will tell you, though, that the old set of textbooks in the back of the room does break it out by the three branches. You might want to look at the material there, and the encyclopedia also has some material on the legislative branch of the government."

As she is talking, Ms. Mason reaches over and opens Derrick's book to the correct chapter. She then continues on over to Margie's group and starts talking to them.

"Derrick, would you go get each of us one of those old textbooks?" Wilma asks.

Derrick looks at her and explodes.

"Who the hell do you think you're ordering around?"

"I'll get them," Karl volunteers, and he gets up and goes to the bookshelves and takes down four copies of the old textbooks. He brings them back and hands one to Sarah and one to Wilma. He drops another one on Derrick's desk. Derrick ignores him and the book.

Ms. Mason has been watching the exchange between Derrick and Wilma. She walks back over to the group.

"Derrick, come up to my desk for a minute," she requests.

Derrick gets out of his chair, saunters up to the front of the room, and sits down in the chair beside Ms. Mason's desk. Ms. Mason takes out her grade book.

"Derrick, I don't want you to fail this course this year. I don't want to be the one who keeps you from graduating along with your friends. You made an F the first six weeks, and so far this semester you haven't done a thing. If you will just carry your share of the load in your group you can still make it. Why don't you give Wilma, Sarah, and Karl a chance? Who knows, you might even enjoy this."

Derrick is looking down at his hands as she talks. When it is obvious that she is not going to say anything else, he shrugs his shoulders, pulls himself up out of the chair, and slowly makes his way back to his desk. The other three members of the group are all reading from the old textbooks.

"We are reading the part about the legislative branch," Wilma says as Derrick sits down. "It starts on page 94."

Derrick looks as though he is going to say something, stops, and opens the book on his desk. He glances over towards Ms. Mason, who is engrossed in helping one of the other groups. He then appears to start reading.

Questions for Reflection and Discussion

1. List different models of classroom instruction.

2. What do you think determines why different teachers use differing classroom procedures?

3. What method of instruction did you prefer when you were in high school? What characteristics of this method appealed to you?

4. Why did Ms. Mason choose to introduce this unit on the Constitution by pretending that she was a police officer? What other ways might she have introduced the unit?

5. Should Ms. Mason have insisted on a reply from Mark when he did not answer her question? Why or why not?

6. What are possible managerial and content-related problems that Ms. Mason might expect to encounter as she makes the change from a teacher-directed to a cooperative learning environment?

7. Describe an alternative to cooperative learning strategies for dealing with the extreme heterogeneity of this class.

8. **Ms. Mason** apparently accepts the fact that **Derrick** is going to sleep and that some of the honors students are going to be working on other projects during her class. What is your reaction to this policy? What are some possible reasons for her decision to accept these behaviors? What are some alternatives to this way of dealing with these students?

9. What appears to you to be the rationale that guided **Ms. Mason** in her selection of the members of the various groups?

Class and Individual Projects

Grouping

Make your own groups for the study of the Constitution. Divide the class into *three* groups with five students in each group. Select a chairperson for each group. For more information about the students, refer to the cumulative folders and biographies in the Appendix.

GROUP 1   GROUP 2   GROUP 3

Chair_____   Chair_____   Chair_____

_____   _____   _____

_____   _____   _____

_____   _____   _____

_____   _____   _____

In the space below, explain the criteria that you used in establishing these groups.

What were some major decision points, which students were involved, and how did you resolve any problems?

Helping Individual Students

Five of the students in **Ms. Mason's** class appear to be in danger of failing political science. For two of these students, make a list of possible factors that may account for their lack of achievement. For each of these factors, indicate whether it is something that is under the control of the teacher. Indicate what additional information you would need to have in order to make a decision about how to improve the situation.

STUDENT 1 _____

    Factor _____ _____

    _____

    Factor _____ _____

    _____

    Factor _____ _____

    _____

STUDENT 2 _____

    Factor _____ _____

    _____

    Factor _____ _____

    _____

    Factor _____ _____

    _____

Additional information needed:

STUDENT 1 _____

_____

STUDENT 2 _____

_____

Establishing Objectives

Using the copy of the Constitution in Appendix II, decide on a list of objectives for a unit on the Constitution of the United States. Classify these objectives as to which domain they are in, cognitive (C) or affective (A). If the objective is cognitive, indicate whether it requires simple recall (R) or a higher level of thinking (H).

OBJECTIVES

DOMAIN LEVEL

C-A   R-H

1. _____   ____ ____

_____

_____

_____

2. _____   ____ ____

_____

_____

_____   ____ ____

3. _____

_____

_____

_____   ____ ____

4. _____

_____

_____

_____

Questions Based on Activities

1. What appears to you to be the rationale that guided **Ms. Mason** in her selection of the members of the various groups? How does the rationale that you used differ from hers?

2. What are some things that teachers and administrators might do about out-of-school factors that affect in-class learning?

3. What groups of people should be involved in setting educational objectives? What role should each group play in this process?

Additional Teaching and Learning Suggestions

1. Locate and share information about the theory, practice, and evaluation of cooperative learning strategies.

2. Imagine that you are a student in **Ms. Mason**'s political science class. Describe your perception of the classroom climate.

3. In small groups, generate ways in which **Ms. Mason** might help **Eduardo** and **Raphael** achieve academically.

4. Share personal experiences from your school days about classes in which you thought group activities were used effectively and classes in which group activities just did not work. In cooperation with your colleagues, generate a list of factors that appear to be conducive to effective group work.

5. Select three or four students from **Ms. Mason**'s class and role-play a conversation following the class session in which she announces the change in class procedure to cooperative learning strategies. Repeat this activity with other students. For example, the first time you might want to have three of the honors students, **Wilma**, **Edwin**, and **Margie**. The next time the group might consist of three "regular" students, **Bobby**, **Gladys**, and **Nancy**. Analyze these discussions in terms of their implications for using group activities.

6. Discuss problems with the evaluation of group work. Find articles on this topic in the literature, and share ways in which these problems might be addressed.

7. Suggest additional ways in which this case study might be used to increase preservice teacher education students' understanding of the effect of classroom climate and of changing teaching methodologies on students' attitudes, behavior, and achievement.

8. Interview teachers about their use of cooperative learning or other group strategies. Ask them about the purposes for which these strategies are most effective, advantages of this approach, and problems that result from these practices.

9. Visit a classroom where cooperative learning strategies are being used. Analyze the differing student behaviors called for in this situation and in a conventional lecture–discussion classroom.

10. Role-play one of the groups trying to complete the assignment **Ms. Mason** has given.

FOR FURTHER READING

Bennett, N., and Dunne, E. (1991). "The nature and quality of talk in co-operative groups." *Learning and Instruction* 1: 103–118.

Davidson, N., and O'Leary, P. W. (1990). "How cooperative learning can enhance mastery teaching." *Educational Leadership* 47: 30–33.

Dishon, D., and O'Leary, P. W. (1984). *A guidebook for cooperative learning: A technique for creating more effective schools.* Holmes Beach, FL: Learning Publications, Inc.

Johnson, D., and Johnson, R. (1975). *Learning together and alone: Cooperation, competition and individualization.* Englewood Cliffs, NJ: Prentice-Hall.

Maltese, R. (1991). "Three philosophical pillars that support collaborative learning." *English Journal* 80: 20–23.

Manning, M. L., and Lucking, R. (1991). "The what, why, and how of cooperative learning." *Social Studies* 82: 120–124.

Nastasi, B. K., and Clements, D. H. (1991). "Research on cooperative learning: Implications for practice." *School Psychology* 20: 110–131.

Rose, R. (1991). "A jigsaw approach to group work." *British Journal of Special Education* 18: 54–58.

Sharan, S., and Sharan, Y. (1989-90). "Group investigation expands cooperative learning." *Educational Leadership* 47: 17–21.

Sharan, Y., and Sharan S. (1987). "Training teachers for cooperative learning." *Educational Leadership* 45: 20–25.

Slavin, R. E. (1983). *Cooperative Learning.* New York: Longman.

Slavin, R. E. (1991). "Synthesis of research on cooperative learning." *Educational Leadership* 48: 71–82.

Slavin, R. E., et al. (1985). *Learning to cooperate, cooperating to learn.* New York: Plenum Press.

Smith, R. A. (1887). "A teacher's views on cooperative learning." *Phi Delta Kappan* 68: 663–666.

Soldier, L. L. (1989). "Cooperative learning and the Native American student." *Phi Delta Kappan* 71: 161–163.

Trottier, G., and Knox, G. (1989). "Active learning in middle school: Grade eight English." *Canadian Journal of English Language Arts* 12: 16–21.

Chapter 3

How Can You Do This to Me?

■

GRADING AND EVALUATION

One of the most difficult tasks that teachers face is that of deciding what grade to give a student on a test, an oral presentation, a project, or any other activity that counts toward the report card grade. A prerequisite, and even more important activity, is deciding what is to count toward the final grade. In other words, each teacher must articulate and operationalize a grading philosophy. This case study gives you opportunities to think about and to experience the problems faced by teachers as they undertake this difficult and extremely important task.

It may be that you, some of your colleagues, or your instructor have serious reservations about the efficacy of the competitive grading system used in the American public schools. The authors of this book certainly do. It would be an interesting and possibly productive activity to discuss radical revisions that might be made in grading philosophy and practice. The reality of the case is, however, that the vast majority of schools do require teachers to evaluate and to grade students competitively. The freedom that teachers have to make assessment decisions varies from state to state, from district to district, and even from school to school within the same district. Some school districts leave the evaluation of students almost totally in the hands of the individual teacher, while others specify a numerical range for each letter grade or in some instances require a district-wide test that must count as a specified percentage of the final grade. For the purposes of most of the activities in this case study, we are assuming that **Ms. Mason** has (you have) almost unlimited freedom to make these evaluation decisions.

■ Grading and Evaluation

Before proceeding, you may wish to briefly review Chapter Two, the chapter in which **Ms. Mason** teaches her class about the Constitution. In particular, you may want to reacquaint yourself with the fifteen students in her class. Additional information about the students may be found by looking in the name index. The student biographies and cumulative folders in Appendix I will also provide data about students' school activities and performance.

Unlike most of the other chapters, this one does not present a narrative case study but rather a set of materials for you to use to simulate some of the most important tasks a teacher faces. The materials include a set of test papers and a grade book. A copy of the main body of the U.S. Constitution without the amendments is found in Appendix II. The tasks you are to perform include grading a test, constructing a test, and developing a philosophy of grading. Then you will be expected to discuss the problems you encountered, explain the rationale for the decisions that you made, and reflect on alternative decisions and possible consequences of those decisions.

It is almost certain that different solutions will be arrived at by different members of the group. For example, there will probably be wide variation in the letter grade given to a particular student, or disagreement about whether a student's answer to a specific question is right or wrong. A valuable activity would be for the participants to attempt to *articulate* the reason for the grade assigned, the *data* that support that reason, and the underlying *philosophy* that guided the selection of these particular data and that supports the reason given.

The questions and activities in this case are highly interactive. You will probably want to use the questions for reflection and discussion to begin thinking about the tasks you are to do, and then revisit them after completing the exercises.

Questions for Reflection and Discussion

1. As you remember it, describe the grading policy of the junior or senior high school that you attended. What do you see as the strengths and weaknesses of that policy?

2. It could be argued that a competitive grading system is inherently discriminatory. Defend or argue against this proposition.

3. What are the relative merits of various forms of tests— multiple choice, matching, true–false, completion, best-answer, and essay—from the standpoint of ease of construction? What are their merits in terms of evaluating important instructional outcomes?

4. Think back to your high school days and describe the kind of test you liked best. Explain what it was about this form of evaluation that appealed to you as a student. How does your perception change as you view this test from the perspective of a teacher?

5. Should the quality of a student's handwriting—penmanship—be a factor in determining the grade? Do you think that penmanship does make a difference in grades assigned? Defend your answer.

6. A doctor does what he does because he believes that it is the most effective action to cure the disease or to alleviate the suffering. Should a teacher use grades in the same way? In other words, should one of the criteria for determining what grade to put on a student's paper be the effect the teacher believes that grade will have on the student's future performance? What might be the consequences of such a practice?

7. How much control over the grading process should a teacher have? The principal of a school? A central administration of a school district? A state legislature?

8. Some school districts, particularly at the senior high school level, have district tests that teachers must use for midterm and final examinations. What are the advantages and disadvantages of this?

Class and Individual Projects

Grading Test Papers

On the following pages are a set of test papers that you are to grade. You are to arrive at a numerical grade and also a letter grade for each student. Make comments to the student on at least five of the papers. Some of the issues that you will need to decide include (1) What weight will be assigned to each question? (2) May a student get partial credit, or is the item either right or wrong? (3) Will your knowledge of the student's academic ability or other information about the student influence your assessment of individual items or your assignment of an overall grade? (4) How will the raw numbers be translated into letter grades? There will probably be other decision points as you go through this process. Do *not* attempt to evaluate the quality of the test itself. You will do this in another exercise. If you are not sure of the answer to one or more of the questions, refer to the copy of the Constitution in Appendix II.

In order to get the maximum benefit from this project, you will need to mentally and emotionally put yourself in **Ms. Mason**'s shoes. Imagine that these are real test papers written by real students; that you must return the papers and react to the pleasure, indifference, or pain experienced by the student receiving the paper; that you are a teacher. Use the grade book below to record your grades. GOOD LUCK!!

GRADE BOOK

Student	Number grade	Letter grade
Abbott, Derrick	_____	_____
Aquilar, Raphael	_____	_____
Booker, Wilma	_____	_____
Drake, Nanci	_____	_____
Farrish, Gladys	_____	_____
Gerrard, Clarise	_____	_____
Handley, Clifford	_____	_____
Hinijosa, Eduardo	_____	_____
Jackson, Mark	_____	_____
Latham, Karl	_____	_____
Laurence, Margie	_____	_____
Scott, Art	_____	_____
Tompkins, Sarah	_____	_____
Utter, Bobby	_____	_____
Zettler, Edwin	_____	_____
Average Number Grade	_____	

Derrick

UNIT TEST ON UNITED STATES CONSTITUTION

I.   Define each of the following words.

1.   bill *a law*

2.   habeas corpus

3.   ratification

4.   impeachment

II. For each of the following, tell which branch has <u>primary</u> responsibility.

5.   To raise and maintain armies._____

6.   To appoint judges._____

7.   To settle disputes between two states._____

8.   To tax and spend money._____

9.   To veto laws._____

III. Write the correct letter in the blank before each of the following.

Use (A) for president, (B) for vice-president, (C) for senator,

(D) for representative, and (E) for judge.

_C_10.   Serves for life.

_C_11.   Is president of the senate.

_B_12.   Is eligible for office at twenty-five years of age.

_E_13.   Serves for six years.

_A_14.   Is responsible for enforcing the laws of the land.

IV. Explain the system of checks and balances in our federal government, and give

examples.

B. Utter

UNIT TEST ON UNITED STATES CONSTITUTION

I. Define each of the following words.

1. bill *Something that somebody owes*

2. habeas corpus *Says you can't keep somebody locked up*

3. ratification *puts it into effect*

4. impeachment *to kick somebody out of office*

II. For each of the following, tell which branch has <u>primary</u> responsibility.

5. To raise and maintain armies. *Leg.*

6. To appoint judges. *Jud*

7. To settle disputes between two states. *Jud*

8. To tax and spend money. *Leg*

9. To veto laws. *Ex*

III. Write the correct letter in the blank before each of the following.

Use (A) for president, (B) for vice-president, (C) for senator,

(D) for representative, and (E) for judge.

E 10. Serves for life.

B 11. Is president of the senate.

B + C 12. Is eligible for office at twenty-five years of age.

C 13. Serves for six years.

A 14. Is responsible for enforcing the laws of the land.

IV. Explain the system of checks and balances in our federal government, and give examples.

It means that nobody can get to much power. The president can veto stuff that the Congress passes. The court can say that a law is no good. The house has to ok who even the president appoint

Raphael

UNIT TEST ON UNITED STATES CONSTITUTION

I. Define each of the following words.

1. bill *a proposed law*
2. habeas corpus *to keep out of jail*
3. ratification *to make happen*
4. impeachment *a trial*

II. For each of the following, tell which branch has <u>primary</u> responsibility.

5. To raise and maintain armies. *legislative*
6. To appoint judges. *executive*
7. To settle disputes between two states. *judicial*
8. To tax and spend money. *legislative*
9. To veto laws. *judicial*

III. Write the correct letter in the blank before each of the following.

Use (A) for president, (B) for vice-president, (C) for senator,

(D) for representative, and (E) for judge.

E 10. Serves for life.

A 11. Is president of the senate.

D 12. Is eligible for office at twenty-five years of age.

C 13. Serves for six years.

A 14. Is responsible for enforcing the laws of the land.

IV. Explain the system of checks and balances in our federal government, and give examples. *They were afraid somebody might try to be KING so They divided up the power. The congress can pass the laws, the courts enforce the laws and the president can veto. The judges are appointed by the President but Congress can say NO.*

C. T. Hardley

UNIT TEST ON UNITED STATES CONSTITUTION

I. Define each of the following words.

   1. bill *a proposed law*

   2. habeas corpus *Latin for "you have the body"*

   3. ratification *to give official sanction to*

   4. impeachment *to challenge or discredit a person*

II. For each of the following, tell which branch has <u>primary</u> responsibility.

   5. To raise and maintain armies. *it is really a joint responsibility of the president and Congress.*

   6. To appoint judges. *Executive*

   7. To settle disputes between two states. *judicial*

   8. To tax and spend money. *legislative*

   9. To veto laws. *executive*

III. Write the correct letter in the blank before each of the following.

   Use (A) for president, (B) for vice-president, (C) for senator,

   (D) for representative, and (E) for judge.

   e 10. Serves for life.

   b 11. Is president of the senate.

   d 12. Is eligible for office at twenty-five years of age.

   C 13. Serves for six years.

   A 14. Is responsible for enforcing the laws of the land.

IV. Explain the system of checks and balances in our federal government, and give examples.

   A symbiotic relationship is established whereby overlapping responsibilities and constitutional constraints limit the power of any one branch to act unilaterally.

MARK JACKSON

UNIT TEST ON UNITED STATES CONSTITUTION

I.   Define each of the following words.

    1.   bill Draft of a law before it is passed

    2.   habeas corpus gets somebody out of jail

    3.   ratification

    4.   impeachment to put a president out of office

II.   For each of the following, tell which branch has <u>primary</u> responsibility.

    5.   To raise and maintain armies. Congress

    6.   To appoint judges. President

    7.   To settle disputes between two states. courts

    8.   To tax and spend money. house of rep

    9.   To veto laws. courts

III. Write the correct letter in the blank before each of the following.

    Use (A) for president, (B) for vice-president, (C) for senator,

    (D) for representative, and (E) for judge.

    _E_ 10.   Serves for life.

    _A_ 11.   Is president of the senate.

    _b_ 12.   Is eligible for office at twenty-five years of age.

    _C_ 13.   Serves for six years.

    _C_ 14.   Is responsible for enforcing the laws of the land.

IV.   Explain the system of checks and balances in our federal government, and give examples.

    Congres can over ride veto
    President appoints judges

UNIT TEST ON UNITED STATES CONSTITUTION

I. Define each of the following words.

1. bill- *a draft of a law proposed to any law-making body*

2. habeas corpus- *an order to bring an individual before a court to decide whether he can be kept in jail*

3. ratification - *to approve or confirm to put into effect*

4. impeachment - *to accuse - its like what a grand jury does*

II. For each of the following, tell which branch has <u>primary</u> responsibility.

5. To raise and maintain armies. *Legislative*

6. To appoint judges. *Executive*

7. To settle disputes between two states. *Judicial*

8. To tax and spend money. *Legislative*

9. To veto laws. *Executive*

III. Write the correct letter in the blank before each of the following.

Use (A) for president, (B) for vice-president, (C) for senator,

(D) for representative, and (E) for judge.

E 10. Serves for life.

B 11. Is president of the senate.

D 12. Is eligible for office at twenty-five years of age.

C 13. Serves for six years.

A 14. Is responsible for enforcing the laws of the land.

IV. Explain the system of checks and balances in our federal government, and give examples. *The founding fathers wanted to make sure that no single branch of the government got too much power. They remembered the problems they had with King George and also the struggle between the large and small states during the constitutional convention. Therefore they built into the Constitution provisions so each branch would have checks on, or power over, the other two branches.*
Examples: 1. The President can veto bills 2. The Congress, by 2/3 vote can over ride the veto. 3. The President appoints judges. 4. The senate can turn down his appointments.

Echde

UNIT TEST ON UNITED STATES CONSTITUTION

I. Define each of the following words.

1. bill _a proposed law that is going to get passed_
2. habeas corpus _to get out of jail oh_
3. ratification
4. impeachment _put out of a job or in trouble_

II. For each of the following, tell which branch has <u>primary</u> responsibility.

5. To raise and maintain armies. _legislature_
6. To appoint judges. _executive_
7. To settle disputes between two states. _judicial_
8. To tax and spend money. _legislature_
9. To veto laws. _judicial_

III. Write the correct letter in the blank before each of the following.

Use (A) for president, (B) for vice-president, (C) for senator,

(D) for representative, and (E) for judge.

_E_ 10. Serves for life.

_A_ 11. Is president of the senate.

_D_ 12. Is eligible for office at twenty-five years of age.

_C_ 13. Serves for six years.

_A_ 14. Is responsible for enforcing the laws of the land.

IV. Explain the system of checks and balances in our federal government, and give examples. _some things one of them can do is put the other out of business like impeaching the president. The president can veto_

UNIT TEST ON UNITED STATES CONSTITUTION

I. Define each of the following words.

1. bill *a law*

2. habeas corpus *keeps police from keeping people in jail without reason /*

3. ratification *?*

4. impeachment *find somebody guilty*

II. For each of the following, tell which branch has <u>primary</u> responsibility.

5. To raise and maintain armies. *Army*

6. To appoint judges. *Country*

7. To settle disputes between two states. _____

8. To tax and spend money. *President*

9. To veto laws. *President*

III. Write the correct letter in the blank before each of the following.

Use (A) for president, (B) for vice-president, (C) for senator,

(D) for representative, and (E) for judge.

e 10. Serves for life.

a 11. Is president of the senate.

c 12. Is eligible for office at twenty-five years of age.

b 13. Serves for six years.

d 14. Is responsible for enforcing the laws of the land.

IV. Explain the system of checks and balances in our federal government, and give examples.

Nobody has too much power. The president vetos laws. and things

Nanci Drake

UNIT TEST ON UNITED STATES CONSTITUTION

I. Define each of the following words.

1. bill – *a suggested law – it must be voted on and passed by both house and senate before becoming a law*

2. habeas corpus – *an order stating that a "body" must appear in a court of law.*

3. ratification – *votes signify their agreement by voting in favor of the proposal or bill or law*

4. impeachment *to charge or accuse (usually the President) an official with something serious enough to cause removal from office*

II. For each of the following, tell which branch has <u>primary</u> responsibility.

5. To raise and maintain armies. *legislation*

6. To appoint judges. *executive*

7. To settle disputes between two states. *judicial*

8. To tax and spend money. *legislative*

9. To veto laws. *executive*

III. Write the correct letter in the blank before each of the following.

Use (A) for president, (B) for vice-president, (C) for senator,

(D) for representative, and (E) for judge.

e 10. Serves for life.

b 11. Is president of the senate.

d 12. Is eligible for office at twenty-five years of age.

c 13. Serves for six years.

a 14. Is responsible for enforcing the laws of the land.

IV. Explain the system of checks and balances in our federal government, and give examples. *The different branches of government were designed to work together so that no one branch would ever get too much power. That is why the President can appoint judges to the Supreme Court and veto laws from Congress. That is why Congress can vote to impeach and remove the president. That is why the Supreme Court (jud) can rule in matters between states.*

Margie

UNIT TEST ON UNITED STATES CONSTITUTION

I.   Define each of the following words.

1.   bill *a proposed law*

2.   habeas corpus *requires that a person have a hearing before a judge in due time*

3.   ratification *approval*

4.   impeachment *the H.O.R. decides if there is enough evidence to bring out a person*

II.   For each of the following, tell which branch has <u>primary</u> responsibility.

5.   To raise and maintain armies. *legislative*

6.   To appoint judges. *executive*

7.   To settle disputes between two states. *judicial*

8.   To tax and spend money. *legislative*

9.   To veto laws. *executive*

III.   Write the correct letter in the blank before each of the following.

Use (A) for president, (B) for vice-president, (C) for senator,

(D) for representative, and (E) for judge.

e 10.   Serves for life.

D 11.   Is president of the senate.

e 12.   Is eligible for office at twenty-five years of age.

C 13.   Serves for six years.

a 14.   Is responsible for enforcing the laws of the land.

IV.   Explain the system of checks and balances in our federal government, and give examples. *The Constitution is designed so that no one branch of the government has too much power. 1. The president appoints judges but the senate has to confirm. 2. The legislature passes laws, but the president can veto.*

UNIT TEST ON UNITED STATES CONSTITUTION

I.   Define each of the following words.

1.   bill – *before its a law its a bill*

2.   habeas corpus – *the body, smething about the body*

3.   ratification – *to vote on*

4.   impeachment – *to gets the presiderts out*

II. For each of the following, tell which branch has <u>primary</u> responsibility.

5.   To raise and maintain armies. *Congress*

6.   To appoint judges. *President*

7.   To settle disputes between two states. *Congress*

8.   To tax and spend money. *Congress*

9.   To veto laws. *Presidents*

III. Write the correct letter in the blank before each of the following.

Use (A) for president, (B) for vice-president, (C) for senator,

(D) for representative, and (E) for judge.

E 10.   Serves for life.

A 11.   Is president of the senate.

B 12.   Is eligible for office at twenty-five years of age.

C 13.   Serves for six years.

A 14.   Is responsible for enforcing the laws of the land.

IV. Explain the system of checks and balances in our federal government, and give examples.

The president has some things he can not do because Congress can keep him from doing it. The S. Court can run over the others because it can say no. Really Congress controls itself because the house can say no to the senate.

Edwin B.

UNIT TEST ON UNITED STATES CONSTITUTION

I. Define each of the following words.

1. bill *The first steps of a law*
2. habeas corpus *Provide for a speedy trial.*
3. ratification *Approval*
4. impeachment *The first stage in removing a person from office*

II. For each of the following, tell which branch has <u>primary</u> responsibility.

5. To raise and maintain armies. *Legislature*
6. To appoint judges. *Executive*
7. To settle disputes between two states. *Judicial*
8. To tax and spend money. *Legislative*
9. To veto laws. *Executive*

III. Write the correct letter in the blank before each of the following.

Use (A) for president, (B) for vice-president, (C) for senator,

(D) for representative, and (E) for judge.

C 10. Serves for life.

B 11. Is president of the senate.

D 12. Is eligible for office at twenty-five years of age.

C 13. Serves for six years.

a 14. Is responsible for enforcing the laws of the land.

IV. Explain the system of checks and balances in our federal government, and give examples.

No one-person or agency can accumulate too much power.

Veto + override
Appoint "fail to approve
Impeachment

Art Scott

UNIT TEST ON UNITED STATES CONSTITUTION

I.   Define each of the following words.

1.   bill *a law before it becomes a law.*

2.   habeas corpus *says you can't keep someone in jail without a reason.*

3.   ratification *to ok something*

4.   impeachment *throw out of office*

II. For each of the following, tell which branch has <u>primary</u> responsibility.

5.   To raise and maintain armies. *Congress*

6.   To appoint judges. *Supreme court*

7.   To settle disputes between two states. *supreme court*

8.   To tax and spend money. *congress*

9.   To veto laws. *president*

III. Write the correct letter in the blank before each of the following.

Use (A) for president, (B) for vice-president, (C) for senator,

(D) for representative, and (E) for judge.

E 10.   Serves for life.

B 11.   Is president of the senate.

D 12.   Is eligible for office at twenty-five years of age.

C 13.   Serves for six years.

A 14.   Is responsible for enforcing the laws of the land.

IV. Explain the system of checks and balances in our federal government, and give examples. *The power is equally divided up so that nobody can become a dictator. They can get rid of the president if they have a good enough reason.*

Test Construction

Teachers not only teach; they must also evaluate the effects of that teaching. One traditional and almost universal way of doing this evaluation is through the use of teacher-made tests. These tests come in many forms—multiple choice, true–false, completion, matching, short answer, essay, and so on. Most programs of teacher education give students information about principles of test construction and also, one hopes, practice in actually constructing these kinds of content coverage tests.

You may have been frustrated as you graded the set of papers by what you perceived to be the poor quality of the examination. We agree that it is not a particularly good test. Test construction is not one of **Ms. Mason**'s strong suits. What we would like you to do is to improve the quality of the test. Either individually or in small groups, construct some sample items that might do a better job of measuring the learning that has occurred in this class.

Once again, imagine that you are **Ms. Mason**. You have just completed teaching the unit on the Constitution and you want to know how much your students have learned. Using the Constitution, construct a test for that purpose. Remember that what you choose to test is a powerful indicator of what you think is important in the unit.

Before you begin, please keep one important fact in mind. The test that a teacher administers speaks more loudly about what his or her real objectives are than anything that teacher might say. Students very quickly learn to concentrate on those things that will help them to get the grade they want. If your tests measure only the ability to recall specific facts—and this is sometimes warranted—then students will learn those facts. If the test measures the ability to see relationships among concepts, then that is what students will focus on.

In Appendix II, you will find a copy of the United States Constitution. Using the Constitution and any other sources, or your own knowledge of the Constitution, construct on the following page the test items that are called for. You may choose to use some forms of questions other than the more traditional ones called for in this exercise. Great! Explain the rationale for your choices.

TEST ON THE UNITED STATES CONSTITUTION

MULTIPLE CHOICE

1.

2.

MATCHING

1. _____   a. _____

2. _____   b. _____

3. _____   c. _____

4. _____   d. _____

SHORT ANSWER

1.

2.

DISCUSSION

Assessment

There are other ways besides tests by which students may be evaluated. Portfolios, interest inventories, and the creation of products are just a few of these alternative forms of assessment. In Chapter Four you will be introduced more fully to some of these assessment techniques. This activity is primarily to get you to recognize the need for using multiple forms of assessment.

Ms. Mason chose to teach this unit using cooperative learning strategies. One of the reasons for this decision was the extreme heterogeneity of the class. She also had concerns about the social relationships among the students. Using the worksheet that follows, name the kinds of behaviors and/or products that would be evaluated, explain how the evaluation would occur, and tell how the various elements in the overall assessment would be combined for reporting purposes. Write a brief paper in which you justify your plan for evaluating this unit on the Constitution of the United States. Remember that the choices you make are a reflection of what you believe about people, about learning, and about the purposes of schooling. Be prepared in discussion with your peers to explicate and to defend your choices.

EVALUATION PLAN FOR UNIT ON THE U.S. CONSTITUTION

Elements to be included and process whereby data are to be gathered and evaluated

1. Element _____

     Process _____

     _____

     _____

2. Element _____

     Process _____

     _____

     _____

3. Element _____

     Process _____

     _____

     _____

4. Element _____

     Process _____

     _____

     _____

Explanation of interrelationships of the elements to the total grade

_____

_____

_____

_____

_____

_____

_____

_____

_____

_____

_____

_____

_____

_____

_____

_____

_____

_____

_____

_____

_____

_____

Questions Based on Activities

1. **Clifford Handley's** definitions of habeas corpus, ratification, and impeachment are all correct definitions of the words, but not as those words relate to the Constitution. What are possible reasons why he answered this way, and what should be **Ms. Mason's** response?

2. One response **Ms. Mason** could make to **Derrick's** paper would be simply to give him an F and return the paper. What are other possible actions that might be taken? What would you do? Explain the rationale for your decision.

3. What would you do about **Bobby Utter's** response to question 12?

4. The activity that asks you to construct a test on the U.S. Constitution contains four types of questions: multiple choice, matching, short answer, and discussion. What are other ways in which the student's understanding of the Constitution might be evaluated?

5. Which students in **Ms. Mason's** class would be most likely to object to an alternative method of assessing classroom work? How would you explain your choices?

6. Compute the mean and the standard deviation of the number grades that you assigned to the test papers.

Additional Teaching and Learning Suggestions

1. Assume that **Sarah, Raphael,** and **Eduardo** all do very poorly on a written exam. In small groups, decide what might be some causes for this poor performance and what steps might be taken to increase the likelihood of success for these students.

2. **Wilma, Clifford, Margie,** and **Edwin** all make perfect scores on an exam. The remainder of the class either fails or does very poorly. Brainstorm possible actions that **Ms. Mason** might take. Rank these suggestions in terms of your perception of their relative effectiveness.

3. Examine and evaluate the literature to find opinions on the advantages and disadvantages of competitive grading.

4. Interview teachers and/or administrators from various school districts to discover the differing grading policies of the districts. Elicit the teachers' reactions to these policies, and share these with your colleagues.

5. Obtain copies of tests that have been used by teachers of a variety of subjects (English, history, biology, and so on). Based on these tests, what appear to be the major objectives of the unit being tested? How do the tests differ? In what ways are they similar?

6. **Derrick's** parents have seen his test paper and your grade. They have requested an interview to see what can be done. They, particularly his mother, feel that you are not doing enough to motivate **Derrick** to achieve. Role-play the interview. You may include both parents or just one. You may choose to include **Derrick** in the interview.

For Further Reading

Canady, R. L., and Hotchkiss, P. R. (1989). "It's a good score! Just a bad grade." *Phi Delta Kappan* 71: 68–71.

Coladarci, T. (1986). "Accuracy of teacher judgments of student responses to standardized test items." *Journal of Educational Psychology* 78: 141–146.

Crooks, F. J. (1988). "The impact of classroom evaluation practices on students." *Review of Educational Research* 58: 438–481.

Deutsch, J. T. (1979). "Education and distributive justice: Some reflections on grading systems." *American Psychologist* 34: 391–401.

Doyle, W. (1983). "Academic work." *Review of Educational Research* 53: 159–199.

Driscoll, M. P. (1986). "The relationship between grading standards and achievement: A new perspective." *Journal of Research and Development in Education* 19: 13–17.

Eliott, O. (1991). "The uses of tests." *American School Board Journal* 178: 33–34.

Ericksen, S. C. (1983). "Private measures of good teaching." *Teaching of Psychology* 10: 133–136.

Fielding, G., and Shaughnessy, J. (1990). "Improving student assessment: Overcoming the obstacles." *NASSP Bulletin* 74: 90–98.

Goslin, D. A. (1967). *Teachers and testing* (2nd ed.). New York: Russell Sage Foundation.

Harris, K. H., and Longstreet, W. S. (1990) "Alternative testing and the national agenda for control." *Social Studies* 81: 148–152.

Herter, R. J. (1991). "Writing portfolios: Alternatives to testing (research and practice)." *English Journal* 80: 90–91.

Hills, J. R. (1991). "Apathy concerning grading and testing." *Phi Delta Kappan* 72: 540–545.

Kirkland, M. C. (1971). "The effects of tests on students and schools." *Review of Educational Research* 41: 303–350.

Linek, W. M. (1991). "Grading and evaluation techniques for whole language teachers." *Language Arts* 68: 125–132.

Madaus, G. F. (1990) "The distortion of teaching and testing: High-stakes testing and instruction." *Peabody Journal of Education* 65: 29–46.

Mehrens, W. A., and Kaminski, J. (1989). "Methods for improving standardized test scores: Fruitful, fruitless, or fraudulent?" *Educational Measurement: Issues and Practice* :14–22.

Milton, O. (1982). *Will that be on the final?* Springfield, IL: Charles C. Thomas.

National Council for the Social Studies. (1991). "Testing and evaluation of social studies students. NCSS position statement and guidelines." *Social Education* 55: 284–286.

Natriello, G. (1987). "The impact of evaluation processes on students." *Educational Psychologist* 22: 155–175.

Quellmalz, E. S. (1985). "Needed: Better methods for testing higher-order thinking skills." *Educational Leadership* 43: 29–35.

Sperling, D. (1993). "What's worth an 'A'? Setting standards together." *Educational Leadership* 50: 73–75.

Stiggins, R. J., and Bridgeford, N. J. (1985). "The ecology of classroom assessment." *Journal of Educational Measurement* 22: 271–286.

Stiggins, R. J., et al. (1986). "Classroom assessment: A key to effective education." *Educational Measurement: Issues and Practice* 5: 5–17.

Weston, P. (1990). "The impact of assessment: Developing a European perspective." *Journal of Curriculum Studies* 22: 489–492.

Wright, D., and Wiese, M. J. (1988). "Teacher judgement in student evaluation: A comparison of grading methods." *Journal of Educational Research* 82: 10–14.

Chapter 4

Is There Always Just One Right Answer?

ALTERNATIVE METHODS OF
INSTRUCTION AND ASSESSMENT

Assessment or evaluation in schools is a constant source of controversy and concern. Students worry about making grades. Teachers worry about giving grades and then being held accountable for those grades. Administrators worry about keeping everyone satisfied *and* making sure that their schools don't have the worst grades in the district.

Standardized and typical one-right-answer tests have traditionally been the primary instruments for measuring student achievement and success. Recent years have seen an increased questioning of the effectiveness of these instruments for really measuring student achievement. Accompanying this questioning has been a shift toward using assessment and evaluation measures that provide a more complete picture of the student's achievement and progress. As a result, evaluation procedures which incorporate portfolio assessment and holistically scored essays or projects have quickly gained popularity.

In many cases, adopting a new system of grading also necessitates a somewhat different approach to teaching and learning—an approach that may tend to digress from the one-right-answer approach to instruction. This case describes some of the dilemmas a teacher faces as he struggles to incorporate some of these less-traditional methods of instruction and assessment.

■ *Alternative Methods of Instruction and Assessment*

During his first year at Edge City High School, all of the horrors that he remembered from his own high school days became a vivid reality for **Coach Elgin Pratt**. The curriculum for Junior English was practically the same as it had been when he was in school, and he fell into the trap of teaching the way he had been taught—probably because he didn't know any other way to do it. As he lectured, he watched the students stare with glassy eyes either at him or at a boring textbook. They turned in boring essays that always consisted of an introduction, three paragraphs of body, and a conclusion. Their grammar and spelling were horrible, but writing the misspelled words over and over didn't seem to help, and the students rarely completed the grammar drills he assigned. He was beginning to hate what he was doing because he knew the students were bored and unhappy and he felt unable to change what was happening in the classroom.

The turning point came with the last formal observation of his first year at Edge City. It was like a nightmare; everything that could have gone wrong did. He decided to lecture about and discuss the story the class had been reading. He thought the students might be more inclined to participate than usual because the story was about "young love," and so he tried to get them to offer their opinions or thoughts. He even decided to use the overhead projector for recording notes from the lecture; he thought it would be easier for them to copy that way.

When his supervisor came in, the class was rowdy, but no more than usual. As he took the roll three or four students persisted in wandering around the room and talking to their friends. He finally started the class and the wanderers sat down, but didn't stop talking to their friends; they just yelled from their seats to their friends' seats. As he talked, the students talked, but not in answer to his questions. Sure, a few students stayed with him, but most of them began to shout that they didn't know how to spell a word, or that they couldn't read his writing. Somehow he made it through the lecture and gave a writing assignment, which only a few students began to work on (and, unknown to his supervisor, only a few turned in).

Elgin was sure that his career as a teacher was over—he had heard that an observation like that could ruin someone. He was surprised to discover that in his conversation with the principal, **Mr. Brownell**, the principal focused on how to address the problems in his class rather than chastising him for letting them occur. In fact, his supervisor suggested that Elgin talk to **Ms. Mason** and a few other teachers about how to restructure his class and his teaching so that the kids became more involved. Listening to that suggestion was probably the most beneficial thing **Elgin** did that whole year.

"You know, **Ms. Mason**, *I* never liked school too much, because what we studied and did in class was really boring. I just did what I had to because I wanted to play basketball. Now I'm sure most of my students feel the same way about *my* class. That 'lit' book is so awful—I mean, the things in it are so foreign to our students. Is there any way to avoid putting them to sleep? I want kids to *like* coming to my classes!"

"**Elgin**, next to poetry, history is probably one of the most disdained subjects in school. I love history, but I didn't love it until it had some meaning for me. It wasn't any good for me until I could make some connection between my own life and what I was studying or reading. So I've tried to help my students make that connection. Sometimes I use a cartoon or an article from the newspaper to stimulate the connection. I've even used real-life instances that students have shared with me. If you can find something that the students can relate to or are interested in and then use it to start helping them make connections to stories or poems, you might find yourself feeling better about your classes."

"That sounds good, but *how* do I find these things that they like or know about?"

"This may sound overly simple, but I just talk to my students and listen to their comments. I ask them about things. There are some interest inventories or scales that would help you get the information, too. They're pretty easy to give, and all you have to do then is read them through for the information you want. Of course, you could talk to Mrs. Gillespie, the Senior High librarian, or you might try at the University. Someone there might be able to put you on the right track."

From his conversations with **Ms. Mason** and a few other teachers, **Elgin** came up with a plan to reshape his class. During the summer he took an adolescent literature course at WSU and spent time in the library and the local bookstore finding groups of books to use in his classes. He decided to pair novels that were labeled modern realistic fiction with the more traditional required literature. He planned his discussions to involve finding similarities between the paired books. He thought that the students might find the modern adolescent literature more to their liking and so would be more inclined to read it; then, he thought, he could convince them to work through the more traditional literature by constantly pointing out the comparisons.

In the adolescent literature class, **Elgin** also learned about the process of holistic scoring and portfolio assessment. So he decided to start small and use some of each of these measures in his classes. He came up with a generic rubric to use in scoring the essays or papers his students wrote. He knew that technically he was supposed to have the students help construct the rubrics, but he wanted something to start with that fall and he was unsure about how much help or cooperation he might get from his classes. He also created a portfolio shell for his class; he just listed a few of the assignments that he had planned for his students to complete. He knew that this wasn't exactly the way a portfolio was supposed to work, but again, he wanted something to start with. He planned to let the students choose some of the work to put into the portfolio and, of course, he would add comment cards to document their progress or achievements. He knew too that he would still have to keep a traditional grade book, because Edge City High was simply not ready to dump numerical grades—the computer couldn't handle any other system.

Toward the end of his second year at Edge City High School, **Elgin** began to experiment with using videos to supplement his classes' studies of novels. Now into his third year, he had built up a whole collection of novels and videos. He had expanded his portfolio approach to include more student choice, and his rubric idea was catching on; he had even developed the generic rubric with his students this year. His classes seemed to enjoy this approach, and he had begun to notice marked improvement in their writing and in their interest in the class. This six weeks his class was reading *The Outsiders* and *West Side Story*.

"OK, class, I asked each group to decide on the issues these two books have in common. Let's identify these issues. Who wants to go first?"

Art Scott, the student who transferred from somewhere in Florida is the first to raise his hand.

"My group felt like there were a lot of things that the books had in common, but there was one really major issue that went on throughout both books. Gangs. I mean, both stories are about what happens to people who are in gangs or around gangs. Really, what the stories seem to be saying is that gangs are bad. Right?"

Another student breaks in. "Hey, gangs aren't bad. They're like your family—they protect you. And think about the books. People started having trouble when they tried to get out of their own gangs. That's what would happen in my neighborhood if you decided to leave your gang. I mean, I'm not in a gang, but in L.A., my Uncle Tomas is, and he says it's the way to be; it's survival. If you're not in you die."

Coach Pratt is stunned. **Eduardo Hinijosa** rarely says anything in his class, and now he has spoken almost a whole paragraph. In addition, he has revealed some of his true feelings and some information about his family. **Pratt** always wondered if **Eduardo** was even listening; maybe he had been wrong about this kid. He smiles at the thought, and then redirects the discussion.

"OK. What about the other groups? What issues did you feel were addressed in both stories?"

Lissa James raises her hand and speaks. "My group actually had a similar idea. We didn't talk about gangs being good or bad, but we talked about how they can affect a lot of people's lives. If you think about it, hundreds of people were affected in both of the cities in the stories, and at the center of it all was the different gangs." She smiles. She finally has agreed with the rest of the group. Now maybe they will all stop making fun of her because she gets good grades all the time. She can't help it, and she doesn't study all that hard; school just comes easy to her. And sometimes, when the other students look down on her, she wishes that she were more like them.

"My group sorta talked about that same idea," says **Mary Beth Anderson**. "But we also talked about how there are some good and bad gangs and that really all of the public seems to think that gangs are bad. We only hear about the bad things that gangs do."

"It's usually the bad things that get put into the paper and it's the bad things that make everyone else scared of the gangs. I've never heard of any good things that gangs do. What kinds of things are you talking about?" asks **Art**.

"Well, it's like the things that **Eduardo** mentioned. If you're in with a gang, even if you're somebody's mother or grandmother, that gang'll protect you. It does seem like a family. And with all of the crime today, some people need that extra protection."

In a way, **Coach Pratt** is pleased that his class has so many different ideas about the books and about the issue of gangs; it shows that they are really thinking about the stories. After polling a few other groups, he announces the follow-up writing assignment.

"I'm pleased that we had so much discussion about these two stories. What I'd like you all to do now is to reflect on the issue of gangs in relation to the books, and then write a couple of paragraphs about the impact that the gangs had on the lives of the people in their communities."

"Say, Coach, if we have some personal examples to make our point stronger, can we use them?"

"Sure, **Art**, examples can make writing more interesting to read and discussions more lively. By the way, class, I'll be asking you to share some of these essays during class tomorrow, so be prepared."

The next day the class shares their paragraphs. The plan is to first share the stories as a whole group, and then to divide into small discussion or editing groups to help one another work on improving the paragraph essays before they have to be turned in for a grade. **Lissa James** raises her hand to be the first one to share an essay.

A Stone in a Pond

Lissa James

The impact that gangs have on others in a community is similar to what happens when a stone is thrown into a pond. What do you see? Ripples and circles flow out over the pond and actually change the texture of the water until time causes the ripples to stop. The same is true for gangs. An argument between gang members causes a series of reactions on the part of the various gangs. Soon a fight breaks out and then an injury or a death occurs. This injury or death doesn't just affect the person involved, it impacts many people. Families may lose a loved one or the person who had a job and kept them in food and clothing. Landlords may then be forced to evict families because they can no longer afford to pay the rent. Then the families have to rely on welfare to help them make it through this crisis. The impact continues on and on; not unlike the concentric circles that appear when a stone is thrown into a pond.

Gangs Are the Family You Don't Have

Eduardo Hinijosa

Gangs are like your family. They protect you and care about you. They take care of you. In the books the gangs really cared for the people. When the one guys got in trouble the gangs came to the rescue and fought the other guys for their honor. If the guys didn't have the gangs then they might have had trouble or died sooner.

The two books prove that gangs are the way to survive. Sometimes somebody has to die to prove a point. I think that is what was going on in both books. The deaths were to prove a point. Really if everyone would just leave the gangs alone they could take care of each other and we wouldn't have so many troubles.

A Similar Ending

Art Scott

The "Gang" has had a tremendous impact on today's society. Some say a gang will bring strength and companionship, love and caring. Others suggest that the gang only brings trouble and hardship. I feel that a gang, any gang, will always bring one thing—a loss.

The two books that we read really are quite like the situation that I was confronted with when we lived in Miami. There were many gangs and, as a result, many problems. The most common solution was a fight which ultimately ended in a loss, usually a death. When the fighting somehow did not end in a death, there was still a loss. Someone went to jail, someone left a family or community, or someone broke up with a loved one. The ending of a gang event is always the same—someone becomes a loser!

A Product of Society

Derrick Abbott

They
Hear
Everything

Groups
Attacking
No
Good
Society

Have We Given Them a Chance?

Mary Beth Anderson

Do we ever stop to *really* think about gangs. The newspapers always print the horrible things that gangs do, like killing someone or harassing someone. The press seldom recognizes any of the good impact that gangs may have on their members and their members families. Is it that there is nothing good or is it because media type people choose to ignore the gangs?

We spent a lot of time in class talking about how the gangs in both books really harmed the communities that they involved. I, on the other hand, would have liked to explore how the gangs were a positive influence on the lives of their members. Did the gangs teach the concept of loyalty? Did the gangs teach the idea of friendship? Did the gangs teach the idea of survival of the fittest? Did the gangs teach the idea of maturity? The answer to all of these questions is yes! Now instead of just pushing them aside and thinking only about the negative, let's give gangs a chance or at least think about it.

Questions for Reflection and Discussion

1. What other kinds of strategies should **Elgin** use in his class to motivate and involve his students?

2. Pretend that you are **Elgin**'s supervisor. Role-play the conversation you might have with him after the observation described in the case.

3. Some would argue that using nontraditional methods of teaching is merely a way of trying to entertain students and is not the job of the classroom teacher. Do you agree or disagree with this thinking? Do you feel a need to try to motivate your students? Explain your answer.

4. Think about the conversation between **Ms. Mason** and **Elgin Pratt**. If you had been in her place, what kinds of suggestions would you have given him?

5. Reflect on the subject of alternative assessment in the classroom. Is it a valid issue for all teachers to explore or just a "passing fad"?

6. What can **Elgin** do to modify his instruction and assessment for his "special students" (ESL, mainstreamed, gifted)?

7. The concept of gangs is a controversial but current issue. What other issues might high school students be motivated to discuss or study?

Class and Individual Projects

Reach the Objective

Following are some of the course objectives that **Elgin Pratt** had to deal with in his Junior English class. Devise some other activities that he could have used to meet the various objectives.

WRITING (SKILLS AND CONCEPTS)

 use the writing process model to plan and generate writing
 refine sentences and paragraphs to exhibit unity, clarity, and coherence
 write longer compositions that use outside sources of information
 use a variety of forms in writing (persuasive, narrative, descriptive, etc.)
 address audience, purpose, and form in writing
 use the forms and conventions of written language
 practice proofreading of original work

LANGUAGE (SKILLS AND CONCEPTS)

 produce simple, compound, complex, and compound-complex sentences
 choose appropriate words to convey meaning
 analyze mechanical structure of sentences
 use oral language effectively

LITERATURE (SKILLS AND CONCEPTS)

 recognize main types of figurative language
 identify irony, tone, mood, and symbolism in literary selections
 recognize characteristics of literary selections
 use literary terminology correctly

WRITING ACTIVITIES:

 Skills—

 Concepts—

LANGUAGE ACTIVITIES:

Skills—

Concepts—

LITERARY ACTIVITIES:

Skills—

Concepts—

Make the Grade

Using the rubric (holistic scoring guide) below, grade the student essays from **Mr. Pratt**'s class. Be sure to write a written response to each student's essay. You may want to read some of the outside resources on holistic scoring before you complete this assignment.

Another activity could involve creating a rubric that would more closely match the assignment given by Mr. Pratt. Try your hand at this!

4   A 4 paper demonstrates a high degree of competence in response to the assignment but may have a few minor errors. A paper in this category:

- is well organized and coherently developed
- clearly explains or illustrates key ideas
- demonstrates syntactic variety
- clearly displays facility in the use of language
- is generally free from errors in mechanics, usage, and sentence structure

3   A 3 paper demonstrates competence in response to the assignment but may have minor errors. A paper in this category:

- is generally well organized and coherently developed
- explains or illustrates key ideas
- demonstrates some syntactic variety
- displays facility in the use of language
- is generally free from errors in mechanics, usage, and sentence structure

2   A 2 paper demonstrates some degree of competence in response to the assignment but is clearly flawed. A paper in this category reveals one or more of the following weaknesses:

- inadequate organization or development
- inadequate explanation or illustration of key ideas
- a pattern or accumulation of errors in mechanics, usage, or sentence structure
- limited or inappropriate word choice

1   A 1 paper demonstrates only limited competence and is seriously flawed. A paper in this category reveals one or more of the following weaknesses:

- weak organization or very little development
- little or no relevant detail
- serious errors in mechanics, usage, sentence structure, or word choice

A Whole Lot More Than Numbers

Using the information from the first activity, now create a portfolio shell (user's guide) for the students in **Mr. Pratt**'s class. You may want to read more about portfolios in some of the outside references before completing this assignment.

Questions Based on Activities

1. Obtain a sample of student essays or projects from your observations. Create a rubric for grading these items in a holistic fashion. Discuss your findings.

2. If you were given a choice in how to be graded in this class, would you choose some form of alternative assessment or a more traditional approach? Discuss the reasons for your choice, and experiment with creating options in both areas.

3. Review the objectives for this class. Which ones are concept-based? Which ones are skills-based? In what ways is your instructor addressing these objectives? In what ways is your instructor assessing these objectives?

Additional Teaching and Learning Suggestions

1. Interview a teacher who uses portfolio or alternative assessment on a regular basis. Bring samples to share with the class.

2. Are there specified objectives for courses in your state? If so, find the ones that apply to your content area. Together with other students in the same content area, brainstorm innovative ways of instructing and assessing these objectives.

3. Research the issue of assessment. Make sure that you read materials addressing both the traditional and alternative forms of assessment. Discuss your findings in a debate format with one side supporting traditional assessment and the other supporting alternative assessment.

4. From your classroom observations, develop a list of teaching practices and assessment measures that teachers regularly use. Compare and discuss your list with others in the class.

FOR FURTHER READING

Bloom, B., et al. (1981). *Evaluation to improve learning.* New York: McGraw-Hill.

Callahan, R. (1962). *Education and the cult of efficiency.* Chicago: University of Chicago Press.

Frederiksen, N. "The real test bias: Influences of testing on teaching and learning." *American Psychologist* 39: 200.

Gillen, J. M. (1992). "A lesson from Macbeth." *English Journal* 81: 64–66.

Haney, W. (1985). "Making testing more educational." *Educational Leadership* 43: 4–13.

Hills, J. R. (1981). *Measurement and evaluation in the classroom* (2nd ed.). Columbus, OH: Merrill.

Jongsma, K. S. (1991). "Rethinking grading practices (research of practice)." *Reading Teacher* 45: 318–320.

Maeroff, G. I. (1991). "Assessing alternative assessment." *Phi Delta Kappan* 73: 272–281.

Popham, W. J. (1987). "The merits of measurement-driven instruction." *Phi Delta Kappan* 68: 679–682.

Reef, L. (1990). "Finding the value in evaluation: Self-assessment in a middle school classroom." *Educational Leadership* 47: 24–29.

Rogers, V. R., and Stevenson, C. (1988). "How do we know what kids are learning in school?" *Educational Leadership* 45: 68–75.

Rousculp, E. E., and Maring, G. H. (1992). "Portfolios for a community of learners." *Journal of Reading* 35: 378–385.

Sheppard, L. A. (1989). "Why we need better assessments." *Educational Leadership* 46: 4–9.

Stiggins, R. J. (1988). "Revitalizing classroom assessment: The highest instructional priority." *Phi Delta Kappan* 69: 363–368.

Wiggins, G. (1991). "A true test: Toward more authentic and equitable assessment." *Phi Delta Kappan* 72: 703–713.

Chapter 5

Do They Have to Be in a Straight Row?

■

CLASSROOM MANAGEMENT

Most educators would readily agree that the first day of school is the most important as far as the establishment of "classroom climate" is concerned. It is during this first day, or first week, that a climate is established that influences, even determines, behavior patterns and attitudes that will prevail for the rest of the academic year. Experienced secondary teachers know that it is unlikely that there will be discipline problems on the first day. But they also know that they must set the tone and convey their expectations or the second day may be chaos. Students use this time to discover what the class is going to be like, what is expected of them and, in some cases, what they can get away with.

The folk wisdom of teaching says "Don't smile until Christmas" and "Start out hard, you can always ease up." Whether or not this is indeed wisdom is moot. What is not arguable is that how the teacher chooses to spend those first days will have important consequences for the rest of the time the class meets. Research evidence from many studies indicates that the public school classroom is a social system, and that behavior patterns in that system are largely a function of the culture of that system. It is also undeniable that the person responsible for the creation of that climate or culture is you, the teacher. Within certain limits, you are the one who decides how the room is arranged, what artifacts are present, what activities will be conducted, who may speak, and so on. The climate is also shaped by the implicit nonverbal messages you send.

Once again we have to say that there are no infallible rules that we can give to neophyte teachers as to how they should go about the process of establishing this climate and making these decisions. The answer is—surprise, surprise—it depends. It depends on the grade level, the subject being taught, the size and dimensions of the teaching area, the resources available, the motivation of the students, your personality and philosophy, and possibly dozens of other variables.

There are, however, research-tested principles of classroom management that can inform the decision-making process. In this chapter you will watch as two teachers go through the first day of school. **Mrs. Georgia Kessler** and **Mr. Royce Goodwin** certainly take different approaches. You are encouraged to see how the practices of these two teachers measure up to what you know about sound classroom management. You will also engage in activities that will give you practice in making and justifying some of the decisions that are necessary at the beginning of a school year.

■ Classroom Management

Mrs. Kessler **Nanci Drake** has always been just a little bit apprehensive when she walks into a classroom for the first time. She doesn't know why. It isn't that she is fearful of failing, or that she expects to get into trouble. Maybe it's just the fact that it's a new experience, and that there is always something of the unknown when you are in a new class with a new teacher and with a different group of students. As she walks down the C hall toward her third-period English class, these old feelings are with her.

She has heard other students talk about **Mrs. Kessler** and she has, of course, seen her in the halls, but this is the first class that she has had with her. As is usually the case, the student reports vary. Nearly all of the students agree that she is "tough." According to the student reports, you have to earn what you get in her class. They also agree that there is no room for fun and games in "old lady **Kessler**'s" room. On the other hand, she also has heard students talking about how much they learned in her class.

Mrs. Kessler is standing beside the door of Room 202. As **Nanci** enters, **Mrs. Kessler** nods her head but does not speak, nor does she smile. **Nanci** finds her way to an empty desk near the windows. She lets her gaze wander around the room. One of the first things that strikes her is how everything appears to be aligned. The desks are in five perfectly straight rows with seven desks in each row. The books are flush with the edge of the shelves. It seems that everything in the room is numbered with the numbers ranging between one and forty. About three feet of the chalkboard nearest the door is divided into two squares. The top square contains what is apparently an assignment for the next day. The bottom square is empty.

Unlike most of the teachers' desks that **Nanci** has seen, **Mrs. Kessler**'s desk is perfectly clear. It contains no books, no papers—nothing. Even the bulletin boards, though tastefully decorated, have a kind of symmetry that matches the rest of the room. **Nanci** smiles as an image of a platoon of marching soldiers enters her head.

Students continue to file into the room, and **Nanci** directs her attention to them. This is a regular tenth-grade English class, and she expects that she will know most of her classmates. She sees **Clarise Gerrard** enter the room with an expectant look on her face. **Clarise** quickly scans the room and appears to be disappointed in what she sees. She makes her way to a desk in the back of the room. **Bobby Utter** has settled into a desk across the aisle from **Nanci**.

"I hear this woman is a real battle-ax," he whispers.

Nanci smiles at him but does not reply. **Bobby** is in her political science class. She has the feeling that he is no dumb bunny, but most of his energy seems to be devoted to trying to get attention and at the same time stay out of trouble.

The bell rings, marking the end of the passing period, and **Mrs. Kessler** walks into the room and closes the door. As she approaches the podium beside her desk, the door opens and three boys burst into the room, find empty desks, and sit down. **Mrs. Kessler** looks at them but says nothing. She stands for a moment, her eyes moving up and down the rows as though cataloging the faces in front of her. She begins to speak.

"I am going to call the roll now. As your name is called, go to the desk that I point to. If someone is sitting in that desk, they are to get up and come to the front of the room and stand until their names are called. When I call your name I will also give you a number. That number will be used by you for the remainder of the year and so you will need to remember it. If there is any question about your ability to remember your number, write it down somewhere. I do not wish to keep reminding you of what your number is. Are there questions about what you are to do? No? Then let's begin. **Andrea Barton**, your number is one. Take this front desk."

Mrs. Kessler points toward the first desk in the first row. A Hispanic student whom **Nanci** does not know gets up from the desk and leans on the chalkboard at the front of the room.

"**Nanci Drake**, number two."

Nanci gets up and walks across to the desk **Mrs. Kessler** is pointing at, the one directly behind **Andrea**. As this ritual continues, **Nanci** directs her attention toward **Mrs. Kessler**.

What she sees is a rather tall, angular woman with a stern, almost forbidding face. **Mrs. Kessler** appears to be in her early fifties. Her dress is conservative, her hair is black and straight with no hint of gray or of curls. It is quite long but pulled straight back into a bun. If she is wearing makeup it is not apparent.

Nanci is fascinated by the sound of her voice. Unlike the almost cold outward appearance, **Mrs. Kessler**'s voice is soft and inviting. Though she speaks quietly, the sound carries to all corners of the classroom. She has been teaching for twenty-four years, and is the overall chairperson of the English Department at Edge City High.

The ritual of assigning the students to desks is almost completed. It has quickly become apparent that students are to sit in alphabetical order in this class and that the numbers, whatever they are for, correspond to the students' position in the alphabet. Four students are still standing in front of the room waiting for their desks to be assigned. **Bobby Utter** and **Darrel Webster** have been talking ever since they were moved from their original desk. The talking has gotten progressively louder, and suddenly **Bobby** bursts out laughing.

Nanci watches as **Mrs. Kessler** turns and looks toward the two boys. Her expression has not changed. She walks toward them and beckons for **Bobby** to follow her as she moves away from the students toward the far corner of the room. **Bobby** has an expression that hovers somewhere between a look of embarrassment and a smirk. Both faces are in profile, and **Nanci** watches **Bobby**'s expression change to a solemn, almost fearful look as **Mrs. Kessler** talks. After a very short period of time **Mrs. Kessler** resumes assigning seats, and **Bobby** stands in the corner of the room trying to assume a more defiant or self-assured look. Finally, his name is called and he takes his seat near the end of the last row.

Nanci quickly counts the number of students in the class. There are fourteen girls and twelve boys, for a total of twenty-six. The chairs are arranged in five rows of seven chairs each, so there are two empty chairs behind **Darrel Webster** and one completely empty row beside the window.

"It looks like we have room to spread out a little bit, so I am going to ask you to move one more time. Maintain your position in relation to the person in front and in back of you." She begins to count, beginning with **Darrel**. "One, two, three, four, five, six. You six people move to the next row over. You are going to have window seats. There will be one empty seat in the back. The next five move to the row they vacated. There will be two empty seats at the end of your row."

Quickly the students are rearranged so that all of the students are sitting in the desks nearest the front of the room.

"This is your home," **Mrs. Kessler** announces. "When you enter the room this is where you go. There will be no exchanging of desks."

The students sit quietly as **Mrs. Kessler** looks up and down the rows of desks and writes names and numbers on a chart. When she has finished writing, she walks out in front of her desk and begins to talk.

"I don't have a lot of rules, but the ones that I do have I expect you to obey. Tomorrow when you have your notebooks I will give you a handout that contains those rules, and we will talk about them again. Today I will be explaining some of my expectations for your nonacademic behavior in and out of my class. Everything that I am going to say to you and everything contained in the list of rules could be listed under one heading, and that heading is respect. I expect you to respect yourself, to respect me, to respect your classmates, to respect your school, to respect the building and grounds. If you do this, you and I will get along fine and you will have an enjoyable and a productive year. Less than this will not be tolerated.

"I also have expectations about your academic behavior. That too is simple and to the point. I expect, and will accept no less than, your best. You must do the assigned work and you must do it promptly and conscientiously. To help you do this there are some specific things that you must do.

"By tomorrow I expect each of you to have a three-ring notebook similar to this." As she talks **Mrs. Kessler** holds up a blue notebook opened so that students can see the inside. "I don't care about the color but it must be three-ring—not two or four—and it must have a pocket on the inside of the front cover."

Mrs. Kessler is walking up one aisle and down the other as she shows the notebook and points to the various features. "Notebooks that meet these specifications may be purchased in the school supply room or at any number of stores around here. Please remember that you must have this book with a packet of paper by tomorrow. Tomorrow I will tell you how the notebook will be used in class."

Laying the notebook on her desk, Mrs. Kessler walks to the chalkboard in the front of the room and points to the two lined-off squares. "In this space tomorrow will be your assignment for the next day. I will show you exactly how that assignment is to be entered into your notebook. What I want to say now, and I will repeat it tomorrow, is that the moment you enter the room each day, not when the bell rings, when you get to your seat, you are to write this assignment in your notebook. If you were absent the day before you will find yesterday's assignment here." Mrs. Kessler is pointing to the bottom square.

Nanci lets her eyes leave Mrs. Kessler for a moment and wander around the room. All the other students have their eyes on the front of the room, and the only sound is the sound of Mrs. Kessler's voice.

Mrs. Kessler continues talking about how the class is to be conducted and what her expectations are. Nanci couldn't believe how detailed the instructions were. Among other things, Nanci discovers at least one of the purposes of the numbers that have been assigned to the students. Each of the sets of reference books in the room—dictionaries, anthologies, and so forth—bears a number. Whenever she has to use one of these volumes she is expected to use only the one marked with a two, her number. She shakes her head in amazement as the instructions for turning in papers are given.

"When you are handing in test papers or homework assignments," Mrs. Kessler is saying as she places her hand on top of a file cabinet in the corner of the room, "they are to be placed on the top of this cabinet. When I pick up the stack of papers after they have all been turned in they must be in numerical order according to your assigned number. To accomplish this, each of you must make sure that your paper is in the correct sequence. For example, if Henry turns his paper in first he just places it on top of the cabinet. If Andrea turns hers in next, she would simply put hers on top of his since her number is one and his is twelve. If Darrel is next, his paper goes on the bottom since his number is twenty-six."

Mr. Goodwin   Nanci had mixed feelings when she discovered that she was assigned to Mr. Goodwin's algebra class. Mathematics is not her best subject, and she was pleased to hear from some students that Goodwin didn't make you work too hard for a grade. Some of these same people told her that they had enjoyed his class and felt they had learned something—on the other hand, Kathy Carr, a close friend of her sister's, who had been in his class, said that she had never known what to expect from day and day and that she had always been anxious because she did not know what grade she was making or what he expected her to be doing.

As she approaches Room 116 she sees a group of boys she recognizes as juniors and seniors grouped around Mr. Goodwin. There is joking and laughter, and as another student approaches she sees the teacher and student greet each other with an animated "high five."

The group is almost blocking her entrance to the door, but she edges her way into the room, now almost full of students, and takes one of the empty seats in the back row. She is struck by the contrast between this room and the one she has just left. Unlike the neat, almost antiseptic atmosphere in Mrs. Kessler's classroom, Mr. Goodwin's room exudes an aura of unlived-in disorder. A few yellowed notices are thumbtacked to the bulletin boards. Textbooks are stacked across the front of the room, ready to be distributed. The custodial staff has cleaned the chalkboards, and the vinyl floors have recently been buffed, but this only highlights the clutter on the teacher's desk and the disarray of the materials on the bookshelves. Stacks of student papers from last year take up one full shelf of the small bookcase adjacent to the teacher's desk.

There is no apparent planned arrangement of the student desks. They almost seem to be randomly distributed in the available space. As students take their seats they move them one way or another, seemingly in an attempt to achieve some kind of order.

Just as **Nanci** is sitting down, the bell marking the end of the previous period rings. She hears **Mr. Goodwin** tell the students outside the classroom to hurry to their next classes and a moment later he walks through the door and sits on his desk facing the class.

"Greetings, salutations, and all that other good stuff, you lucky creatures. You were fortunate enough to have been assigned to me for your induction into the intricacies of algebra. Some of you are probably scared to death and think that algebra is some kind of voodoo, but it really isn't. Learning algebra can be a lot of fun if it's done right, and we're going to do it right. I don't believe in long faces and I don't think that school has to be a dull and dismal place, so we are going to have fun in here.

"One of the first things that I have to do is to learn your names, so I am going to start on that right now. When I call your name hold up your hand. **Grace Aronson**."

A slightly built young lady with auburn hair tentatively raises her hand.

"Welcome to 166, **Grace**. I will remember your name by thinking *graceful—grace full—grateful—*get it? Grateful that I have a beautiful red-headed lady in my fourth-period class. **Tommy Bustamonte**."

The tall, dark-featured Hispanic boy sitting in the desk across from **Karl Latham** has his elbow resting on his desk, with his arm in an upright position. He lazily lifts his index finger and waggles it a couple of times.

"Yo, man. I'm here," he informs **Mr. Goodwin**.

"I won't have any trouble remembering *your* name," replies **Mr. Goodwin**. "All I have to do is think about the track meet last spring. First time a freshman ever won the high jump. How high are you going to go this year?"

Tommy shrugs his shoulders but does not reply.

"**Rachael Dodd**," he continues. A large African-American girl in the front row raises her hand. "Hi Rachael. Tell me something about yourself that will help me remember your name."

"That's *your* problem. *I* know my name and I know your name."

"Great! Just what I needed. **Rachael Dodd** is the girl who knows her name and knows my name."

This procedure continues until he has called everyone's name and engaged them in some kind of conversation. This takes nearly the entire period. When he has finished teasing **Jake Waldrip**, the last student on his list, he stands and looks at each person in the class for a moment.

"Watch this," he says. He starts down the row nearest the door and, pointing at each student in turn, he calls out their names. When he has finished, he glances at his watch.

"Well, it looks as if we only have about 5 minutes left, so let's just sit and talk quietly. We will start on the algebra tomorrow."

Nanci looks around the room. She knows quite a few of these students, and it occurs to her that **Mr. Goodwin** may have his hands full teaching this bunch. There are no really bad apples that she knows about, but several of them have spent considerable time in detention. She is also disappointed that more of her close friends are not in the class.

For a minute or two the class is quiet. Then **Clarise** and **Karl** start talking and giggling. Before the bell rang the noise level has risen, and several students are out of their desks talking to other students. She hears **Karl** say to the three other boys he is talking with, "Hey, I think this class is going to be a blast!"

Questions for Reflection and Discussion

1. Some high school or junior high school students may find **Mrs. Kessler**'s "tight-ship" approach security-giving, while at the same time limiting. Some may find **Mr. Goodwin**'s more easygoing approach likable but may suspect his style and find it is not conducive to their learning. Discuss the kinds of responses different students might give to these two teachers. What implications might these responses have for classroom management? For student learning?

2. **Mrs. Kessler** requires students to buy a particular kind of notebook to be used solely for her class. Does this discriminate against **Raphael**, **Mark**, and other less-affluent students? Justify or argue against this position.

3. Which teacher, **Mrs. Kessler** or **Mr. Goodwin**, do you predict will have the most classroom management problems as the year progresses? What elements of their classroom procedures cause you to made this prediction?

4. Assume that you are **Nanci Drake**. What is your impression of **Mrs. Kessler** at this moment?

5. Describe some alternative ways **Mrs. Kessler** could have used these first moments with her students. What is the rationale for these ways of beginning a semester?

6. List the advantages and disadvantages of seating tenth-grade students alphabetically.

7. What do you think **Mrs. Kessler** said to **Bobby**? Write this down and share it with the class.

8. What are possible repercussions, both positive and negative, of **Mr. Goodwin**'s behavior, such as giving his ex-students the "high five" and sitting on his desk?

9. How would you characterize **Mr. Goodwin**'s remarks to **Grace** (p. 67)? What might be the reaction of students, administrators, and parents to a teacher addressing a student in such a way?

10. What are additional things that you feel **Mr. Goodwin** should have done on the first day of school? What about **Mrs. Kessler**?

Class and Individual Projects

Where Do I Sit?

1. On the next page is a diagram of **Mrs. Kessler**'s or **Mr. Goodwin**'s room (they are the same). You have had a description of the furniture arrangement in these two classrooms. Assume that you are teaching an academic subject—English, history, mathematics—not a lab or activity course. Using the symbols below, indicate how you would arrange the desks in your room. You have twenty student desks in the room.

 = student's desk, with the arrow indicating the direction in which the student is facing

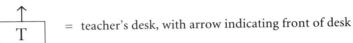 = teacher's desk, with arrow indicating front of desk

= podium (if you would use one)

2. Explain the reasons for your room arrangement.

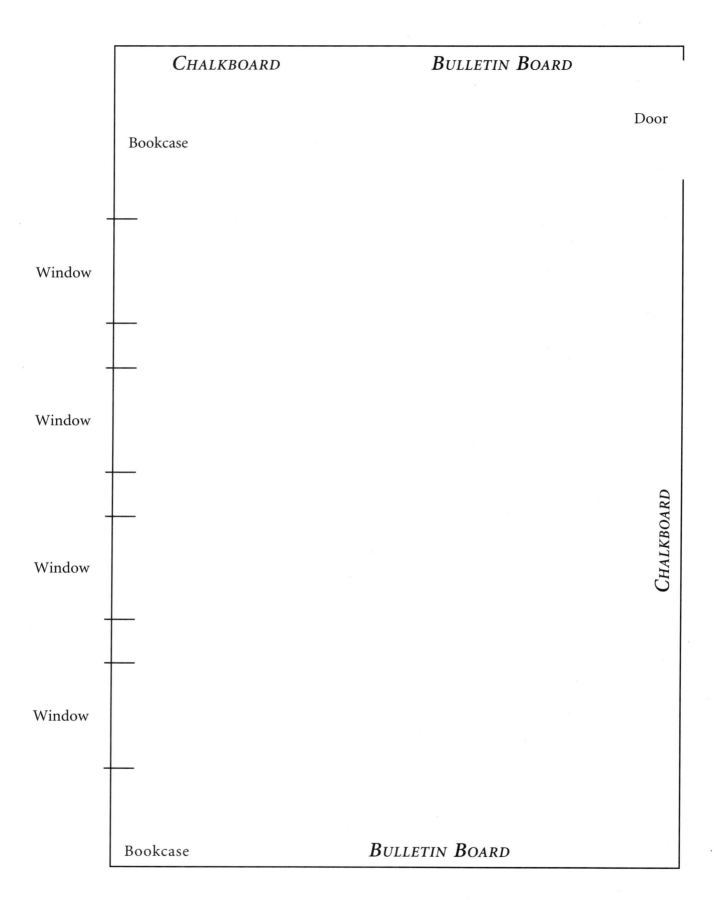

You Have to Start Somewhere

During the crucial first few days of class, different teachers stress different facets of the classroom culture. **Mrs. Kessler** gives most of her attention to organization and management, **Mr. Goodwin** appears to be attempting to establish a "fun" climate. Some teachers emphasize the importance of the discipline being taught and get almost immediately into instruction. There are many other possible emphases or combinations of emphases.

Choose a subject and a grade level, and indicate in outline form the kinds of things you would do during the first two days of the school term.

1st day 1st 15 min. _____

_____

_____

1st day 2nd 15 min. _____

_____

_____

1st day 3rd 15 min. _____

_____

_____

1st day 4th 15 min. _____

_____

_____

2nd day 1st 30 min. _____

_____

_____

2nd day 2nd 30 min. _____

_____

_____

To Choose or Not to Choose—That Is the Question

Give arguments for and against seating students alphabetically as opposed to letting them choose their own seats. You may also propose alternative methods of seat assignment.

_____

_____

_____

_____

_____

_____

_____

_____

_____

_____

_____

_____

_____

_____

_____

_____

_____

_____

_____

_____

_____

_____

Questions Based on Activities

1. In the room arrangement activity, assume that you have the option of any kind of furniture—tables, couches, and so on. What would you choose to use? Explain the reasons for your choices.

2. Explain the rationale for your discussion about how you would introduce yourself and your subject to your class.

3. Describe the general atmosphere you would like to create in your classroom through the manipulation of the physical environment (room arrangement, pictures, bulletin boards, and so on).

Additional Teaching and Learning Suggestions

1. Brainstorm with your peers ways in which teachers may quickly learn the names of students in their classes.

2. Using professional journals, find and annotate articles that discuss effective classroom management practices. Share these in either small-group or total-class formats.

3. **Bobby Utter, Nanci Drake**, and **Clarise Gerrard** are eating lunch together and discussing their feelings about their teachers, **Mrs. Kessler** and **Mr. Goodwin**. Role-play this discussion. Stop at an appropriate time and discuss the implications of the differing reactions to the same situation.

4. Interview a teacher or teachers and ask them to describe how they spend the first day of class. Share these descriptions with your colleagues. Discuss some possible reasons for the varying practices.

5. Write a paper describing one of your high school or junior high school classes that suffered from poor classroom management practices. Analyze this class in terms of possible reasons for the lack of organization and order.

6. Visit a school after school hours and look at the physical arrangement of several rooms. Describe similarities and differences in furniture arrangement, decoration, cleanliness, and any other factors that appear to influence the climate of the room.

7. As trivial as it may seem, teachers must make a decision about whether and how students are going to be allowed to leave the classroom to go to the bathroom, to get a drink of water, or for any other reason. In small groups, list and discuss how teachers in your classroom experience handled this problem. Brainstorm additional ways in which this might be done. Discuss how the age of the students might affect your procedure.

8. Just as the arrangement of furniture, the use of pictures, and other manipulations of the physical environment of a classroom affect the perceptions of people in that environment, so does the external appearance of the school. Visit several school sites, and through the use of snapshots, videotapes, or written notes, compare the physical appearance of the schools and describe the feelings evoked by each setting.

For Further Reading

Allen, J. D. (1986). "Classroom management: Students, perspectives, goals and strategies." *American Education Research Journal* 23: 437–459.

Boostrom, R. (1991). "The nature and function of classroom rules." *Curriculum Inquiry* 21: 193–216.

Bossert, S. (1977). "Tasks, group management and teacher control behavior: A study of classroom organization and teacher style." *School Review* 45: 552–565.

Brophy, J. E. (1986). "Classroom management techniques." *Education and Urban Society* 18: 182–195.

Clifford, M. M. (1990). "Students need challenge, not easy success." *Educational Leadership* 48: 22–26.

Cohen, E. (1987). *Designing groupwork.* New York: Teachers College, Columbia University.

Downing, J. A., et al. (1991). "Using reinforcement in the classroom." *Intervention in School and Clinic* 27: 85–90.

Duke, D., and Meckel, A. (1984). *Classroom management.* New York: Random House.

Emmer, T., et al. (1984) *Classroom management for secondary teachers.* Englewood Cliffs, NJ: Prentice Hall.

Good, T. L., and Brophy, J. E. (1991). *Looking in Classrooms* (5th ed.). New York: Harper-Collins.

Kierstead, J. (1985). "Direct instruction and experiential approaches: Are they really mutually exclusive?" *Educational Leadership* 42: 25–30.

Kierstead, J. (1986). "How teachers manage individual and small group work in active classrooms." *Educational Leadership* 44: 22–25.

Lasley, T. J. (1989). "A teacher development model for classroom management." *Phi Delta Kappan* 71: 36–38.

Prawat, R. S. (1992). "From individual differences to learning communities—Our changing focus." *Educational Leadership* 49: 9–13.

Schmidt, F., and Friedman, G. (1987). "Strategies for resolving classroom conflicts." *Learning* 15: 40–42.

Shrigley, R. L. (1986). "Effective discipline: A positive approach to self-direction and personal growth." *NASSP Bulletin* 70: 65–71.

Stallion, B. K., and Zimpher, N. L. (1991). "The effects of training and mentoring on the inductee teacher's behavior." *Action in Teacher Education* 13: 42–50.

Part II

Issues in Education

Do You Call This Being Creative?

■

SEXISM IN THE CLASSROOM

One of the coauthors' first teaching assignments, long ago, was three classes of eighth-grade American history and two classes of seventh-grade world geography. When one of his friends, a high school principal, heard the classes he would be teaching, he declared, "If you can teach eighth graders, you can teach anyone!"

That statement implies that there are unique challenges associated with teaching thirteen- and fourteen-year-old boys and girls. This is undoubtedly true, but there are, of course, unique challenges to teaching *any* age group or subject field.

Many of the problems associated with teaching middle school or junior high school students are a result of the physiological and psychological realities of this age group. Growing sexual awareness, the earlier maturation of the girls, abundant energy, and the need to establish independence from adult authority all contribute to a dynamic classroom environment fraught with opportunity—and with the potential for disaster.

Potential disaster turns into actual tragedy in hundreds of thousands of cases each year. The United States has one of the highest rates of teenage pregnancy and venereal disease of any industrialized nation. The number of children having children bodes ill for the future.

Coming to understand their sexuality and learning to exhibit responsible sexual behavior is an essential task for boys and girls entering adolescence. It is a task that American society has generally chosen to ignore. Throughout the nation, community after community has agonized over the relative roles of the home and school in providing sex education. Even with the threat of AIDS, quite frequently it is decided that this is an inappropriate topic for discussion in schools. Middle school teachers must frequently make decisions about what constitutes appropriate and inappropriate behavior between the sexes. A recent poll by *Seventeen* magazine (LeBlanc, 1993) reports that more than 90 percent of girls between the ages of twelve and sixteen indicate that they have been the victims of sexual harassment in school. This harassment ranges from suggestive looks, gestures, and comments to forced sex.

The sexual awakening of early adolescence, the reluctance of adults to recognize and deal with this phenomenon, the tragic AIDS epidemic, the prevalence of teenage pregnancy, abortion, and venereal disease, and the recognition of sexism and sex discrimination in school and society—all of these impinge upon the public schools and present numerous problems for teachers and administrators. This case describes the dilemma faced by one teacher as she attempts to decide what to do about an incident of possible harassment.

Cassie Hudgkins is a new eighth-grade English teacher at Hooker Middle School. She was hired at midterm and it is now the middle of April. This is **Cassie's** first teaching assignment and she has found teaching to be a stimulating and rewarding activity. With considerable help from other teachers, particularly **Rose Ragsdale**, she has learned the necessity of having consistent expectations for student behavior. Her students know that if they exceed the limits of acceptable behavior they will suffer the consequences. At the same time, she has been able to create a relaxed, pleasant atmosphere in which banter and joking are almost the rule rather than the exception.

Her self-confidence has increased with the passage of time. She likes teaching. She thinks that she is going to be happy in Edge City. But what is she going to do about **Maurice?**

■ *Sexism in the Classroom*

Cassie is standing by the window looking at the students in her fourth-period class. This is unquestionably her favorite class. She knows that she is not supposed to have favorites, but these kids are so alive, so alert, so full of energy. And so bright. For the first time ever, the middle schools in Edge City have established "honors" classes in English and mathematics. This is one of the two eighth-grade honors English classes. When she thinks about it, it bothers **Cassie** that there is only one African-American and two Hispanic students in the class, but most of the time she does think about it. She knows that the students were selected primarily on the basis of the scores they made on a nationally standardized English achievement test, on last year's grades, and on teachers' recommendations. The system has worked in identifying students who are capable of doing the work required of them and who, unlike many of the students in her other classes, usually do their work without excessive prodding from her.

There are twenty-four students in the class—fourteen boys and ten girls. They are exceedingly "normal," energetic, mischievous thirteen- and fourteen-year-olds. They come to class in a rush, they leave in a rush. If she let them, they would all talk at once and would be constantly in and out of their seats, punching each other, passing notes, and doing all of the things that make life at this age enjoyable.

Part of the contentment that **Cassie** feels comes from the fact that while they *could* act that way, they seldom do. The room right now is almost devoid of sound. The students are busily working at their desks, making a list of possible topics for a paper that they are to write. The activities, in addition to the choice of a topic, include prewriting, rough sketching, peer-editing, final copying, and then a clocking routine in which each student's work is checked by four other students to see that all parts are complete.

"OK, class. You should have a fairly long list of possible topics now. What I want you to do now is to look your list over and circle the one that you want to write on. Remember that what we are trying to do is to explain to the class how to *do* something. Make sure that you know how to do the thing yourself, and that it is something that can be explained to the others. I will come around to your desk and, if the subject is acceptable, give you the go-ahead to get started on your paper."

Moving to the end of the row of desks near the window, **Cassie** stops by **Sandra**'s desk and looks at the page and a half of topics listed. *How to Get and Keep a Baby Sitting Job* is the first on the list, and is also the one that **Sandra** has circled.

Sandra Atkins, a petite, freckle-faced young lady with waist-length blonde hair, looks at her anxiously.

"Is that all right?" she asks.

"I think it could be a very interesting paper," **Cassie** replies. "Remember that you want to talk about the steps that you go through and you want to make it interesting."

Cassie moves on around the room, approving most of the selected topics, giving assurances, and making suggestions for improvement. **Maurice Yeatts** sits at the front desk in the third row. He is a small, dark-haired young man who is quite evidently looked up to by most of his peers. He tends to overparticipate in class discussions, and is usually the leader in any caper that occurs in class. A capable student, he usually does his work and does it well. As she looks down at his paper she notices that he has written only five possible topics and that he has circled two of them. The first circled topic is *How to Draw a Cartoon*. The other is *How to Irritate Girls*. **Cassie** smiles at **Maurice** as she remembers the incident that occurred a month or so ago.

Not too long after **Cassie** had taken over the class, it became apparent to her that **Maurice** seemed to really like her. He was very cooperative in class. One day when she walked into the classroom, **Cassie** saw a very well-drawn cartoon projected on the screen from the overhead projector that was right beside **Maurice**'s desk.

"How nice," she exclaimed. "Who did this?"

"**Maurice**," replied several students. "He's always drawing stuff."

"Well, I think it's very well done. Thank you, **Maurice**."

A new cartoon appeared each day after that, and **Cassie** continued to respond positively to **Maurice**'s efforts. Then one day instead of a cartoon there was a large heart, an arrow, and the words, I LOVE YA, BABE.

Cassie erased the picture and words from the projector and looked at **Maurice** who was watching her with a sly grin on his face.

"I think we will dispense with the art work for a while, **Maurice**. It seems that you have run out of ideas."

Maurice appeared to be disappointed at her reaction, but he shrugged his shoulders and offered no argument.

"You need to select one topic," **Cassie** says to him now.

"Yeah, I know . . . but what if you can't decide?" he asks.

"Well, **Maurice**, to be honest with you, I kind of miss your cartoons. You are really very good at it. I think I would enjoy reading about how you go about drawing the way you do. It might even improve my own artistic endeavors."

"Uh-huh. I *am* getting bored with your smiley faces on the chalkboard and on our papers," he grins.

Cassie laughs and says, "You see, your paper could end up saving my future students from boredom."

Cassie continues moving around the room reacting to the students' choices of topics.

It is the next day, and the students are working in groups of four. Their instructions are to exchange their rough copies and peer-edit each other's work with comments and suggestions. The work is proceeding quietly and efficiently. **Cassie** moves from group to group offering her own suggestions and encouraging the efforts that are being made.

Suddenly, **Nathan** interrupts the quiet with a raucous laugh. **Cassie** approaches the group of four boys and looks over **Nathan**'s shoulder at the paper he is reading. She immediately recognizes **Maurice**'s handwriting.

"I'm sorry, **Ms. Hudgkins**, but this is really funny!" **Nathan** says.

"Well, you're disturbing your classmates, so please hold it down," **Cassie** says without stopping to read the paper.

The paper is exchanged a second time, and **David** is the next student who starts to laugh uproariously. **Cassie** quickly approaches the group and takes the paper from **David**'s hand. She is disappointed as she sees that **Maurice** has written only one paragraph when he was supposed to write four. She quickly reads the paper. It is cleverly written, describing how to irritate girls by tying their shoestrings together. Turning to **Maurice** she asks, "Why do you have only one paragraph?"

"Oh, I thought you said we were only to write one paragraph," he answers with a shrug.

"Well, you need to expand this into an acceptable paper. You did not write the logical steps that should be a part of a how-to paper."

"Yeah, I know. I'll have it ready tomorrow."

"By the way, what happened to your other topic? I was looking forward to it."

"Well," he says, "I tried to write on cartoon drawing, but I couldn't."

"What do you mean?" **Cassie** asks.

"Well, it's just hard to explain. I mean, I taught myself how to draw and it's just too hard to explain."

"OK. You do understand that you need to expand on how to irritate girls by tying their shoestrings together?"

"Uh-huh. I'll add some steps tonight in my final copy."

The next day, **Cassie** collects all the students' process papers—the prewriting activities, the peer-edit sheets, and the rough draft that was to reflect the final copy almost word for word. She does not look at any of the final copies until the next day, when several girls from her third-period class approach her.

"**Ms. Hudgkins**, have you graded **Maurice**'s process paper?" **Angela** asks.

"No, I have not read any of the process papers."

"Well, he read it to a bunch of us before school today and I think he ought to get a zero!"

"We all think that!" exclaims **Janet**. "It's a sexist paper and he shouldn't get a good grade for it."

The other girls in the group nod their heads in agreement, but from the smiles on some of their faces **Cassie** suspects that they have not all been totally turned off by the paper.

David is the first person in the room at the beginning of the fourth period. He has an almost smirking grin on his face.

"Have you read our process papers yet?" he asks.

"No, I haven't read any of them yet. Why do you ask?"

"I just can't wait for you to read **Maurice**'s paper. It's really funny."

By now **Cassie**'s curiosity is really aroused, but she has a class to teach.

Cassie feels lucky to have the fifth period as her planning period. She could eat a leisurely lunch and then spend the rest of the time either grading papers or getting ready for the next day's classes. Today, she decides to carry the fourth-period process papers with her to lunch. She wants to see what **Maurice** said that has the girls so worked up.

The teachers' lounge and workroom is nearly full by the time **Cassie** arrives. She goes to the refrigerator, removes her lunch, and finds herself a seat in the crowded room. Looking through the papers, she finds **Maurice**'s and begins to eat and to read.

How to Irritate Girls

Maurice Yeatts

One of the neatest things about being a boy is that you can irritate girls. Girls are like a very complicated piece of machinery. They can break at a moment's notice, and you can never figure out how to fix them.

Tying their shoestrings together will always get a laugh. It works best when their mind is on something else, like watching a movie or being goo-goo over a boy. To do this you must be very quiet and smooth. Gently move your hand to her foot. Make sure you are in a good position and her feet are not underneath her. That could pose problems. If either or both her feet are under her, forget the laces and go to plan "B". Untie one lace at a time, and then gently tie them together. They don't have to be tied tightly as the effect will be there whether they are loose or tight. Now sit back and watch her fall, but make sure you can run fast as she will chase you after she unties them.

Are you ready for another irritating trick? This one you'll love! This must be done in the halls, between classes. Walk the hall looking cool and keep your eyes open for a cute sweetie. Once you have her in sight, get her within range of the right hand or left, if you are a leftie. Slowly reaching for the middle of her gluteus maximus open the thumb and index finger. Then grab the gluteus maximus with those fingers and shut them. This will produce a pinch effect. Do not try this until you have had proper instruction.

My final and most perfected irritation for girls is the snapping of the "ole training bra." This one is quite complicated, so pay attention. There are two basic types of bras, front snap and back snap. Stay away from the back snap. Just kidding! Go to the attic and get your sisters or brothers old doll. Next you will need a rubber band and two peanuts. Carefully place these on the doll in the appropriate place. If you're not sure where to put them, look in the Sears catalog, under lingerie. Take the doll and stand it up so it will be around your height. Then practice by casually walking by and reaching for the rubber band. Pull it back and let it snap. With a little practice you can become an expert in very little time. If your mother catches you, tell her you are doing an experiment for Mrs. Hudgkins class.

Irritating a girl is not for everyone, so if you feel you can't do it, don't feel bad. I was lucky enough to be born with that talent and have spent many hours perfecting it. Being a boy does have its advantages.

Cassie chuckles several times as she reads the paper. This is just further evidence that **Maurice** is a clever and creative young man.

Evelyn Waters, a biology teacher, sees her smiling to herself and comments. "You don't usually see a teacher smiling when she's reading papers."

"This is **Maurice Yeatt**'s paper," **Cassie** says. "He let some of the girls see it and they're acting as if they're upset. Here, read it if you like."

Cassie is surprised to see a frown cross **Evelyn**'s face as she reads.

"No wonder they're upset," **Evelyn** says. "This is a clear case of sexism and of advocating sexual harassment if I have ever seen one. That kid has always been a wise-ass—I had him last year and again this year. If there's any opportunity to stir up trouble, he's going to do it. I really think that somebody needs to take him down a peg. I think that you should show this paper to **Darlene**."

George Arnett, biology teacher and football coach, looks up from the newspaper he is reading. "Let me see that, **Cassie**," he says as he reaches for the paper.

He quickly reads **Maurice**'s essay. "You people have to be kidding!" he exclaims. "This is totally harmless. It has gotten to the point where you can't say or do anything anymore without offending somebody. This is absolutely nothing but normal behavior. And don't kid yourself, those girls love it."

Evelyn's face is red, and her voice is shaking.

"That's what I would expect *you* to say. Isn't that one of the defenses at a rape trial?—'But, Judge, she really enjoyed it!' "

Cassie is upset by the incident. When she gets back to her classroom she has difficulty reading the other fourth-period papers because her mind keeps coming back to **Maurice**. She had thought that the paper was clever. His interest in the female anatomy is totally normal and there are really no offensive words in the paper. It meets the general criteria she had specified. It has few grammatical or other writing errors. But **Evelyn** really reacted negatively to it. And so did the girls. She didn't know how serious they were. Had they really been offended, or was this just their way of trying to get **Maurice** in trouble? Her inclination is to simply make some appropriate comments on the paper and to ignore or at least play down the significance of the entire incident. On the other hand, she is a beginning teacher, and it couldn't do any harm to at least ask **Darlene Doyle**, the eighth-grade English Department head, what *she* thought should be done. Maybe she is naive because she hadn't really even considered the possibility that the behavior described in the paper might be sexual harassment.

Darlene is a good teacher. She has been teaching for fourteen years. She keeps up with changes in her field and with the latest in instructional strategies. She works hard planning her lessons, and she expects students to put forth the same kind of effort in completing the requirements set forth in those lessons. There is no room for foolishness in her classes. She does not dislike students, but she deliberately keeps herself from getting close to any of them. She does not want her feelings about a student to affect her decisions regarding that student. She knows that she is referred to as "sourpuss **Doyle**" but she tells herself that this no longer bothers her at all.

Students in her classes know what is expected of them and they generally perform well academically for her. She gives unstintingly of her time, and spends many hours before and after school helping students who are having difficulty. She also has the respect of the other teachers at Hooker. She has been unanimously elected department chair for the past six years. One of the reasons for her success as a department chair is the fact that she does not try to enforce her philosophy or her methods on the other teachers. She knows that there is great variation in the way the English classes are taught. She really thinks that the other teachers would all do well to emulate her, but she realizes that this will not happen, so she maintains harmony in the department, provides opportunities for the sharing of ideas, and is always open if a teacher seeks her advice.

She is glad that the new teacher, **Cassie Hudgkins**, feels free to come to her. **Cassie** has not had any major problems, but **Darlene** feels that she has been particularly effective in helping **Cassie** organize some of the materials and in helping her to construct valid and reliable tests. She smiles as **Cassie** walks into her room during their planning period.

"I don't like to bother you," **Cassie** apologizes. "But one of my students turned this paper in, and it has caused a stir among some of the girls in at least two of my classes, and I wonder what you would do if you were in my place."

Darlene takes the paper and quickly reads it.

"You have to do something, and it should be pretty decisive," she says. "I would call his parents and tell them about the paper and send it home for them to read. I would announce in class that you do not approve of the way **Maurice** responded to your assignment. I would require him to write another paper and I would give the new paper a grade no higher than a C."

"I don't think he was being mean or malicious," **Cassie** argues. "He is just naturally mischievous. What if I just talked to him about it? We really have a pretty good relationship."

"You do what you think is proper," **Darlene** answers. "I would never allow one of my students to get away with such a prank. What you have to keep in mind is that other students have read it and they are going to be watching to see what you do. One other suggestion is to just send him along with the paper to the office and let the principal deal with it. That's what they get paid for."

"I'll think about it," **Cassie** says as she heads for the door. "Thank you for listening."

"How can something that starts out so simple end up being so complicated?" she asks herself. "What am I going to do about **Maurice**?"

Questions for Reflection and Discussion

1. How would you define sexual harassment?

2. What special academic and social problems are created by the extreme physiological differences to be found in the typical middle school classroom?

3. What principles will guide you in making discipline-related decisions in cases of possible sexism, racism, or other forms of discrimination?

4. This case presents some evidence that **Maurice** might have a "crush" on **Ms. Hudgkins**. What are some general principles that should guide teacher behavior in such cases?

5. How do you account for the different attitudes toward the incident with **Maurice** taken by **Cassie**, by **Evelyn Waters**, by **Darlene Doyle**, and by **George Arnett**?

6. What response do you predict would have been forthcoming if **Cassie** had referred the matter to the central administration and **Martin Quincy**, the principal, had become involved?

7. How might **Maurice**'s parents have reacted if **Cassie** had talked to them about his paper?

Class and Individual Projects

Is It Right or Is It Wrong?

Businesses, universities, professional organizations, and other entities are struggling with the problem of defining appropriate behavior between the sexes. It could be argued that a clear policy concerning appropriate sex-related behavior is needed at all levels of public schooling. Indicate which in-school behaviors would fall into each of the categories listed below.

Clearly unacceptable (example: fondling)

_____

_____

_____

_____

Questionable (example: holding hands in hallways)

_____

_____

_____

_____

Acceptable (example: smiling at a member of the opposite sex)

_____

_____

_____

_____

■ *Put Up or Shut Up*

What actions would you take if you were in **Cassie**'s shoes?

_____

_____

_____

_____

_____

What effect do you predict these actions would have on **Cassie**'s relationship with the following people?

Maurice

_____

_____

_____

Darlene Doyle

_____

_____

_____

The other students in her fourth-period class

_____

_____

_____

You've Got to Start Somewhere

Teachers, in the final analysis, determine what kinds of behavior are acceptable in their individual classrooms. Imagine that you are teaching your discipline at an eighth-grade level. In the space below, describe your policy regarding sex discrimination and sexual harassment. How would students be informed of your policy?

_____

_____

_____

_____

_____

_____

_____

_____

_____

_____

_____

_____

_____

_____

_____

_____

_____

_____

_____

_____

_____

Questions Based on Activities

1. Assume that **Cassie** (you) have returned **Maurice**'s paper with an A and no comment. **Sandra**, **Angela**, and **Janet** stop by after school and ask why you didn't reprimand him and give him a low grade. How would you respond to them?

2. Describe a discipline sex-related incident from your school days that you feel was handled particularly well. Describe one that was poorly handled.

3. Discuss the advantages and disadvantages of having rules governing specific behavior as opposed to more general rules.

Additional Teaching and Learning Suggestions

1. Gather information on court cases dealing with sex discrimination and/or sexual harassment. Discuss the implications of these cases for public school classrooms.

2. Assume that **Ms. Hudgkins** follows **Darlene Doyle**'s suggestion and calls **Maurice**'s parents in for a conference. Role-play that conference with and without **Maurice** present. Repeat the role play assuming that the parent takes a different stance.

3. Interview several teachers and ask them what they would do in a similar situation. Ask why they would choose this particular action.

4. Let some junior high school students read **Maurice**'s paper. Ask if they would turn in such a paper themselves. Once again, get at their reasons.

5. Interview vice-principals in charge of discipline in one or more schools. Ask them to describe the procedures that a teacher follows if she wishes to refer a student to the administration for some infraction. Ask them to describe the procedures followed when the student reports to them. Finally, ask them what they would have done if **Ms. Hudgkins** had referred **Maurice** to them.

6. Examine student handbooks and other relevant documents to determine the official policy of school districts in the area of sexual harassment.

FOR FURTHER READING

Banks, T. L. (1988). "Gender bias in the classroom." *Journal of Legal Education* 38: 137–146.

Cantor, L., and Cantor, M. (1976). *Assertive discipline—A take charge approach for today's educator.* Santa Monica, CA: Cantor and Associates, Inc.

Dowling, P. (1991). "Gender, class, and subjectivity in mathematics: A critique of Humpty Dumpty." *For the Learning of Mathematics: An International Journal of Mathematics* 11 (1): 2–8.

Eccles, J. S., et al. (1991). "Control versus autonomy during early adolescence." *Journal of Social Issues* 47: 53–68.

Eccles, J. S., et al. (1991). "What are we doing to early adolescents? The impact of educational contexts on early adolescents." *American Journal of Education* 99: 521–542.

Finley, P., and Kleinfeld, J. (1990). *Gender wars at John Adams High: A case study: Teaching cases in cross-cultural education* 6. Fairbanks, AK: Alaska University Center for Cross Cultural Studies.

Grahame, P. R., and Jardine, D. W. (1990). "Deviance, resistance, and play: A study in the communicative organization of trouble in class." *Curriculum Inquiry* 20: 283–304.

Le Blanc, A. N. (1993). "Harassment at school: The truth is out." *Seventeen* May, 134–135.

McBride, R. E. (1990). "Sex-role stereotyping behaviors among elementary, junior and senior high school physical education specialists." *Journal of Teaching in Physical Education* 9 (4): 249–261.

Merrion, M. (1990). "How master teachers handle discipline." *Music Educators Journal* 77: 26–29.

Riger, S. (1991). "Gender dilemmas in sexual harassment policies and procedures." *American Psychologist* 46 (5): 497–505.

Romatowski, J. A., and Trepanier-Street, M. (1987). "Gender perceptions: An analysis of children's creative writing." *Contemporary Education* 59 (1): 17–19.

Short, R. J., and Short, P. M. (1989). "Teacher beliefs, perceptions of behavior problems and intervention preferences." *Journal of Social Studies Research* 13: 28–33.

Stitt, B. A., et al. (1988). *Building gender fairness in schools.* Carbondale, IL: Southern Illinois University Press.

Strauss, S. (1988). "Sexual harassment in the school: Legal implications for principals." *NASSP Bulletin* 72 (506): 93–97.

Wall, A. N. (1992). "Gender bias within literature in the high school English curriculum: The need for awareness." *English Quarterly* 24 (2): 25–29.

Chapter 7

How Was Your Breakfast This Morning?

■

SOCIOECONOMIC, ETHNIC, AND
CULTURAL DIFFERENCES

According to some individuals and groups, the answer to many of the schools' most perplexing problems lies in the home. They say that if the home were doing its job we would not have to be concerned about readiness for school, about sex or drug education, about motivation, discipline, or gangs. It is true, of course, that the school is only one of society's institutions concerned with the acculturation of the young. The home, religious institutions, the media, and government assume vital and, in the case of the home, primary responsibility in this process. The problem for teachers and administrators is that the lines of responsibility and accountability are blurred, or in some cases do not exist. We have moved from a time when the school was seen solely as a place where students were taught to read and write to a time when schools are multipurpose institutions that provide for career preparation, offer instruction in home and family living, and sponsor many kinds of extracurricular activities. As an accompaniment to this increased role, schools and are often blamed for many of the ills facing today's world.

Today one may not speak about "the home" or "the church" as though they were identifiable, unitary entities. In the United States there are a multiplicity of religions with differing agendas, beliefs, and practices. What might be acceptable, even desirable, to one would be repugnant to another. This diversity is multiplied when one speaks of the home. Homes differ in make up, in what constitutes a "family," in how much money is available, in power relationships, in values, in race, in ethnicity, and on and on. Like snowflakes, no two families are alike.

While this diversity is inevitable and even desirable, it does pose problems for the school and for the individual teacher in the school. While it is well and good to say that parents should provide their children with information about, and healthy attitudes toward, their sexuality, the fact remains that many cannot and will not do this. Children who are read to from infancy, who have a wealth of print and nonprint educational materials available, who travel and are exposed to a wide variety of educational stimuli, usually come to school better prepared for the tasks that school presents. But many do not have these advantages. It is a fact that the most powerful variable in determining school success in the United States today remains the socioeconomic status of the parents.

One of the most perplexing tasks facing any teacher is how to accommodate this diversity. How much and what kind of allowance should be made for the student who must work in order to remain in school? Whose values should be taught? What affirmative actions, if any, should be taken to make up for past discrimination? What effect does the teacher's own cultural history have on her approach to teaching?

Edge City is in some ways a microcosm of our larger culture. This case introduces you to the homes of several of the students in the district's secondary schools. What accommodations should teachers make for the differences in these students' out-of-school experiences?

■ *Socioeconomic, Ethnic, and Cultural Differences*

Summer is hot in Westland. You can never be sure of what *kind* of hot, though. Sometimes it is 98 degrees with 55% humidity, a New Orleans or a Savannah hot. Or it might be 105 degrees with 15% humidity, a Santa Fe or a Las Vegas hot. Regardless of what kind of hot it is, when the first cold front comes through in late September or early October with its breezes whistling through the post oak and elm, the relief manifests itself in various ways. Dogs jump higher, bark more, and run faster; smiles replace frowns; and dreams that withered along with the roadside grasses in August suddenly spring back into consciousness, enlarged and suddenly attainable.

That front came through Edge City late last evening and now, at 7:15 on the morning of October 9, is working its magic on families in all parts of the town.

Raphael

Conchita Aquilar is preparing breakfast for herself and her four children. The kitchen windows are open to let in the cooling wind that is still blowing from the north. When she comes into the kitchen from the bedroom that she shares with her two youngest children, she stands for a moment in front of the screen door and inhales deeply. A smile almost creases her lips. The two youngest girls, **Maria** and **Alecia**, are sitting at the kitchen table and are squabbling over which one is going to get to wear the big red bow to school today. **Anita**, her nineteen-year-old daughter, has just left for her job in the tractor plant, and **Raphael** wanders into the kitchen from the small living room where he slept.

(*In Spanish*) "Don't I have any clean jeans?" he asks. "I wore these yesterday and the day before."

"I told you last week when you came in with the leg nearly torn off your pants that you were down to your last three pairs," **Conchita** says resignedly. "If you want some more clothes you are going to have to get them. I tell you and I tell you that you need to get yourself a job in the afternoon and on the weekend to help out around here. They are looking for a full-time stock boy at Piggly Wiggly. **Mr. Miller** told me he would hire you if you quit school and went to work full time. He pays four and a half dollars an hour, and you could work at least fifty hours. That's over two hundred dollars a week."

"And I told you that I can't quit school," **Raphael** responds. "They got laws that say you have to go to school."

"Those laws are for them, not for us," his mother argues. "If you didn't show up over there nobody would ever say a word."

It is obvious that this is not the first time this conversation has taken place. Many of the Hispanic boys **Raphael**'s age have, indeed, left school, even though only a very few of them have jobs. They hang out together at the park and on the K-Mart parking lot.

"Just wear those one more day," **Conchita** says. "When I get home tonight I will wash them."

The half smile has long since left her face, and **Conchita** swears softly as she glances up at the clock on the stove and realizes that she will have to rush to get to her job in time. **Raphael** is not smiling, either, as he slams the door behind him, leaving without eating any breakfast at all. But as he walks along the sidewalk toward the Seven-Eleven where he plans to buy doughnuts and coffee, the coolness of the fall morning has its effect and he begins to whistle softly to himself.

Clarise

That same coolness surrounds **Buster Gerrard** as he walks from the barn back to the farmhouse. He has just finished milking the small dairy herd that is his principal means of income. He sits on the back steps and removes his boots before entering the kitchen, where his wife, **Clara**, is preparing breakfast for him and their two children, **Clarise** and her younger brother, **Ethan**.

He walks through the door into the shabby living room and calls from the bottom of the stairs that lead to the upstairs bedrooms. "You kids git on down here. You're gonna miss the school bus and I ain't about to take you into town agin."

He turns back and sits down at the kitchen table, and **Clara** pours a mug of coffee and puts it down in front of him. This is followed moments later by a plate containing eggs, bacon, and grits. **Buster** immediately begins eating.

Clara, with a sigh, goes to the stairs and calls.

"**Clarise**, **Ethan**, you'all come on. It's getting late."

As she turns back toward the kitchen, fourteen-year-old **Ethan** comes tearing down the stairs and past her into the kitchen where his father is finishing his breakfast. Moments later, **Clarise** saunters into the room. They both sit down and start eating the food that **Clara** places before them. Neither of them has spoken.

Clarise has on a plain brown skirt and a stiffly starched white blouse. Her honey-blonde hair hangs all the way down to the small of her back. She wears no makeup, no jewelry, no nail polish, no body powder or perfume. She does not look at her mother or father as she eats. As soon as she finishes she gets up and walks out of the room, picks up a small satchel, an English textbook, and a notebook, and continues on out of the house.

She hurries down the dirt road and around a bend in the road, then stops, puts the books down, and reaches into the satchel. Lipstick, powder, rouge, and perfume are quickly applied. Just as she is putting the last touches on her makeup **Ethan** rounds the bend.

"You know what they're going to do to you when they catch you!" he says to her.

"If you keep your mouth shut they won't catch me," she replies. "They're so busy going to church and reading the Bible they don't have any idea of what's going on around them. Besides, it's too pretty today to think about getting caught."

Nanci The **Drakes** live in a four-bedroom, three-bath, ranch-style brick home on Idiot's Hill, a quiet, tree-lined section of the city just west of downtown. The area got its unofficial name from the locals, who said years ago when the subdivision was being developed that only idiots from the college would pay that kind of money for a quarter-acre lot. **Adam Drake** bought the house from its original owner eleven years ago when he was hired by the sociology department of the University. He was the first black professor in the department, and at that time, the first black homeowner in this section of Idiot's Hill. In the intervening years, two more African-American families have moved within four blocks of the **Drakes**. The **Drake** family consists of **Adam**, his wife **Hilda**, a twenty-year-old son who is in his sophomore year at Georgetown University, an eighteen-year-old daughter in her senior year at Edge City High, and **Nanci**.

Hilda has prepared the family's breakfast on the large screened porch that looks out on a spacious yard that is completely covered with post oak trees except for the space occupied by the swimming pool. Pitchers of orange juice and milk, an assortment of dry cereals and pastries, and a carafe of coffee sit on a wicker table. **Adam**, dressed for work in a gray pin-striped suit, is scooping oak leaves from the surface of the pool, and **Hilda** is standing beside him sipping coffee.

The two girls, **Deidra** and **Nanci**, come out onto the porch from the house.

Nanci, wearing a fashionable skirt and sweater ensemble, hugs herself and shivers. "I can't believe it's this cool. Doesn't it feel wonderful?" she asks as she sits down at the table and pours a glass of orange juice.

Adam puts down the scoop, puts one arm around **Hilda**'s waist, and they walk back onto the porch. "It's days like this that make you wish you didn't have to go to school, either to teach or to learn."

Each of them kisses their daughters before sitting down at the table.

Edwin   The palatial two-story house is almost obscured by the large oak trees that completely cover the spacious front yard. Located in the southwestern section of Edge City, the area couldn't be called a housing development, but the street on which the house is located contains other similar houses. They differ in design, in building materials, and in decor, but they all have one thing in common: they are expensive. The cost of the least expensive exceeds $250,000.

Edwin Zettler walks down the winding staircase from his upstairs bedroom and into the large kitchen. The full-time maid, an elderly black woman, sees him coming and begins preparing a place for him on the island counter.

"Good morning, **Lillian**," **Edwin** says.

"Good morning, Mr. **Edwin**," she replies. "You better go back up and get a sweater. We had a norther blow through here last night. It isn't real cold but it sure is nippy out there. Feels good!"

"OK. I'll check before I leave. I guess he's already gone?" **Edwin** asks.

"Yes. Your daddy left more than an hour ago. Wouldn't even wait for me to fix his food. Said something about having to find another driver. That man is going to kill himself one of these days."

"How about mother? Is she awake?"

"Yes sir. I carried her up some coffee a while ago. She said she slept better last night. Maybe you ought to go up and see her for a minute if you have time."

Carrie Zettler, who is paralyzed from the waist down, seldom leaves her room. She is also almost totally withdrawn from what is going on in the world, in Edge City, and even in her family. She spends much of the time in a chair by the window, looking out over the beautifully landscaped backyard.

Edwin knows that he should go up and talk to her but he also knows that he would feel bad when he got through. He always does. He is convinced that his mother could lead a much happier life if she would just try. He also blames his father for not making more of an effort to get her out of her room and doing something.

"Thanks, I'll do that as soon as I finish eating," he replies.

A few minutes later he walks out the door with a sweater slung over his shoulder. He walks to the brand new sports car, parked in the driveway, and before getting in, stops to put on the sweater. The weather is nippy and it feels good. He wishes he had someone besides Lillian to share it with.

Karl   "Why don't you just mind your own business? If I've told you once I've told you a hundred times—what I do and when I come home is none of your damn business anymore!"

Karl Latham lies in bed and listens to the loud, angry voice coming from the kitchen. He stayed up last night with his mother, not knowing whether to wish for his father to come home or to stay away. He knew that if he came home there would be a fight, and he wasn't sure that he could handle it anymore. The shouting and the cursing were bad enough, but he knew that he couldn't stand to see his mother hit again, and he knew that if he intervened he would end up getting hurt. Why didn't his father just go away? He and his mother could get along just fine. He would quit school and get a job. His mother wasn't allowed to work, but if the old man was gone she could, and **Karl** was sure that she would enjoy doing something other than just staying in the house all day.

He can remember when he was very small and how happy they all were. But during his early elementary school days his father started drinking more and more. He lost one job after another and with every new setback things got worse and worse at home. **Karl** really can't understand why his mother doesn't leave, except that she has always been somewhat shy and withdrawn, and now, he believes, she lives in mortal terror of her husband. **Karl** spends many hours fantasizing what he would do to his father and how he could rescue them from this situation. But even though he is sixteen years old, he is late in maturing and has his mother's small frame. His father, on the other hand, is over six feet tall and a muscular 210 pounds.

As he finishes dressing he hears the front door slam. He walks into the small kitchen where his mother is washing the dishes his father used for his breakfast.

"One of these days I'm going to kill him," he says.

The look on his mother's face stops him.

"I didn't mean that," he assures her. "But I *am* going to get us away from him somehow."

"**Karl**," his mother says with a wan smile, "he can't hurt us any more than he has already. All I really feel for him is pity. If he didn't have us, I don't know what he would do. I keep praying that something will happen to bring back the man I once knew. If he would just stop drinking, he could get and keep a job and things would be all right."

Karl has heard all of this many times before. He does not share his mother's optimism. Finishing his breakfast, he goes out the front door. Almost immediately he comes back in the house. "Have you been outside?" he asks. "It's almost cold out there. I think I had better get a jacket. Why don't you walk down to the shopping center and do some shopping or have lunch or something? It's too nice to just stay inside."

Questions for Reflection and Discussion

1. Many educators and authors of reform programs for education advocate greater parental involvement in school. Discuss this proposal in the light of the five homes in this case.

2. What are some ways in which knowledge of home conditions might aid in developing teaching strategies for the secondary school classroom?

3. How might the schools in general, and Edge City School District in particular, respond to the issue of cultural diversity?

4. What are some ways in which the schools can help students be more understanding and more accepting of students with differing cultural, ethnic, racial, and socioeconomic status?

5. One function that many have suggested is important for the teacher to perform is that of a role model for his or her students. Is this realistic in the light of the cultural diversity of the school population? Explain.

6. **Karl** has the potential of being classified as abused. What is the proper role of the school and of the teacher if evidence reveals that this is indeed the case?

Class and Individual Projects

Why Can't They All Be Alike?

Select two of the students whose home lives have been described and list facets of their culture, ethnicity, or socioeconomic status that might contribute to or adversely affect their successful participation in the program of the school.

STUDENT _____

1. _____

2. _____

3. _____

What, if anything, might the school do to improve the situation?

_____

_____

_____

_____

STUDENT _____

1. _____

2. _____

3. _____

What, if anything, might the school do to improve the situation?

_____

_____

_____

_____

▨ *I Know and I Care*

List specific ways in which knowledge of the variability in the home life of these students might help you in your relationship with them and in planning and implementing more effective instructional programs.

1. _____

_____

_____

_____

2. _____

_____

_____

_____

3. _____

_____

_____

_____

4. _____

_____

_____

_____

5. _____

_____

_____

_____

Look Homeward, Angel

Write a brief paper in which you describe those elements of your home life that have affected your ability, either positively or negatively, to successfully perform the role of classroom teacher.

Questions Based on Activities

1. After completing "Why can't they all be alike?" brainstorm additional agencies, sources, and/or individuals who might be involved in providing resources to assist in meeting the needs of economically deprived students.

2. What are some ways in which teachers and other school personnel might become more knowledgeable about and sensitive to the home environment of students?

3. Share with your colleagues specific examples of students overcoming adverse home conditions. What factors appear to be important in explaining this phenomenon?

Additional Teaching and Learning Suggestions

1. Imagine each of the students in this case having difficulty with a homework assignment. Discuss the support and help that they could expect from family members. What, if anything, does this have to say about the issue of equity?

2. In small groups, brainstorm the characteristics of a home that you think would be related to success in school. List them in order, from most important to least important. Compare your list to the research literature on the influence of the home on school success.

3. Using a still camera or a video camera, document differences in residential areas in your town, city, or school district.

4. Interview school officials and/or teachers concerning the differential behavior patterns of students coming from different residential areas in the district. Determine from the interviews what actions the school takes to accommodate these differences.

5. Interview teenagers who have dropped out of school to determine the major causes for their failure to remain in school. Compare these reasons with the literature on school dropouts.

FOR FURTHER READING

Bain, J. G., and Herman, J. L., eds. (1990). *Making schools work for underachieving minority students*. Westport, CT: Greenwood.

Craig, S. E. (1992). "The educational needs of children living with violence." *Phi Delta Kappan* 74: 67–71.

Cummins, J. (1986). "Empowering minority students: A framework for intervention." *Harvard Educational Review* 56: 18–36.

Eitzen, S. D. (1992). "Problem students: The socio-cultural roots." *Phi Delta Kappan* 73: 584–590.

Fordham, S. (1988). "Racelessness as a factor in black students' school success: Pragmatic strategy or pyrrhic victory?" *Harvard Educational Review* 58: 54–84.

Heath, S. B. (1983). *Ways with words: Language, life, and work in communities and classrooms*. New York: Cambridge University Press.

Hilliard, A. G. III. (1992). "Why we must pluralize the curriculum." *Educational Leadership* 49: 12–14.

Inkeles, A. (1968). "Social structure and the socialization of competence." *Harvard Educational Review*: 50–68.

Lareau, A. (1987). "Social class differences in family–school relationships: The importance of cultural capital." *Sociology of Education* 60: 73–85.

Levine, D. U., and Havighurst, R. J. (1992). *Society and education.* Needham Heights, MA: Allyn and Bacon.

Molnar, A., and Gliszcinski, C. (1983). "Child abuse: A curriculum issue in teacher education." *Journal of Teacher Education* 34: 39–41.

Pellicano, R. R. (1987). "At risk: A view of 'social advantage.'" *Educational Leadership* 44: 47–49.

Peshkin, A., and White, C. J. (1990). "Four black American students: Coming of age in a multiethnic high school." *Teachers College Record* : 21–29.

Price, Hugh B. (1992). "Multiculturalism: Myths and realities." *Phi Delta Kappan* 74: 208–209.

Ravitch, D. (1992). "A culture in common." *Educational Leadership* 49: 8–11.

Stone, J. C., and DeNevi, D. P., eds. (1971). *Teaching multi-cultural populations: Five heritages.* New York: Van Nostrand Reinhold.

Vandergrift, J. A., and Greene, A. L. (1992). "Rethinking parent involvement." *Educational Leadership* 49: 57–59.

Chapter 8

Can't I Learn Too?

■

MAINSTREAMING
THE EXCEPTIONAL STUDENT

Almost everyone would agree that the most effective teaching takes place in a one-on-one or tutorial situation. In other words, the ideal teacher–pupil ratio is one to one. Except for some exceptional situations such as private music lessons, some special education instruction, and remedial tutoring sessions, this ideal is seldom achieved in a public school setting. The more common ratio is in excess of fifteen or twenty to one. One solution to the instructional and management problems created by the diversity of students found in these classrooms with many students is to make sure that each class is composed of students who are alike in ability, interest, and motivation. Unfortunately—or fortunately, depending on your point of view—"homogeneous grouping" has proved to be an elusive goal. Some would also argue that in a culturally diverse, democratic society it is an inappropriate goal.

As our society has become more sensitive to the implications of the racial, ethnic, and cultural differences in our population, it has demanded that our schools take these differences into consideration in what and how we teach. Bilingual education and multicultural awareness programs, as well as the mainstreaming of special education students, are all examples of legislative mandates that encourage schools to be open and accessible to all children.

An individual may be totally in accord with the implied goals of these programs and yet recognize the special problems that the implementation of such programs may present to classroom teachers. How much time should a teacher spend with newly arrived Hispanic students who have minimal skills in the English language? With an extremely bright student who learns much faster than her classmates? With a multiply handicapped student who cannot speak, read, or write his response to a question? What special financial and organizational problems do these students present to a district? How do the exceptional children and their parents react to the different proposals for integrating them more fully into the life of the school?

This case describes a series of events that accompany the mainstreaming of a multiply handicapped student into three "regular" high school classes. **Sarah Tompkins** is a sophomore and has, until this year, been confined to the district's special education classes. This year, at the urging of the high school counselor, **Mr. Kelly**, and her parents, she is being mainstreamed into **Ms. Mason**'s political science class, **Mr. Simpson**'s computer education class, and **Miss Richland**'s sophomore English class.

■ Mainstreaming the Exceptional Student

"Thank you all for coming here on your planning periods," begins **Paul Kelly**, the counselor. "What I'd like to do today is tell you a bit about **Sarah Tompkins**, who will be mainstreamed into your classes this year. **Sarah** is what we would now call an exceptional student; you might be more familiar with the term 'disabled.' As a result of a childhood swimming accident, she has minimal use of her legs and is confined to a wheelchair. She has been diagnosed as learning-disabled. This disability primarily affects her reading. The wheelchair should present few problems, since our buildings and classrooms have all been renovated or designed to accommodate them. The learning disability is something we all should be concerned with, because of the amount of reading that students are required to do in high school. Let me tell you that **Sarah** is a good student; her IQ is average, but the disability causes her to not process the printed text exactly the way other students do. As a result, she reads at a slower pace and may have trouble comprehending the material the first time around. She may, at times, seem inattentive, but can be redirected back on task. She also has to listen very carefully to oral presentations, whether it be a lecture, directions, or an assignment; as a result she may need to hear things repeated. So her situation is not terribly drastic, but it is one that we all need to take into consideration when working with her. I guess at this point I should try to answer any questions you may have."

Ms. Mason is first to speak. "From what you've said, **Sarah**'s situation, other than the wheelchair, doesn't seem to be so much different from some of the other students that I deal with in class. But what can I do to help her? Remember, I have perhaps twenty other students to deal with that period."

"I don't recall that you have any other learning-disabled students in your classes, but you are somewhat right; **Sarah** will remind you of some students who may seem slow when it comes to reading or confused when you give directions. What you need to remember is that this doesn't mean that she is not trying or that she can't understand. What it should indicate to you is that you need to make some adaptations in your instruction, especially when you deal with her. For instance, you might overcome the potential problem with directions or assignments by writing them on the board in addition to giving them orally. Then you can redirect her questions to those written instructions instead of constantly repeating yourself. Actually, that's a rather good technique for teachers to use with any student."

Miss Richland looks concerned and asks, "But what about the reading? You know we read several novels this year; how is she going to handle that?"

"Yes, that is a problem and there are a number of ways to approach it. Because **Sarah** is formally diagnosed as learning-disabled, she is eligible for assistance from a number of sources. One source provides books on tape for individuals in her position; this organization will, with enough lead time, put textbooks on tape for students to use throughout a school year. I'm sure most of the novels that you read are already on tape, so **Sarah** simply needs to contact this organization and request the materials. **Ms. Mason**, we might want to provide **Sarah** with the name of the textbook for the political science class so that she can look into requesting it as well. In addition to using the Books on Tape connection, **Sarah** can use a tape recorder to keep track of lectures or discussions, and we might try pairing her with one of our senior peer tutors so that she can engage in some extra discussion or conversation about the novels and other assignments."

Mr. Simpson has been silent throughout the meeting, but now he suddenly interjects, "Well, you've got the reading and lecture business covered, but how will her problem affect keyboarding skills? Is she going to have trouble reading the keys or what?"

"It is quite possible, **Mr. Simpson**, that **Sarah** may make errors in her keyboarding. After all, it is a class in learning and she will be learning to keyboard like the rest of the students, but you may also notice that she will reverse letters occasionally. What we need to do is make her aware of how the word or words *should* look and just call her attention to it when she makes the inversion. She may or may not be slower in learning to keyboard. Her parents have told me that she does have a computer at home, so she will be able to practice any exercises or assignments that you may give. I think what we all need to remember is that **Sarah** is not a slow or retarded individual; as I stated before, her IQ is average and she is more than capable of doing satisfactory work in any of your classes. None of you need be worried about her causing tremendous problems in your classes; you simply need to be aware of her situation and, when the time calls for it, provide the necessary support. For instance, we need to remember that this will be **Sarah**'s first experience in classes other than special education, so she might be a bit apprehensive or nervous. Perhaps you might offer a bit more attention or reassurance in the beginning—at least until she begins to feel more comfortable with the regular classes.

"Oh, one other bit of information—the secondary special ed teacher, **Ms. Dillon**, is available to provide you with advice and assistance. **Sarah** will be working with her when she is not in one of your classes, so if you need some help, please ask **Ms. Dillon**. She may also end up consulting you about **Sarah**'s progress, because she is responsible for completing the IEP or individualized education plan required by the Westland Education Agency. I'm confident that if all of us work together we can make this a workable situation for everyone, don't you think so?"

As **Sarah**'s parents sit waiting for the three teachers to arrive, **Mr. Kelly** tries to reassure them that their decision is a good one.

"I'm sure that **Sarah** will be much better off attending classes with the rest of her friends. We find that when we isolate students too much it has a tendency to promote withdrawn behavior and discourage normal socialization. Besides, she's a bright girl, and there is really no need for her to be confined to the regular special ed classes. You know there is really no reason that she should not consider going to college to pursue a career of her choice. Has she spoken to you about going to college?"

Sarah's father begins to squirm in his seat as he confronts **Mr. Kelly**. "Are you serious? We have never really thought about letting **Sarah** go to college. We—I mean, she's in a wheelchair and she has that disability; what kind of career could she have? I've made financial arrangements to provide for her—at least I'm putting into a fund to do that. Now you're telling me that she can take care of herself. She can't do that at home now, how can she do that away at some college?"

"You know, **Mr. Tompkins**, your wife and I have discussed this issue before, when you weren't able to get away from your office. **Sarah** is just not as disabled as you seem to perceive. Mrs. Tompkins agreed that you both try to help **Sarah** quite a bit and that she might be able to do more around the house and here at school than you realize. The disabilities that she has are not insurmountable. Legislation throughout the country has mandated that public places address the needs of the handicapped. **Sarah** can go just about anywhere today and she can use public transportation to get there; she could learn to drive a car, once it has been adapted for her. A physical disability isn't the problem that it once was. Her learning disability is also something that she can learn to deal with. There are many successful people who have learning disabilities. Many people have learned to deal with their disability; **Sarah** can too! But we have got to give her the chance to try. That's why I'm so excited about your decision to let her move into a more normal high school experience."

Mr. and Mrs. Tompkins nod their heads in agreement. **Mrs. Tompkins** says, "Well, we do want to do what's best for **Sarah**. We just don't want her to get hurt, you know, with the other kids making fun of her because she can't do some things."

"I know, **Mrs. Tompkins**. But I think that **Sarah** will be just fine. She may be a bit anxious at first, but I think she'll begin to enjoy her high school years more by being able to be more like the other students. And the reason I've asked you to meet with her teachers is to reassure you both that everyone here at school will be doing all that we can to help **Sarah** when she needs it. Ah, here they come. **Mr.** and **Mrs. Tompkins**, let me introduce you to **Ms. Mason**, **Sarah**'s political science teacher, **Mr. Simpson**, **Sarah**'s computer education teacher, and **Miss Richland**, **Sarah**'s English teacher.

Sarah has been a bit apprehensive about this "big" move and expresses this in a telephone conversation with her friend, **Lissa**.

"I'm scared, **Lissa**. It'll be great being in class with you, but I'm still scared about all the other kids. People are really funny about this wheelchair; my parents practically drive me crazy worrying about oiling the wheels or if the battery is charged up enough. I don't want the kids to think I'm some kind of monster or something and I sure get tired of people acting like they feel sorry for me."

"**Sarah**, none of the people that I know think you're a monster—that's bogus. We do have some dweebs who will act dumb and say stuff. Just blow them off! Those kids even make fun of teachers who have greasy hair or wear the same outfit twice in the same week. It'll be fine once they get to know you; we'll have good times. We can go the ballgames and dances and shows and stuff—just like we do now, only then you'll know most of the kids and that'll be better. Don't you think?"

"I guess, but I'm also kinda worried about the teachers. My mom said that she met the three of them and that **Mr. Kelly** told them what was wrong with me. Mom said he was trying to help them figure out how to help me. You know sometimes I get real tired of everybody trying to *help* me. It's not like I can't do it; it just takes me longer sometimes. Anyway I heard that **Mr. Simpson** is tough; I can just see me messing up on a paper that I have to type; I'm glad that I have a computer here so I can practice."

One afternoon **Mr. Simpson** catches **Miss Richland** alone in the teacher's lounge and "unloads" on her.

"I tell you, having that wheelchair kid in my class is going to create all kinds of problems for me. You know, I've got a student teacher this time, and how can I deal with trying to get her under control when I have to worry about this handicapped kid? They sure do expect a lot from us in this district!"

"I didn't get the idea that **Sarah** was going to be that much of a problem, **Greg**. I mean, sure we might have to explain things more, but **Paul** made a good point about putting the directions and assignments on the board. That makes a lot of sense. I'm just worried that if she can't get the novel on tape from that company, that I'll be expected to read it onto a tape for her and I just don't have time for that."

"That sounds just like something the people downtown would want us to do. As if we don't have enough to do with the regular kids. You're too nice. You got to learn to get tougher or else this district will use you up."

"Oh, come on. But you know, **Paul** did mention that we would have to help with that IEP, whatever that is. I don't know anything about that, do you?"

"Typical, it's just more work. A lot more work. Work that the special ed people are supposed to do and are trying to foist off on us. I'm not doing it, that's for sure!"

At the end of class one day **Ms. Mason** asks **Sarah** to stop by right after school. **Sarah** worries about this the rest of the day and is a nervous wreck by the time she arrives at **Ms. Mason**'s room.

"Gosh, **Ms. Mason**, I know I had to ask some questions today, but . . ."

"Wait a minute, **Sarah**, you're not in trouble! I just wanted some private time to talk with you. I wanted to let you know that I will help you as much as I can, but I don't want to make you feel uncomfortable in class. So you will have to let me know when I've gone too far or when you need some additional help. I just want you to know that I'm here for you, but I don't want you to feel like you're so different from the other kids."

"Well, I *am* different and they all know that I've been in those special ed classes. Some of them act like I'm a baby or something. I'm not, you know."

"Oh, I know you're not. You did better than most of the class on that last quiz. I'm not trying to stir up unpleasant feelings, because I wanted our little talk to be good for both of us. From what I see, you seem to fit in with most of the kids. If there is anyone in my class who is bothering you so much that you can't concentrate, let me know. That's a discipline problem that I can handle. OK?"

"Sure **Ms. Mason**. It's real nice of you to try and help me learn. I like your class and I'm gonna work real hard for you."

"No, **Sarah**, actually you're going to work really hard for *yourself*!"

At lunch with **Lissa**, **Sarah** overhears some students talking.

"Man, that **Sarah** sure has those teachers under her control. Old man **Simpson** hovers over her like a mother hen. She doesn't have to think in that class. He does all the work for her. She's got an A in the bag. And **Miss Richland**, she's so . . ."

"Come on, **Jason**, she's just trying to help. Give **Sarah** a break. I'll bet *you* wouldn't have the guts to come around here in a wheelchair. Besides, she's smarter than both of us. Didn't you see her answering all the questions in **Ms. Mason**'s class yesterday? Are you jealous or what? Hey, if you want me to, I'll ask **Mr. Simpson** to stand by *your* chair tomorrow."

"See, **Lissa**?" says **Sarah**. "Did you hear **Jason**? Why are they like that? You'd think that I asked **Mr. Simpson** to do all that work for me. I'd be glad if he just left me alone. I'm the only one he ever talks to since he has **Miss Munos**, the student teacher, in there. He even told her to leave me alone because I was too big of a problem for her to handle. I wonder if he knows that *he's* the problem. Oh well, maybe he'll be absent a lot."

"I wouldn't count on it, **Sarah**. Simpson's got 'one life to live' and that's school; he's never absent. But you're right; he is weird and hanging around you, that would sure make me nervous. Isn't there someone you can tell?"

"I don't know. I have **Ms. Dillon** after lunch and she's pretty cool. Maybe she can give me some advice about how to deal with him. You know he's the only teacher that I seem to have trouble with. **Miss Richland** even came to talk to **Ms. Dillon** about getting me some books on tape, and the ones that we can't rent from that company in New York, she's gonna have one of her cheerleaders read into a tape for me. That's pretty nice. And **Ms. Mason** treats me like everyone else; I even get to sit in the back of the room and *not* by her desk. Simpson, though, he's another story."

"You better talk to somebody. I don't think you have to take that from teachers. There might be some law or something . . ."

"Oh, **Lissa** . . ."

That afternoon, **Sarah** asks **Ms. Dillon** for help in dealing with **Mr. Simpson** and with some of the other students who seem to view her as so very different from themselves. **Ms. Dillon**'s advice is to simply "be herself." She encourages **Sarah** to try as hard as she possibly can in her classes. That way her other teachers will begin to realize how good a student she really is. As far as her peers are concerned, **Ms. Dillon** tells **Sarah** to ignore the ones who make fun of her; her "real friends" won't do these kinds of things and eventually the other kids won't either.

Questions for Reflection and Discussion

1. What does **Mr. Kelly**'s conversation with **Sarah**'s parents reveal about him?

2. What does the conversation with **Sarah**'s parents reveal about them?

3. Did **Mr. Kelly** provide enough (and appropriate) information to the teachers to help them deal with having **Sarah** in their classrooms? If you were one of these teachers, what other kinds of information would be helpful to you?

4. What do **Sarah**'s conversations reveal about her feelings toward being mainstreamed? Do you think these feelings are typical of most students in the same situation?

5. As a classroom teacher, how would you have reacted to **Sarah**'s being placed in your classroom?

6. If you were in **Miss Richland**'s place, how would you have reacted to **Mr. Simpson**'s conversation?

7. What kind of help could **Ms. Dillon** give to the regular classroom teachers? (Brainstorm or use another text to help find information.)

8. To what extent should regular classroom teachers be expected to provide input for IEPs? What kinds of input should they have to provide?

9. Was **Ms. Mason** wise in asking **Sarah** to return for their private conversation? How could she have handled this situation differently?

10. How should **Sarah** handle her problem with **Mr. Simpson**?

Class and Individual Projects

What's the Plan?

Individually, with a partner, or as a group, complete an individualized education plan for **Sarah**. Use the two-page form that follows to complete this activity.

In the space below, identify any problems that you had in trying to complete the form. Then indicate how the problems were resolved.

PROBLEM   RESOLUTION

_____   _____

_____   _____

_____   _____

_____   _____

_____   _____

_____   _____

_____   _____

_____   _____

_____   _____

_____   _____

_____   _____

_____   _____

_____   _____

_____   _____

_____   _____

_____   _____

Individualized educational program. Form 1

IDENTIFICATION INFORMATION

Name _____

School _____

Birthdate _____ Grade _____

Parent's Name _____

Address _____

_____

Phone: Home _____ Office _____

_____

CONTINUUM OF SERVICES

Hours per week

Regular class _____

Resource teacher in regular classroom _____

Resource room _____

Reading specialist _____

Speech/language therapist _____

Counselor _____

Special class _____

Transition class _____

Others: _____

_____

_____

YEARLY CLASS SCHEDULE

1st Semester

Time	Subject	Teacher

2nd Semester

Time	Subject	Teacher

TESTING INFORMATION

Test Name/Date	Interpretation

CHECKLIST

___ Referred by _____

___ Parents informed of rights; permission obtained for evaluation

___ Evaluation compiled

___ Parents contacted

___ Total committee meets and sub-committee assigned

___ IEP developed by subcommittee

___ IEP approved by total committee

COMMITTEE MEMBERS

Teacher _____

_____

Other LEA Representative _____

_____

Parents _____

_____

_____

_____

Date IEP initially approved _____

HEALTH INFORMATION

Vision _____

Hearing _____

Physical _____

Individualized educational program. Form 2

Student's Name _____ Subject Area _____

Level of Performance _____ Teacher _____

Annual Goals: 1. _____
                2. _____
                3. _____

Date Initiated	Objectives	Materials	Evaluation	Date Achieved	Person Responsible

Get to Know the Student

Divide the class into groups of similar content areas. As a group, brainstorm ideas about the following:

Problems **Sarah** might have in your class
Ways you would address these problems
Additional information you might need about **Sarah**

Questions Based on Activities

1. Obtain several sample IEP forms from your observations. Compare these forms with the ones in the activities. How are they alike? How are they different? Share your findings in class.

2. Divide the class into groups of mixed content areas. Compare the findings from the activity titled Get to Know the Student. What similarities do you find? What differences do you find? How would you explain these similarities and differences?

Additional Teaching and Learning Suggestions

1. Examine the literature relating to Public Law 94-142. Discuss its provisions, implementation, and impact on the educational community.

2. Examine any additional literature that you can find on the issue of mainstreaming or inclusion. Discuss your findings in a debate format, with one side supporting the issue of inclusion and the other arguing against it.

3. Discuss the issue of inclusion with a special education teacher and a regular content area teacher. Compare your findings with those of the others in the class.

4. In your observations, talk with some students who have been mainstreamed into regular classrooms. How are their attitudes and feelings similar to **Sarah**'s? How are they different from **Sarah**'s?

FOR FURTHER READING

Armstrong, T. (**1985**). "How real are learning disabilities?" *Learning* 14: 44–47.

Brandt, R. (1990) "On learning styles: A conversation with Pat Guild." *Educational Leadership* 48: 10–13.

Brunner, C. E. and Majewski, W. S. (1990). "Mildly handicapped students can succeed with learning styles." *Educational Leadership* 48: 21–23.

Candler, A. (1983). "The differences among children with learning problems." *Education* 104: 219–223.

Evans, R. (1990) "Making mainstreaming work through prereferral consultation." *Educational Leadership* 48: 73–77.

Friedrich, D., et al. (1984). "Learning disability: Fact and fiction." *Journal of Learning Disabilities* 17: 205–209.

Margolis, H., and Tewel, K. (1990). "Understanding least restrictive environment—A key to avoiding parent–school conflict." *Urban Review* 22: 283–298.

Ohanian, S. (1990). "P.L. 94-142: Mainstream or quicksand?" *Phi Delta Kappan* 72: 217–222.

Slate, J., and Saudargas, R. (1986). "Differences in learning disabled and average students' classroom behaviors." *Learning Disabilities Quarterly* 9: 61–67.

Smith, C. (1985). "Learning disabilities: Past and present." *Journal of Learning Disabilities* 18: 513–517.

Traver, S. (1986). "Cognitive behavior modification, direct instruction and holistic approaches to the education of students with learning disabilities." *Journal of Learning Disabilities* 19: 368–375.

Walberg, H. J. (1984). "Improving the productivity of America's schools." *Educational Leadership* 41: 19–27.

Wang, M. C., et al., eds. (1987). *The handbook of special education: Research and practice.* Oxford, England: Pergamon Press.

Wang, M. C., et al. (1986). "Rethinking special education." *Educational Leadership* 44: 26–31.

Will, M. C. (1984). "Let us pause and reflect—but not too long." *Exceptional Children* 51: 11–16.

Williams, D. (1990) "Listening to today's teachers: They can tell us what tomorrow's teachers should know." *Teacher Education and Special Education* 13: 149–153.

Zigmond, N. (1990). "Rethinking secondary school programs for students with learning disabilities." *Focus on Exceptional Children* 23: 1–22.

Chapter 9

Now Just Exactly What Did I Do Wrong?

■

A CASE OF CHEATING

The way students look at school differs greatly from the way teachers look at school, from the way parents look at school, from the way taxpayers look at school, ad infinitum. That is not to imply, of course, that all students have the same perceptions—or that all parents, teachers, or taxpayers do. This is one of the characteristics of teaching that make it interesting. There is never a dull day!

The issue raised in this case has to do with how the people involved react to what the school would call deviant behavior, or misunderstood directions, or cheating. As you read about these eighth-grade girls, **Sandra**, **Janet**, and **Veronica**, try to remember your junior high school days. What would you think about what they did? When you read about the dilemma that **John Luttrell** faces, ask yourself if the way the situation is viewed by the girls has any relevance at all. You will hear how various individuals in the school setting react to the action taken by **John**. Do you agree with one of them or do you have a still different perspective?

The issue here is related to other issues in this book—issues like classroom management, cooperative learning, climate setting, and cultural differences. Questions to ask yourself as you read include: Could this incident have been prevented? What should be the overriding concern as you consider probable reactions to whatever action you take? What potential teaching opportunities exist in this situation?

■ A Case of Cheating

John Luttrell is an animated teacher. Five feet ten inches tall, 160 pounds, with light brown hair and an almost continual grin on his face, he enjoys teaching. He has fun with his students. He loves them and he loves history. His leisure reading is almost entirely devoted to biography and history. When he was assigned to Hooker Junior High after having been hired to teach at the high school, he was so disappointed that he considered quitting, but that was three years ago now, and he doubts that if they offered him a transfer back to senior high he would take it. He loves these eighth graders. They are full of life and energy, and he can see real changes occur in the short space of one year.

"OK, you people, listen up," he says as he stands in the middle of his second-period American History class near the end of the period.

The class does not quiet down immediately. He moves toward three boys who are talking to each other and lightly taps them on the tops of their heads.

"Cool it, boys—this is important."

After all of the talking has finally stopped and the students are all looking at him, he begins again.

"We've had a ball studying the Civil War. From our class discussions, from the activities that you have completed, and from my conversations with you, I think that most of you are at least beginning to grasp the phenomenal importance of this majestic, tragic period in our history. You are beginning to see how many of the issues in our country today have been shaped by that experience. Before saying goodby to the Civil War I want you to do one last thing. I want you to look at our country, the United States of America, and I want you to imagine what it would be like today if instead of the North, the South had won the war."

As he pauses, **Veronica Crouch** immediately begins to talk.

"For one thing, we wouldn't be having the Super Bowl Sunday. Buffalo would be in a different country from Dallas."

"You've got the right idea, but this is not something we are going to talk about in class. I want all of you to think about this and write me a paper."

Almost before he could get the word "paper" out of his mouth a groan went up from the class.

"Man, don't you know what all is going on this week? We wrote a big paper just two weeks ago. Let's just talk about it in class."

This outburst comes from **Maurice** and **Mr. Luttrell** walks over and puts his face right next to **Maurice**'s.

"Poor, poor baby. He's going to be overworked," he says.

He walks back to the front of the room and his face gets serious.

"Forget the con job, it's not going to work. You have the entire week to do this. I don't want a book. The paper should be at least three but not more than five pages. Obviously, you can't talk about all of the ways the country would be different, so just select the ones that you think are most important, or most interesting. We have done a lot of cooperative learning exercises this year but this one is *not* one of those. I want your own work, I want to see how and what each of you is thinking. The papers are due at the beginning of the class period on Friday. Remember your reading assignment for tomorrow."

It's Thursday night at the **Atkins** house. **Sandra, Janet,** and **Veronica** are all lying on **Sandra**'s bed chatting away. They are talking about all of the things that are of most importance to extremely bright, popular, happy young women of thirteen. All three are cheerleaders at Hooker; all are in the school's honor society; all come from homes where school is important. They are the kind of students most teachers like to have in their classes—polite, cooperative, and capable. They have several of their classes together, including **Ms. Hudgkins** for English and **Mr. Luttrell** for history.

For the moment the conversation had turned to school, and **Sandra** was saying, "Really, most of what we do in school is a drag and I can't really see much sense in it. But **Mr. Luttrell** is at least interesting. You never know what he's going to do next."

As she is speaking, a look of dismay crosses the faces of **Janet** and **Veronica**.

"Oh, my gosh! That paper is due in the morning," **Veronica** says. "I haven't thought about it!"

"Rats, I haven't either," **Janet** says. "What can we do? He'll kill us if we tell him we haven't done them."

"Have you done yours?" **Veronica** asks, looking at **Sandra**.

"Yes," she replies. "I came home on Monday and started thinking about it and just sat down and wrote it. It took a couple of hours."

"Let me see it," **Veronica** requests.

Sandra goes to the rolltop desk and picks up a three-ring binder labeled "American History." She extracts four pages and hands them to **Veronica**, who begins to read.

"Hey, this is good. Listen," she says to **Janet** as she begins to read aloud.

When she has finished reading she says, "We can use some of these ideas and write these papers in a few minutes."

Janet looks a little skeptical, and **Sandra** says, "I don't know. He did say that we were each supposed to do our own work."

"He won't ever know," **Veronica** insists. "He has five classes of American history with twenty-five or thirty students in each class. Besides, all semester long he has been talking about us being a 'community of learners'—that we are always supposed to learn from each other. We're just practicing what he preaches."

Her argument wins the day, and she and **Janet** begin composing their assignment, using **Sandra**'s paper as a guide. Occasionally they stop and the three of them talk about ways to make changes so that the papers are not identical. After an hour the work is done and they each breathe a sigh of relief.

This is one aspect of his job that **John Luttrell** really doesn't like—grading papers on the weekend. It isn't that he doesn't like grading papers. With the kinds of assignments that he gives, he often enjoys reading the papers. What he doesn't like is giving up his weekend. He has two young daughters, three and five, and he would like to be spending this time with them, but the three-year-old is taking her nap and the five-year-old is playing outside, so he is using this time so that he can finish before it gets too late. He has finished reading his first-period class's papers and has read four from his second period. A smile crosses his face as he picks up **Janet**'s paper. **Janet** is one of his favorite students. Vivacious, creative, and with a great sense of humor, she is a joy to be around. He knew that she would have an interesting paper and he is not disappointed. It is cleverly written, grammatically correct, free of errors, and well thought out. He puts an "A" on the bottom of the last page and reaches for the next paper.

Several minutes later he picks up **Sandra**'s paper. Once again he feels a sense of anticipation, knowing from past experience that he will be reading a quality paper. As he reads, a slight frown crosses his face. This sounds familiar. The more he reads, the more concerned he becomes. Finishing the paper, he begins to leaf through the other papers he has read. Coming to **Janet**'s, he picks it up and begins to reread it, comparing it to **Sandra**'s as he goes along. When he has finished, he lays the two papers aside, shakes his head and returns to his task.

The very next paper belongs to **Veronica**. This time there is no question. This paper is too much like the other two not to have a common ancestor. There is no question in his mind now that there has been considerable collaboration in the writing of these papers. He knows that the girls are inseparable but he is also totally surprised that they would plagiarize a paper or violate his explicit instructions that this was to be an individual and not a group project. His day is ruined. He will have to decide what to do.

It is near the end of the second-period class on Monday. The class has had an animated discussion of some of the policies followed during Reconstruction, and of the formation of the Ku Klux Klan in the South.

"Tomorrow we will continue this discussion, and I have a short video I want you to see. Tonight's a night off. No homework. **Veronica**, **Janet**, and **Sandra**—Please stay for just a moment after the bell. Yes, **Maurice**?"

"Aren't we going to get our papers back? I want to see what you thought about mine."

"I apologize for not giving your papers back today. You will get them tomorrow."

The bell rings and the students file from the classroom, except for the three girls. Each of them has an almost stricken look on her face.

After the last student has left **Mr. Luttrell** motions for the girls to come to him.

"I have talked to **Ms. Hudgkins**," he says. "She said that you could be a little late for your English class. Please come back here instead of going to her class the fourth period. I need to talk to the three of you."

The girls just stand, not looking at him or at each other.

"Go ahead. I'll see you fourth period," **Mr. Luttrell** says.

Each of the three girls has different classes during the third period, and therefore they have no time to talk. It is with a great deal of apprehension that they approach **Mr. Luttrell**'s classroom. **Janet** is the first to arrive, and **Mr. Luttrell** smiles as she enters the room.

"**Mr. Luttrell** I . . ." she starts to say, but **Mr. Luttrell** holds up his hand.

"Let's wait until the others get here, **Janet**," he says.

Presently **Veronica** and **Sandra** walk in.

Mr. Luttrell sits down in one of the student desks and motions for them to take the seats that he has arranged in a circle. Removing three papers from the manila folder that he holds in his hands, he says, "Girls, I've got a problem."

Before he has spoken, **Janet** has begun to cry. **Sandra** also has tears in her eyes, and **Veronica** sits white-faced and grim.

"We cheated. I know that we shouldn't have done it but we have been so busy. **Sandra** didn't do anything wrong. She wrote the paper and it was good. We should have done our own work." The words are tumbling almost uncontrollably from **Janet** between sobs.

"We didn't really cheat," **Veronica** argues. "You have always told us that we learn from each other. I don't see what was so wrong about it."

"**Sandra**, what about you? Did you let them use your paper?"

"Yes, sir. I guess I am as guilty as they are."

"Well, help me out. You have given me a problem, now help me solve it. What, if anything, should I do?"

"Could you just give us another paper to do?" **Janet** asks.

"I could, I guess. But tell you what. You girls haven't done anything like this before, have you?"

Three heads shake a negative response, and he continues.

"What is important here is that you realize what you did wrong and why you should not do it again. To me the problem is that you clearly understood what the intent of the assignment was. If you had come to me on Friday and said that you had done a cooperative paper, we would have still had a problem, but a different one. How you behave and what you believe is more important to me than what you learn about history. I think you *have* learned, and so we are just going to forget this. None of you will receive a grade on this assignment, and needless to say any other incidents like this will be dealt with in an entirely different manner. OK?"

Sandra and **Janet** nod their heads. **Veronica** sits with a defiant look on her face and starts to say something, but stops.

"I'll see you in class tomorrow. Hurry to your English class."

John Luttrell, Royce Goodwin, Darlene Doyle, and **Rose Ragsdale** are sitting in a classroom at the high school waiting for the other members of their committee to arrive so they can begin work. **John** has shared with them the incident involving the three girls in his history class and what action he took.

"You mean that's it?" **Darlene** is saying. "You're going to let them get away with cheating without any penalty at all? I really can't believe this. This is what's wrong with us today. People know that they can get away with anything. They should have gotten zeros on those papers and had to write another one."

"Aw, come on, **Darlene**. Get real," **Royce** says. "It's not a capital crime. I wouldn't have said anything at all. They're good students. It doesn't do any good to just stir up a hornet's nest about something that unimportant."

"You're just too lazy to do anything, **Royce**," **Rose** cuts in. "You have a tendency to take the line of least resistance. I'm not sure what I would have done, but what really tees me off is how you all keep talking about the fact that they're 'good' students. What the hell does that mean? What's a 'good' student? Little white, rich girls who say 'yes ma'am' and 'no ma'am'? I wonder what you would have done, **Royce**, if these hadn't been 'good' students."

Questions for Reflection and Discussion

1. Discuss incidents from your school days that reflect the problem of students copying other students' work.

2. There is considerable survey research that suggests that the incidence of "cheating" in schools is extremely high. What are possible reasons for this? Are there things that the schools might do to improve the situation?

3. **Sandra** wrote the paper, **Veronica** suggested that they use it, and **Janet** reluctantly went along. **Janet** and **Sandra** are very repentant, while **Veronica** appears to be much less so. Are the girls equally culpable? Should they be treated the same? If not, in what ways should their treatment differ?

4. **Rose Ragsdale** contends that how students are treated depends on factors other than merit. Does the concept of the "good" student imply differential and unfair treatment? How would *you* define the "good" student?

5. In several places in this case it becomes obvious that **John Luttrell** has healthy, friendly relationships with these three girls. Discuss the implications of teachers having "favorite" students.

6. In what ways did **John Luttrell** utilize this incident as a "teachable moment"? What are other ways in which he could have capitalized on this incident?

7. **John Luttrell** appears to be very "laid-back" in his relationships with the students. Examples of this relaxed behavior include tapping the boys on the tops of their heads, saying "cool it," and calling **Maurice** "poor, poor baby." What are possible advantages and disadvantages of this approach to teacher–pupil relationships?

Class and Individual Projects

It's My Turn

With which of **Mr. Luttrell**'s actions do you agree and think that your behavior would have been similar?

1. _____

2. _____

3. _____

4. _____

What things would you have done differently, and how?

1. _____

_____

_____

2. _____

_____

_____

3. _____

_____

_____

4. _____

_____

_____

What principles appear to have guided **Mr. Luttrell**'s behavior in this case?

_____

_____

_____

_____

Birds of a Different Feather

Assume that instead of **Sandra**, **Janet**, and **Veronica** the individuals involved in this incident had been three of your most incorrigible, unproductive, unreliable students—**Roger**, **Alvin**, and **Walter**.

Explain exactly how you would have handled the situation.

_____

_____

_____

_____

_____

_____

_____

_____

Explain how your actions in this case reflect your beliefs about adolescence and about the purpose of schooling.

_____

_____

_____

_____

_____

_____

_____

_____

An Ounce of Prevention

List principles that you would follow in cases of suspected cheating. Share with the class.

1. _____

_____

2. _____

_____

3. _____

_____

4. _____

_____

List behaviors that you would practice during in-class testing and other individual work to lessen the incidence of unwanted cooperation among students.

1. _____

_____

2. _____

_____

3. _____

_____

4. _____

_____

Questions Based on Activities

1. If you would have handled the incident differently, explain what you would have done and tell what you see as the advantages to your approach.

2. What principles should inform decisions made in an incident such as this?

3. Defend or refute the statement, "The same treatment is not necessarily equal treatment."

4. What relationships exist between classroom management practices and discipline procedures?

Additional Teaching and Learning Suggestions

1. Role-play the conference between **John Luttrell** and the three girls, but instead of having them admit their guilt, have them deny it.

2. Assume that **Luttrell** had followed **Darlene Doyle**'s advice and had simply given each of the girls a zero on her paper. Role-play a conversation between the girls immediately after they learn of his action.

3. Interview school personnel, teachers, and administrators to learn what their policies are when they suspect that a student has copied another student's work. If there are discrepancies in these policies, discuss the differences and attempt to account for them in terms of educational philosophy.

4. Role-play a situation in which the teacher is administering a midterm examination and it appears that one of the students is copying answers from a student beside him.

5. Get student handbooks or other printed material from several school districts and compare any statements of policy or rules related to cheating.

6. Interview several students and ask them about the incidence of cheating in their schools and their perception of the school's reaction to this behavior.

FOR FURTHER READING

Bellezza, F. S., and Bellezza, S. F. (1989). "Detection of cheating on multiple-choice tests by using error-similarity analysis." *Teaching of Psychology* 16: 151–155.

Calabrese, R. L., and Cochran, J. T. (1990). "The relationship of alienation to cheating among a sample of American adolescents." *Journal of Research and Development in Education* 23: 65–72.

Cook, J., and Gracenin, C. (1981). "When is copying cheating?" *Early Years* 12: 29–32.

Evans, E. D., and Craig, D. (1990). "Teacher and student perception of academic cheating in middle and senior high schools." *Journal of Educational Research* 84: 44–52.

Fowler, D. H. (1986). "Cheating: A bigger problem than meets the eye." *NASSP Bulletin* 70: 93–96.

Houser, B. B. (1982). "Student cheating and attitude: A function of classroom technique." *Contemporary Educational Psychology* 7: 113–123.

Kuhmerker, L. (1988). "Dialog: Mark May talks with Lisa Kuhmerker." *Moral Education Forum* 13: 9–13.

McBryde, N. M. (1987). "Realities of cheating: Preventing, not cures." *American Secondary Education* 15(4): 19–20.

Miller, H. L. (1986). "The fine line between cheating and helping." *Early Times* 17: 104–105.

Pactor, H. S., et al. (1990). "Students' ethics require new ways to cope with cheating." *Journalism Educator* 44: 57–59.

Schab, F. (1980). "Cheating in high school: Differences among the sexes." *Adolescence* 15: 959–965.

Schab, F. (1991). "Schooling without learning: Thirty years of cheating in high school." *Adolescence* 26: 839–848.

Chapter 10

Don't You Have Any Religious Values?

■

SEPARATION OF CHURCH AND STATE

Schools, both public and private, are places where values are practiced and taught. Cleanliness is preferred to dirtiness; promptness is preferable to procrastination; respect for the documents and the symbols of our democratic system is cherished. What is not clear at times is whose definition of particular values is to be advanced. For example, although most people would not argue against teaching the concept of "good citizenship," one person might believe that a good citizen is someone who questions and actively demonstrates against government actions such as the Vietnam or Gulf wars, or government's failure to adequately provide for the homeless. Another person might contend that a good citizen, especially a child or adolescent, is someone who gives unquestioned obedience to constituted authority. Two sets of parents holding these disparate views, or any of the dozens of other views between and on either sides of these positions, might disagree with particular content or methodology being taught or practiced in the schools.

Even more problematic is the place of religion in the public schools. A plethora of court cases at all levels of the judiciary have attempted to define what may or may not be done in the schools in the name of religion. A general statement summarizing these cases might assert that schools may teach "about" religion but acts of group worship may not be practiced in the schools. It must be stressed that while this may be a statement of the general tenor, there are exceptions. Some schools allow their athletes to pray before a basketball or football game. Christmas, a Christian holiday, is usually observed in the public schools. Generally, questions of religious beliefs and religious practice do not intrude into a teacher's classroom. When they do, in most cases teachers respond to the question or deal with the situation and move on to the next activity. Occasionally, however, individual parents, an organized group of parents in an individual school, or an entire school community becomes embroiled in a controversy concerning some content in the curriculum, some statement by a teacher, some outside assignment, or some other activity that they see as violating the dictum of separation of church and state or as violating some important religious conviction of the individual or the group.

How a teacher, a principal, or a school board responds to parental concerns about religious issues has important consequences for how the school is perceived and supported in the community. In this case, two high school teachers, **Mr. McKinney** and **Mrs. Rodriguez**, must decide how they are going to deal with a value-related problem that may also have religious connotations. As you read, think about similar situations you have experienced or have read about. Do you think these two teachers acted wisely? If not, what would you have done instead? Try to understand the ramifications of this controversy from the point of view of the teachers; of **Mr. Brownell**, the school principal; of **Bryan**; and of his parents.

This case describes a series of events that ensue from a previously good student's refusal to complete assignments that address issues which conflict with his family's religious and personal beliefs.

■ *Separation of Church and State*

Edge City School District has not always been known for its progressive nature, but it has consistently supported activities or programs that seem to promote higher achievement and learning among its students. Its career ladder program rewards the further education of its teachers, and so teachers regularly attend classes at the local university. Two high school teachers attended a summer institute that focused on correlating curriculum throughout the school. As a result of their participation in this institute, **Mr. McKinney**, an American history teacher, and **Mrs. Rodriguez**, who teaches biology and environmental issues, decide to experiment with correlating certain segments of their courses. Their first task is to find a common ground on which to begin.

"I really want to try this integrated approach, but we have to find a topic that we both can deal with in enough detail to warrant devoting a whole unit to—I guess about two or three weeks, don't you think?"

"Yeah, **Lisa**, we need to find some topic of substance. What do you plan to teach about during the next two grade periods?"

"You know, **Paul**, I did have one idea. I want to talk about how certain political events impact the ecological balance in the world, and there just isn't anything in the text on that, so I will have to pull together materials from newspapers and magazines. Do you have anything left to teach that might fit in with this kind of discussion?"

"Well, I do try to take my classes up to the present in terms of historical events, and the text is fairly weak once we get past the early 1980s. I wonder if . . . hey, I've got an idea. I could use the idea of wars and review the text in terms of World War I and World War II, Korea, and Vietnam, and then go to magazines and newspapers to find information on the most recent global conflicts, all the way up to Desert Storm. Can we work out something along those lines?"

"You know, we might be able to, because Desert Storm is certainly having an ecological impact in the Middle East and around the world. If I just dig a bit, I'll bet I could find enough on the impact that the other wars have had. Yeah, let's try it!"

One afternoon in a planning session, **Paul McKinney** and **Lisa Rodriguez** discuss their progress thus far.

"Well, **Lisa**, how do you think the unit's working?"

"I'm really pleased. I think the kids like the kinds of things that we're doing and are really interested in the topics and information. At least I've noticed a lot more enthusiastic participation and a much higher energy level in my students. How about you?"

"Yeah, I tell you it's sure a lot easier to teach about the wars this way. If I had continued teaching all those wars the way I had been taught, these kids would have zoned out weeks ago. I even have some kids going to the library to read some of the articles that I've recommended *and* they're not just trying to impress me, they're really interested. All except one. Have you been having any trouble with **Bryan Limb** lately?"

"Now that you mention it, yes. He's always been such a good student, always so interested and never late with a homework assignment. But you know, I haven't received homework from him in over a week. He's been absent for the last four days, so I just thought that he'd been sick and would make up the assignments later. Do you think there's a problem?"

"I can't be sure. You say he's been absent from your class for four days? That's strange, because he's been in mine, but as I look through my grade book, I see that he's missed my classes, but only on days that I'm collecting work. Do you think we should look into this thing any further?"

"Yes, I certainly do! He's too good a student to let fall by the wayside. He was my aide for part of last year and until now we seem to have had a good relationship. Why don't I just talk to him and find out if there is a problem? You know—let him know that we're concerned and offer to help if he has a problem."

"Fine. Just keep me informed and let me know what you do. In case he continues to miss your class, do you want me to send him down to see you when he shows up in mine?"

"No. Let me catch him during homeroom or in the hall. I don't want to make a big deal of this. I mean, he's not failing yet, but he could be getting into serious trouble if things are not corrected soon. I'll let you know as soon as I catch him."

Later that week **Mrs. Rodriguez** sees **Bryan** after school in the parking lot.
"**Bryan**, got a minute?"

"Uh, sure, **Mrs. Rodriguez**. What can I do for you?"

"I was just concerned, **Bryan**. You've missed a lot of class these last two weeks and you're really falling behind in your homework grades. Are you ill?"

"Well, um, yeah. I've had this flu thing and all I seem to do at night is want to sleep. I can't eat too much and I just go to bed when I get home. I can't seem to make myself do any homework."

"**Mr. McKinney** said that you had missed his classes and had fallen behind in his class, too. The only problem we have is that the days that you miss my class you are in his class and the days that you have missed his class you came to my class. Is there something that we're not aware of here, **Bryan**?"

"Yeah. I have a real problem with what we're doing in your classes now. I mean a *real* problem. I mean, I can't do those classes. I mean, I'm not *allowed* to do those classes."

"What do you mean 'not allowed,' **Bryan**?"

"I mean that my parents don't want me to study the stuff that you're doing in class now. I had the same problem a couple of years ago in **Mr. Shapler**'s class when we studied evolution. My parents said I couldn't study that, and I had to sit in the office while the rest of the class did the work. That was embarrassing. I thought that I could slip by with a couple of missed homeworks. Is it really that big of a deal?"

"I just don't understand why your parents don't want you to study the kinds of things that we're studying in class these three weeks."

"We belong to a religion where there are certain kinds of things that you're not allowed to talk about. Evolution is one of them, and all this business about war and ecological crimes is another. I guess you could call my dad a pacifist. I tried to do some of the homework, but my mom and dad really take an interest in what we do at school, and when he saw me working on that stuff about the problems being created by the oil fires from Operation Desert Storm, he just blew up. He threatened to call you and **Mr. McKinney**, but I told him I would handle it. I guess that I really didn't handle it, did I?"

"Well, you handled it in a way, but there must be another way to deal with this. I don't want your good grades to suffer, and I really thought you found this unit interesting."

"**Mrs. Rodriguez**, there isn't any other way. And it's not a question of whether I like the stuff. My parents have forbidden us kids to deal with certain things, and as long as I live with them, I gotta do what they say. They're real strict about that. If you want, I can bring a note from my mom or dad. I just don't want them to call up here again. That was so awful the last time. What can I do?"

"**Bryan**, let me think about this and talk with **Mr. McKinney**. I'll get back with you, but you must promise that you'll come to both classes, even if you don't do the homework, until we figure out some course of action. Deal?"

"Yeah, I'll be in class. Thanks, **Mrs. Rodriguez**."

That night **Lisa Rodriguez** telephones **Paul McKinney** and relates the details of her conversation with **Bryan**.

"**Lisa**, do you really believe that his parents have forbidden him to participate in our classes? I find that *very* hard to believe."

"I just don't know, **Paul**, I have heard of situations where parents got involved in the curriculum. You know, where they tried to censor certain books that were used. I remember a case that we talked about when I was still in undergraduate school in Austin. A fairly new teacher, up north somewhere, had her class reading *The Lion, the Witch, and the Wardrobe* by C. S. Lewis. The class was really enjoying it, and this teacher, who was really into reader response, decided to capitalize on their interest. She let them write plays about the novel and got permission from the school authorities to perform the plays in a schoolwide assembly. I think it was on the night of dress rehearsal when the principal came into the auditorium and told the teacher that the students would *not* be performing their plays and that she could *not* continue their study of this novel. No explanation, nothing. Just that they were to stop the play rehearsal and study of the novel at once.

"The next day the teacher was called into the office and informed by the principal that an angry group of parents had stormed into his office the day before and demanded that he fire the teacher who was teaching their kids about the devil and witchcraft. These parents had heard the children rehearsing and made the assumption that the novel was about witchcraft, and that instruction in the novel was instruction in witchcraft. The parents were very adamant in their demands. Well, the teacher did discontinue her study of the novel, but her contract was not renewed the next year, *and* a community group was formed to approve of all literature to be used in the district's schools. I sure don't want this situation with **Bryan** to escalate into an incident like that!"

"I hardly think that will happen, **Lisa**. The people in this district are more intelligent than that. I still think **Bryan** just doesn't want to do the work, for some reason. Maybe he's got a new girlfriend or something, but for some reason he's not the same **Bryan** we think we know. What we need to do is decide how to handle the fact that he's not coming to class and not doing the homework. If this were any other student, what would you do?"

"But, **Paul**, the point is, **Bryan** *is not* just any other student. He's probably got the highest grade in my class up until this point. If you had seen him and heard him talking, you might be more convinced. I honestly don't think he's lying, but I sure don't know what to do if he isn't. I just can't see failing him."

"All right, then, we have to do two things. First, find out if what he's telling is the truth. And second, if it *is* the truth, we have to figure out what we're going to do about his grades. But if he's *not* telling the truth, we also need to decide what to do about the absences and missing grades, *and* I think that we need to agree that we will both do the same thing. I sure don't want to come out of this situation looking like some kind of monster teacher or something! So what do we do?"

"I really don't know, **Paul**. Do we talk to **Mr. Brownell** or perhaps **Mr. Kelly**? I don't know if this is a situation for the principal or the counselor. Or should we just contact his parents? And if we contact them, what do we say about how to handle their son's Biology and History grade this six weeks? What a hassle! I'll tell you what, let's think about this tonight and talk tomorrow during planning period. Whatever we do, we have to do it soon, and I have a feeling that it could be a very involved solution."

The next day, **Lisa Rodriguez** decides to discuss the situation with the counselor, **Mr. Kelly**, who offers to contact **Bryan**'s parents and let them know how the situation is impacting his performance in both classes. After talking with the parents, **Mr. Kelly** strikes a deal with both **Mrs. Rodriguez** and **Mr. McKinney**. Because the parents are so vehemently opposed to their son's participation in this unit of study, both teachers agree to let **Bryan** make up the missed assignments by creating a more conventional, but less interesting, series of tasks to be completed in the library during the periods he is scheduled for their classes.

Questions for Reflection and Discussion

1. Discuss the issue of parents refusing to allow their children to participate in school activities. How do you feel about this? Where does parental control stop and the teacher's begin?

2. Discuss the role that parents and/or the community should play in curriculum development.

3. If you found yourself in a situation similar to either **Mrs. Rodriguez**'s or **Mr. McKinney**'s, what would you have done?

4. Try to imagine yourself in **Bryan**'s situation. How would you have reacted or acted?

5. Try to recreate **Mr. Kelly**'s conversation with **Bryan**'s parents.

6. Think about how this issue was resolved. How appropriate was the resolution? How else could it have been resolved?

Class and Individual Projects

Now What?

Identify the series of problems that **Mrs. Rodriguez** and **Mr. McKinney** had to deal with in this case. Indicate how they resolved the problem. Then speculate how you might have solved the problem differently.

PROBLEM 1 _____

    Their solution _____

_____

    Your solution _____

_____

PROBLEM 2 _____

    Their solution _____

_____

    Your solution _____

_____

PROBLEM 3 _____

    Their solution _____

_____

    Your solution _____

_____

It's All Pieces of the Same Cloth

Divide into groups of mixed content areas. Select a common but current topic of study and then brainstorm information from each of your content areas that would relate to the topic. Speculate on different ways in which you could integrate these topics of study into your content area instructional units.

TOPIC _____

CRITICAL INFORMATION _____

_____

_____

_____

_____

_____

_____

_____

_____

WAYS TO INTEGRATE _____

_____

_____

_____

_____

Questions Based on Activities

1. Reflect on your classes in high school. Did any of your teachers ever work together on correlated or integrated lessons? How did these lessons work? Did you and your classmates like them? What was your reaction to them? Why did you feel this way?

2. Think about your answers to the activity titled "Now What?" Were you surprised by the problems you found? How do you feel about the way they were handled? Discuss the rationale behind your alternate solutions.

3. Besides the problems you identified in the "Now What?" activity, what other problems might have confronted **Mrs. Rodriguez** or **Mr. McKinney**? What prevented these problems from actually occurring?

Additional Teaching and Learning Suggestions

1. Research the topic of correlated/integrated curriculum. Report your findings to the class.

2. Find a school or group of teachers who use a correlated approach on a regular basis. Talk with the involved teachers about (1) how they decide on topics, (2) how they plan, (3) specific concerns they have for instruction and/or evaluation. Share and compare your findings with the rest of the class.

3. Using the information from the "It's all pieces of the same cloth" activity, create a unit of instruction that is correlated or integrated across a number of content areas. In creating this unit, be sure to provide (1) objectives for each content area, (2) any necessary content material, (3) procedures for instruction, and (4) guidelines on how evaluation of the unit will be conducted.

4. Interview several teachers and administrators about situations where they have experienced a conflict between parents and the school over religious issues. Find out what prompted the conflict and how they worked to resolve it. Share your findings with the class.

FOR FURTHER READING

American Association of School Administrators (1986). *Religion in the public schools.* Rosslyn, VA: AASA.

Benninga, J. S. (1988). "An emerging synthesis in moral education." *Phi Delta Kappan* 69: 415–418.

Crockenberg, V. (1990). "In the courts: Teacher judgement concerning controversial issues." *Teacher Education Quarterly* 17: 97–100.

Daly, J. K., and Roach, P. B. (1990) "Reaffirming a commitment to academic freedom." *Social Education* 54: 343–45.

Evans, C. B. (1991). "The bias-free classroom. Learning environments must embrace diversity of students." *Vocational Education Journal* 66: 22–23.

Gates, B. (1991). "Religion, morality and education—constitutionally incongruent?" *Journal of Moral Education* 19: 147–158.

Jenkinson, E. (1986). *The schoolbook protest movement: 40 questions and answers.* Bloomington, IN: Phi Delta Kappa Educational Foundation.

Jenkinson, E. (1988). "How an imaginary movement is being used to attack courses and books." *Educational Leadership* 46: 74–77.

Kirschenbaum, H. (1992). "A comprehensive model for values education and moral education." *Phi Delta Kappan* 74: 771–776.

Kohlberg, L. "The cognitive-developmental approach to moral education." *Phi Delta Kappan* 66: 670–677.

Meyer, J., et al., eds. (1975). *Values education: Theory, practice, problems, prospects.* Waterloo, Ontario: Wilfred Laurier University Press.

Provenzo, E. F. (1990). *Religious fundamentalism and American education.* Albany: State University of New York.

Raths, L., et al. (1966). *Values and teaching: Working with values in the classroom.* Columbus, OH: Merrill.

Schott, J. C. (1989). "Holy wars in education." *Educational Leadership* 47: 61–66.

Simonds, R. L. (1983). *Communicating a Christian world view in the classroom.* Costa Mesa, CA: National Association of Christian Educators.

Smith, E. (1972). *Religious liberty in the United States.* Philadelphia: Fortress Press.

Spiro, D. A. (1989). "Public schools and the road to religious neutrality." *Phi Delta Kappan* 70: 759–763.

Chapter 11

Whose Paper Is This Anyway?

■

STUDENT RIGHTS AND RESPONSIBILITIES

In recent years, students have increasingly begun to challenge the authority of school officials to exercise control over issues, activities, or behaviors that they feel are really protected under the Constitution of the United States. This challenge has repeatedly created problematic situations for the school officials who are ultimately charged with maintaining effective operation of the school system. While not wanting to discourage creativity and involvement on the part of students, they nevertheless feel a responsibility to exercise the control necessary to preserve the effectiveness of their schools.

One source of considerable conflict has involved schools' attempts to regulate the content of student publications. In general, recent court rulings have relegated the "burden of proof" to the school district, which must show that it has acted fairly and that its action is necessary for maintaining order in the school or district. Increased student awareness and activism continue to make this an area of on-going concern and conflict for school officials. For some districts the response has been to abandon many worthwhile student-centered activities simply to avoid potential problems.

This case describes a series of events surrounding a high school newspaper faculty advisor's censorship of what she believes to be a potentially offensive editorial and cartoon. **Denise Ellis** has been the sponsor of the *Hilltopper* for over ten years and has yet to encounter a case for total censorship. Now she is faced with some student-authored material that is highly sensitive and must deal with a potentially volatile situation.

■ *Student Rights and Responsibilities*

Denise Ellis is fifty years old and proud of her graying hair; she is also quite sure that her quotient of gray hair is just about to multiply several times over. She has always known that this day would come, but this time she has been caught unaware. Before her is the final copy for this month's *Hilltopper*. As sponsor of the high school newspaper, she usually finds that reading the final copy is one of her easiest tasks; she rarely has to make any changes and actually looks forward to reading this copy before anyone else. This time, however, she is sickened by what she sees on the editorial page. The first thing to catch her eye is the cartoon. The staff artist, **Daniel Jacobs**, has outdone himself. He is a good sketch artist and this time he has created an unmistakable likeness of **Reverend Matheson**, the Baptist minister. That in itself might offend a few people, but the fact that the cartoon depicts **Matheson** spread-eagled across a young girl on an operating table in an abortion clinic while shouting "Repent, you sinner! Bring your bastard children to our congregation. We'll tell you how to collect food stamps and AFDC. Just make sure you drop the change in the offering."

The accompanying editorial, although not quite as vivid, is equally shocking. It definitely expresses a pro-choice position and provides lots of detail about various cases in which local girls have been denied, for one reason or another, the option of having abortions. It goes on to describe their present horrid living conditions and miserable existence. It then relates how various church officials have mistreated these girls and rejected their pleas for help. It closes by describing a situation far worse than what she remembers seeing on the news clips about the famine and rioting in Somalia. This, the writer asserts, is the future for our country if we continue to deny the freedom of choice to our citizens.

Denise knows the copy can't go to print with these two pieces in it. She is definitely offended by the editorial and cartoon, but that is to be expected. She was raised to be a staunch Catholic and her beliefs about abortion are known. She doesn't get involved in local movements or protests, but she has repeatedly tried to support her beliefs with logical reasoning. She thinks that her students appreciate and understand these discussions and, most of all, respect her beliefs, just as she has tried to do with theirs. But even this rather controlled liberal attitude will not permit her to allow the students to become embroiled in the controversy that is sure to follow the publication of this editorial page. **Clifford Handley** has to be behind this!

As **Clifford** saunters down the hall to **Miss Ellis**'s room, he smiles. She had told him on the phone that she was concerned about the nature of the lead editorial and cartoon in this month's final copy of the *Hilltopper*—so concerned that she believed that he, as editor, should pull the pieces and substitute something else. Right! Those pieces were the best things to happen to that dying newspaper. **Miss Ellis** was too old to be in charge of a high school newspaper. She had lost her grip on reality and her courage to challenge the old guard. He was tired of doing boring editorials and his father had told him that if he wanted to make it as a journalist, he would have to confront the "issues of the day." This was definitely an issue of the day; it had been spread all over the newspapers during the last presidential election campaign; everyone had read about it. He was just glad that some of his friends had told him about those girls who were denied abortions. They really made good stuff for his piece and what **Reverend Matheson** had supposedly done was great material for the cartoon. Well, **Ellis** would just have to swallow this. The copy was going to stay; his father had already said their lawyer would support his freedom of speech. He was home free.

"**Cliff**, we simply cannot run the copy as is! Now do we have anything else to substitute?"

"**Miss Ellis**, that's good stuff. It's current and it's true. Isn't that what a newspaper is supposed to do, report the facts? I say it stays; the other students want it to stay."

"**Cliff**, the other students have nothing to do with this decision. This is a high school newspaper, not the *New York Times*. You are the senior editor of this newspaper and you were placed in that position because the committee felt you had the maturity to handle all the responsibility that comes with the position. Part of that responsibility involves being able to make decisions about inappropriate copy. I'm telling you that these two pieces are inappropriate for a high school newspaper, and I'm asking you to execute your authority as an editor and pull them."

"**Miss Ellis**, can't you put your personal feelings aside and look at the issue? We study this stuff in government, it's on the news every night, some of us have friends who have gone through it. We are not little babies. High school students can stand to read this kind of stuff. If you would stop being so provincial and focus on the reality of the issue, you'd see how important it is that this paper begin to tackle issues of greater consequence than the speech club's next public debate."

"**Clifford**, I *have* put *my* feelings aside! I am considering the impact that material of this nature will have on all of the people who read it. You do realize that this paper has a much wider audience than the population of this high school. It is read by the parents of the students and by any number of community residents, including city officials. It is filed as a public document in the library and in the state capitol. It is a high school newspaper, and as the sponsor I must take responsibility for judging the appropriateness of the material. These two pieces are inappropriate for a high school newspaper because they deal with issues that may have tremendous repercussions throughout the community, including the possibility of legal action. Now, will you pull these pieces or do I have to?"

"**Miss Ellis**, my father expected you to have this reaction and he has suggested that I consult our attorney about the matter, since it involves my constitutional rights as a citizen of this country. I won't pull those pieces, so you'll have to. But if you do, I'll have to take the matter to legal counsel."

"Legal counsel!! You mean a high school senior is going to try and sue over two articles in the school newspaper? How did this maniac get in charge of the thing?"

"**Mr. Brownell**, **Clifford Handley** was selected as senior editor by a committee of individuals, who did so after careful review of his records and a forty-five minute interview. He is not a maniac, but he is extremely goal-oriented. He has mentioned a number of times that he wants to be a journalist. He has applied at a number of universities with strong journalism programs. He has also confided in several of the students that his father insists he make a name for himself while still in high school journalism. I believe that **Clifford** feels publication of these editorials will help him make that name for himself.

"I'm not even sure that he will consult the attorney. He said that his father had suggested that course of action and he indicated he would follow it if I chose to remove the editorial and cartoon from this issue of the *Hilltopper*. I do not intend to let these two pieces be published in this issue, so I felt it necessary to let you know the possible repercussions ahead of time."

"Well, **Miss Ellis**, let's do a couple of things to head **Clifford** off at the pass. First, let me see the editorial and cartoon to decide if the material is really as offensive as you believe it to be. Then, if it is, I'll talk to **Clifford** and let him know I support your decision. I will also inform him that should he choose to seek legal counsel in this matter, he might find that his rights as a student are somewhat more limited than those of an adult citizen and his case may not warrant a legal investigation. If this doesn't satisfy him, then I will call in his parents. If they have to come in for consultation, then I'll need you to present the situation to them. Is that all right?"

"I have the pieces in question right here, **Mr. Brownell**. They are offensive and really potentially slanderous to **Reverend Matheson** as well as to the girls identified in the editorial. But you decide, and let me know as soon as possible because I have a deadline to meet. The paper is to go to print tomorrow afternoon. If it doesn't, we won't have the paper for distribution this Friday, and a number of articles and advertisements are dependent upon a Friday distribution."

"**Clifford**, I've called you here to discuss this business of the editorial and cartoon. **Miss Ellis** tells me that you are refusing to pull these pieces from the current issue of the *Hilltopper*. Son, you must realize the volatile nature of the material in these two pieces. Why are you insisting on including them in the newspaper?"

"**Mr. Brownell**, that stuff isn't a lie. I can document everything that is in the editorial and cartoon. I don't understand why a school would want its students to lie about things!"

"Son, we're not asking you to lie, we're asking you to think beyond the immediate community of this high school. Do you realize that all of the people you mention or target in these pieces stand to be impacted by your article? How will these articles affect their lives? But even beyond this, you seem to have missed the whole point of having a school newspaper. This school activity is not intended to have the same mission as a daily newspaper. We are more concerned about the process of creating a newspaper; the journalism that goes into its creation. It's an opportunity for individuals like yourself to get involved in the business of journalism and discover if you have the talent or interest to pursue a career in the field. Sure you need to report valid and interesting information, but there are clearly areas where a school-related function does not need to go. This is one of those instances; the *Hilltopper* simply has no business addressing an issue of this nature. Do you understand that?"

"My dad said you all would look at things this way. He said that you all are scared to look at the reality of the situation. Well, I'm not scared. And I have the support to stand up for the things I believe in. How are we students supposed to get a real education here if you all try to keep all of the real stuff from us? I told **Miss Ellis** all of this. She's just so old that she can't understand the kinds of things that are necessary in today's world."

"**Clifford**, the question here is not **Miss Ellis**'s age or ability to relate to issues that you feel are relevant or important. The important issue is your awareness of the inappropriate nature of the material that you insist on printing in the *Hilltopper* this time. You just seem unable or unwilling to accept the fact that this material has no place in a school newspaper. As head official of this institution I support **Miss Ellis**'s decision to leave both pieces out of this issue. I will support this decision wholeheartedly and, if need be, legally.

"I have encouraged **Miss Ellis** to help you reexplore the issue and perhaps rewrite the material in a less inflammatory manner. Perhaps then the material can be published in the paper. If you believe so strongly in your material, I would encourage you to contact the local paper and pursue its publication there. You might find, however, that even in the public domain, news stories need careful documentation and support to avoid legal ramifications.

"**Clifford**, I'll let you know that I intend to contact your parents about this whole matter. My intentions are to make them aware of the situation and how it is viewed and has been handled here at school. I hope this won't present a problem at home, but I do feel that your parents have the right to be informed of all that has transpired. Do you understand all that I have said?"

"Sure. It won't present a problem at home because they understand the provinciality of this community, but it may present a problem here, because as of now, the *Hilltopper* needs a senior editor. I just won't be involved with a group or activity that directly conflicts with my beliefs."

Questions for Reflection and Discussion

1. If you were in a situation similar to the one **Miss Ellis** found herself in, how would you choose to act? Why would you make that decision?

2. What, if any, basic student freedoms were violated in this situation? What constitutes a basic student freedom?

3. What characteristics are important for the sponsor of a student organization?

4. Reflect on the argument between **Clifford** and **Miss Ellis**. Whose argument was stronger? Explain your answer.

5. How do you feel about **Mr. Brownell**'s argument concerning student activities? Do you believe his thinking is in line with that of most principals or administrators?

6. Suppose that **Clifford** had decided to take this issue to the other members of the *Hilltopper* staff. How would he have approached them? What would he have said to them? How do you think they would have reacted?

7. What do you think would have happened if **Miss Ellis** had contacted **Clifford**'s parents about this situation?

8. Suppose that, somehow, the article and cartoon had ended up being printed in the *Hilltopper*. What kinds of repercussions might their publication have prompted?

Class and Individual Projects

This Is the Limit

List four guidelines that could be used for determining the appropriateness of the content in a student newspaper at the senior high school level.

1. _____

_____

2. _____

_____

3. _____

_____

4. _____

_____

In groups of four or five, share your guidelines and select the four that you agree are the most important.

1. _____

_____

2. _____

_____

3. _____

_____

4. _____

_____

Can I or Can't I?

As a group or with a partner, brainstorm a list of student rights and responsibilities. Compare your list with those of others in the class and with outside reading sources.

RIGHTS

_____

_____

_____

_____

_____

_____

_____

_____

RESPONSIBILITIES

_____

_____

_____

_____

_____

_____

_____

_____

She's Got Her Problems, Too!

Identify some possible areas of conflict between a sponsor of a student organization and the members of that organization. Suggest a way of dealing with each of these conflicts.

Questions Based on Activities

1. Is there actually a difference between student rights and student responsibilities? If so, how would you describe the difference?

2. Reflect on your high school days. Can you remember any conflicts between activity sponsors or faculty advisors and students? Discuss these with the rest of the class.

3. Think about the areas of conflict that you brainstormed in "She's got her problems, too!" Try to devise a single or standard approach to use in dealing with these kinds of conflicts.

Additional Teaching and Learning Suggestions

1. Explore the topic of student rights and responsibilities with actual junior and senior high students. Share their comments with the rest of the class. Compare these comments with the lists you created in "Can I or can't I?"

2. Explore the literature addressing the issue of student rights and responsibilities.

3. Think about the issue of teacher rights and responsibilities. Brainstorm what you feel those rights and responsibilities are.

4. Examine the literature addressing the issue of teacher rights and responsibilities.

5. Talk with teachers, administrators, parents, and students about teacher rights and responsibilities. Compare their statements with what the literature says and with the lists that you have created.

6. Explore the similarities and differences between student rights and responsibilities and teacher rights and responsibilities.

FOR FURTHER READING

"Censorship: A continuing problem (the round table)." (1990). *English Journal* 79: 87–89.

Gill, A. M. (1991). "Renewed concern for free speech on campus." *ACA Bulletin* 75: 24–31.

Hahn, C. L., and Tocci, C. M. (1990). "Classroom climate and controversial issues discussions: A five nation study." *Theory and Research in Social Education* 18: 344–362.

Hresan, S. L. (1992). "Process methods of teaching the news writing class." *Journalism Educator* 46: 61–65.

Robbins, J. C. (1990). "Public school and public forums." *Phi Delta Kappa*, Bloomington, IN.

Rose, L. C. (1988). "'Reasonableness'—the high court's new standard for cases involving student rights." *Phi Delta Kappan* 69: 589–592.

Strahan, R. D. and Turner, C. L. (1988). *The Courts and the Schools.* New York: Longman.

Walsh, M. (1991). "Student activism forces schools to revisit free-speech policies." *Education Week* 1: 12.

Part III

Foundations: Teaching as a Profession

■

Chapter 12

Is It Really Me You Want?

■

AFFIRMATIVE ACTION IN ACTION

The purpose of this case study is to get you to think about the impact of race, ethnicity, culture, and socioeconomic status on schools, with particular emphasis on affirmative action hiring. A young African-American woman, **Cassie Hudgkins**, has come to Edge City to interview for a position as a middle school English teacher. Through her eyes you will get what are essentially two views of the same city. You will meet the principals of the high school and the middle school, and one of the teachers.

Cassie gradually comes to realize that her race is probably an important variable in her being offered the position. As you read, try to place yourself in her shoes. How do you think you would react to this knowledge? Would this be an important factor in determining whether you would take the job? How do you think a more qualified Anglo teacher might feel about your being offered the position?

Important legal and value-oriented issues are implied in this description of an event and its setting. You will be given specific tasks to help you understand the impact of the physical and human context on the profession of teaching.

■ Affirmative Action in Action

It has been a long drive. **Cassie** has never been any further south than Louisville, Kentucky, and here she is pulling into Edge City, Westland, after three days on the road.

"I must be out of my mind," she thinks. "What in the world made me think that I wanted to move this far away from my friends and family? I could get a job in Evanston, I know."

It had been a series of coincidental events that had bought her here. **Margie Brower**, a high school classmate she had not seen for years, had been home for Thanksgiving vacation. They had run into each other in Penney's and had decided to have lunch. In the course of the conversation, **Cassie** had told **Margie** that she was graduating from Ball State with a degree in secondary education and an English teaching certificate.

Margie had immediately tried to talk her into coming to Edge City to teach. **Margie** was employed in the Social Security office in Bowie, a city about thirty miles north of Edge City, but she lived in an apartment in the northern section of Edge City. She told **Cassie** that she knew there was an opening for a middle school English teacher beginning in January.

A few days after Thanksgiving, **Cassie** had received a letter from **Farley Brownell**, the principal at Edge City High School.

Ms. Cassie Hudgkins
4445 Airline, Apt. 231
Evanston, Illinois

Dear Ms. Hudgkins,

I have been informed that you are considering applying for a teaching position in the Edge City Independent School District. We do have an opening for an eighth-grade English teacher at Hooker Middle School. I am chairperson of the minority recruitment committee and I would like to encourage you to apply.

I am enclosing an application blank. Please complete this and return it immediately. If it is in any way possible for you to come to Edge City I would like to talk to you and to show you our town and our schools.

We are proud of the quality of life in our city and the quality of education we provide our students. I believe that you would enjoy living and working in Edge City. I will expect to hear from you soon.

Sincerely,

Farley Brownell, Principal
Edge City High School
Edge City, Westland, 76206

Without really considering it too seriously, she had returned the completed application and within a week she had received a phone call from **Mr. Brownell** practically offering her the job. So here she was, two weeks before Christmas, in a strange town, about to make a decision that could, and probably would, change the rest of her life.

Cassie has spent the night with **Margie**, and when she leaves the apartment the next morning she is greeted by a wind that changes the actual temperature of 38 degrees to a wind chill of 18. She hurries to her car, and after getting the engine running she studies the map that **Margie** has drawn for her. **Margie**'s apartment is in the far northwestern part of the city and is located just off of a major north–south freeway. The school, according to the map, is on the western outskirts of the town about two miles southwest of the apartment house.

Not wanting to be late for her appointment with **Mr. Brownell**, **Cassie** stays on the freeway, looking for the Hickory Street exit that will take her to the school. Several large apartment complexes line each side of the road. The area to the east is undulating and covered with what she is later to learn are scrub oak trees. Dotted among the trees are the rooftops of large, luxurious houses.

As she turns west on Hickory Street she notes that the trees abruptly disappear, and between the buildings she can see gently rolling prairie land stretching to the horizon. She passes small strip shopping centers and an occasional office building, and then almost directly in front of her she sees the campus of Edge City High School.

Pulling into the visitors' parking area, **Cassie** gets out of the car, pulls her coat closer and looks around. She is impressed with the size of the campus and with the architecture of the buildings. The school appears to consist of four modern brick buildings connected by covered walkways, some at ground level and others connecting the buildings at higher levels. The building directly in front bears a sign that says ADMINISTRATIVE OFFICES, and she hurries in to get out of the cold.

Just as she enters, a bell sounds loudly, causing her to jump. Doors open down each of the four halls that radiate from the foyer and disgorge hundreds of students, who chat and laugh as they hurry to their next class. She observes that the majority of the students are Anglo, with a substantial admixture of African-Americans and Hispanics. Clusters of black and brown seem to form in the sea of white faces as the students move up and down the halls. The halls empty as quickly as they had filled, and when the next bell rings after about seven or eight minutes, one lone student remains by his locker.

Cassie enters the glassed enclosure that is marked ADMINISTRATION and approaches the long counter. One of the women behind the counter looks up from her computer.

"May I help you?" she asks.

"I have an appointment to see **Mr. Brownell** at ten o'clock," **Cassie** replies.

"Just a moment and I will check," the woman says as she rises from her desk and moves toward a closed door marked PRINCIPAL.

Cassie is almost shocked by the appearance of the man who immediately emerges and comes toward her with his hand extended. What surprises her is his age. He appears to be no more than twenty-five or thirty. The closely cropped, thick brown hair and boyish grin add to the youthful appearance.

"Good morning. I am **Farley Brownell**. I am pleased to meet you. Welcome to Edge City and to the Edge City Independent School District. Would you like some coffee?"

"Thank you. Black will be fine."

Mr. Brownell nods to the secretary and motions for **Cassie** to come past the counter and into his office.

The office is spacious and furnished with a large light oak desk with a matching chair on the left side. Behind the desk is a leather chair. In the middle of the office is a grouping of a small couch and two chairs around a glass coffee table. A bench containing fifteen or twenty African violet plants stand by the window. **Mr. Brownell** motions for **Cassie** to sit in one of the chairs and he sits in the other. Before anything is said, the secretary returns bringing two mugs of coffee on a tray.

Cassie had not expected to be nervous because she really had not thought that she wanted to leave home, but now that she is here she wants to make a good impression and at least be offered the job.

"When did you get in?" **Mr. Brownell** asks.

"Late yesterday afternoon."

"Then you haven't seen our town. After we talk a while I would like to drive you around and show you the other schools and some of the town," says **Mr. Brownell** as he opens the manila folder he has brought with him from his desk.

"I see that you're graduating next week. Have you applied for other jobs?" he asks.

"No. I really wasn't planning on going to work until next fall. I have been working part-time for a florist in Evanston and they would let me work as much as I wanted to. I had thought about taking a couple of ESL courses and taking my time in job hunting."

"This is your first job interview, then?"

"Yes, it is," **Cassie** replies with a nervous smile.

Mr. Brownell gets up, and goes to a file cabinet and takes out a large, brightly covered envelope, which he hands to **Cassie**. "Here is a packet of information about the school district and about the community. Our starting salary with a bachelor's degree is $22,600 for ten months. We have a good package of health and dental care and life insurance. The Westland state retirement system is one of the best. Tell you what—let's look around the building and then see some of the town, and you can ask questions as we go along."

Cassie takes a last sip of her coffee and follows him out of the office. Lockers line each side of the hall they are walking down. The highly polished tile floors are totally free of debris. The woodwork looks freshly painted.

"Most of the required academic subjects—math, English, science, and social studies—are taught in this building," **Mr. Brownell** says as they start down one of the long halls. "All of the science labs are on the first floor of hall B. All of the English and social studies classes are on the second floor. As I told you on the phone, the opening is for eighth grade at Hooker Middle School, but it would probably be possible for you to move up here in a few years."

Cassie realizes that she has been very quiet ever since she met **Mr. Brownell**, but for some reason she feels self-conscious and isn't sure what to say. As they turn the corner and start back toward the office she asks, "How old is this school? It looks brand new."

"We moved in six years ago," he replies. "The high school used to be housed in a building erected in 1927. After we moved out we completely remodeled the inside of that building, and that is now Hooker Middle School. That's where you will be teaching. In fact, why don't we go on over there now? You can meet the principal and one or two of the teachers you will be working with."

As they approach his car in the parking place reserved for the principal, **Mr. Brownell** stops. He points to the large structure to the south of the building they have just left. "That's the sports facility. It has two full-sized basketball courts, handball courts, a swimming pool, offices for the PE faculty, and a band hall and practice rooms."

Pointing to the building to the north, he continues. "That's the fine arts building. It has a large auditorium, art labs and classrooms, and also some general purpose classrooms. That building behind the main classroom building is an industrial arts complex with equipment for teaching electronics, auto repair, woodworking, welding, and agriculture. The football stadium is on the campus at Hooker Middle School."

They get into the car and as they are pulling out of the parking lot **Cassie** realizes what is happening: **Brownell** appears to be assuming that he will offer her a job and that she will accept it. She also realizes that so far he has not mentioned her credentials or conducted anything like a formal interview.

They are driving east down a tree-lined street. Near the campus the houses are modest, well-kept single-family homes, mostly of brick veneer. They also pass an occasional small apartment complex. As they come closer to the downtown area, the houses are larger and older. Some are two- or three-story colonial-style buildings with massive columns. Most of them are of wood siding painted white. Large trees shelter them from the street. **Brownell** turns left onto a side street and almost immediately they approach a three-story red brick building with steps across its entire front. The brick has been recently cleaned and all of the trim is freshly painted. Etched into the concrete on one corner of the building are the words EDGE CITY HIGH SCHOOL, but a large marquee in front argues that this is HOOKER MIDDLE SCHOOL.

"Isn't this an awfully big building for a middle school?" **Cassie** asks.

"We also have some other programs here—special education, cooperative education, and our adult education classes. The third floor is mostly unused. Our other middle school is out close to the high school and it was built just seven years ago."

They get out of the car and walk up the steps. A row of six doors faces them. Pulling one open, **Mr. Brownell** motions for **Cassie** to enter the building. The first thing that strikes her as they enter is the smell. Now *this* is a school! The high school she attended was about the same age and had a very similar smell. The floors are wooden and have a deep glow from years of polish. Display cases filled with trophies line the wall on either side of the large glass enclosure labeled OFFICE.

"Is **Mr. Quincy** in?" **Brownell** asks one of the women behind the counter.

"I am expecting him back any minute," she replies. "He went down to talk to one of the math teachers last period and he isn't back yet."

"Which room? We're going to walk around the building for a while. If we miss him, tell him we'll stop back by the office."

"He went to see **Mr. Jackson**, seventh grade math. Room 202, right above this office."

Brownell thanks her and they leave. A wide staircase is at either end of the corridor. As they emerge on the second floor, a short, stocky man with snow-white hair is approaching them.

"Hello, **Martin**. I've got someone here I want you to meet. This is **Miss Cassie Hudgkins**. I think we're going to talk her into joining your faculty here at Hooker. **Cassie**, this is **Martin Quincy**, principal of Hooker."

Cassie thinks she sees a flash of anger on **Quincy**'s face, but if so he quickly recovers and greets her cordially.

"Welcome to Hooker, **Miss Hudgkins**. We think we have the finest middle school in this part of the country. Let me show you around the building."

As they move along the hallways, **Cassie** can see students busily at work through the occasional open door and hear the sounds of teachers' and students' voices behind those that are closed. **Mr. Quincy** asks her about her college and about her hometown. He glances at his watch. "We're about to get run over. Why don't we step into **Ms. Ragsdale**'s room?" he suggests. "**Ms. Ragsdale** is one of our English teachers, and her planning period starts now. You might want to ask her some questions."

Before he finishes speaking, a bell sounds and students spill into the corridor. **Cassie** did her student teaching in a junior high school but she is still amazed at the differences in size and maturity among the students. Some, especially among the boys, are obviously still children. Others are in that awkward in-between stage, and some, particularly the girls, have reached their adult size. They stand aside to allow the students to leave **Ms. Ragsdale**'s room and then they enter.

Cassie is relieved. **Ms. Ragsdale** is the first African-American teacher she has seen since arriving on the high school campus. Small, wiry, with light brown skin, **Ms. Ragsdale** appears to be in her late fifties or early sixties. She comes across the room to greet them.

"**Rose**, I'd like you to meet **Cassie Hudgkins**," **Mr. Brownell** says. "**Rose** is one of our finest teachers. We're proud of her."

"Hi, **Cassie**," says **Ms. Ragsdale** as she takes both of **Cassie**'s hands into hers. "I'm sure they say that about all of the teachers. What are they trying to hook you into?"

A look of annoyance crosses **Brownell**'s face. "We're not trying to hook her into anything, but we *are* trying to hire her to replace **Jared Davis**," he says.

Ms. Ragsdale laughs. "She's bound to be an improvement over him!"

Once again **Mr. Brownell** has to struggle to suppress a frown. "I need to talk to **Martin** for just a few minutes," he says to **Ms. Ragsdale**. "Why don't you two visit for a few minutes? Tell **Cassie** about our English program and show her the computer lab. Bring her back down to the office in about fifteen minutes. I want to show her a little bit of the town before lunch."

After the two men have left, **Rose Ragsdale** motions for **Cassie** to sit in one of the students' desks and she takes her place in another.

"Where are you from?" she asks abruptly.

"Evanston, Illinois," **Cassie** replies.

"That figures. We aren't exactly having a flood of African-Americans from around here applying for jobs in Edge City School District. The few that are graduated from Westland State are gobbled up by Bowie or Crockett. They both pay more and have benefit packages that are better than ours. Have you talked to either of them?"

"No, I haven't." **Cassie** explains the set of circumstances that has led her here. "So you see, I wasn't really job hunting at all," she concludes.

"This is not a bad district. The community generally supports the schools, and Edge City is not a bad place to live. I enjoy teaching sixth graders and I can work with the other English teachers. At the same time, there is a lot you won't be told and places you won't be shown. Here, let me give you my phone number and you can give me a call about five or five-thirty. We'll get together and I'll tell you some things about the district and show you some parts of the town you probably won't see otherwise. Come on, let me show you the administration's pride and joy, the computer lab."

They are on their way back to the high school when **Brownell** says, "I really haven't asked you much about your educational philosophy or your career ambitions, but I have seen your credentials and we would like you to sign a contract before you go back home. You may be wondering why the principal of the high school is hiring someone for the middle school. Ordinarily I would not be doing this, but because of my position as chair of the minority recruitment committee I can recommend you to the board and I am positive that they will approve you. Of course, I have shown your credentials to **Mr. Quincy** and he would be delighted to have you as a member of his faculty. We would really like to have you join our staff. What do you think?"

Cassie doesn't know what to say. She feels that she is being pressured, but everything she has seen and heard causes her to think that if she accepts the position she will be making the right decision.

"I just don't know," she says. "This is all so fast. Let me study the material you gave me and call and talk to my folks. I will try to let you know before I leave town tomorrow."

Cassie gets back to **Margie**'s apartment about two-thirty in the afternoon after lunch in the huge mall north of town. She spends an hour studying the information contained in the packet of materials **Brownell** has given her. From what she saw on her drive she is somewhat surprised to read that the population of Edge City is 12 percent African-American and 16 percent Hispanic—but then she remembers the students at the high school and at Hooker. There is also information on Bowie and Crockett, and on the shopping facilities and the cultural advantages of living in a growing, economically prosperous area.

She calls and talks to her mother, who urges her to not make a decision until she gets back home—but **Brownell** has told her that he has several applications for the position and that if she really wants the job she probably needs to decide immediately. She suddenly remembers the telephone number she has in her pocket. **Ms. Ragsdale** had sounded sincere when she suggested that she call. She will talk to her, and with **Margie** when she gets in from work. Maybe then she will be able to decide.

The phone is answered on the first ring. "**Ms. Ragsdale**, this is **Cassie Hudgkins**. What can you tell me about the school or the town that might help me decide what to do?"

"Forget the **Ms. Ragsdale**. I'm **Rose**. Where are you now?" **Ms. Ragsdale** asks.

"I'm at my friend's apartment at Windward Oaks."

"I know where that is. What's the apartment number? I'll come over and we'll talk."

Thirty minutes later she is sitting listening as **Cassie** describes the morning she has spent with **Farley Brownell**. Occasionally **Rose** shakes her head and a frown crosses her face.

"It's just what I suspected," she says when **Cassie** has finished. "You're getting the royal treatment. Tell me, how does your academic record look? Were you an outstanding student?"

"Hardly," **Cassie** laughs. "I could have done better, but my grades were just above what it takes to graduate. I was having fun in college."

"What about your student teaching?"

"That was fine, I think. My teacher and college supervisor gave me good recommendations."

"But **Brownell** offered you the job? Right?"

"Yes. I think he wanted me to sign a contract today."

"I don't know whether this will affect your decision or not, but I think you ought to know. He has a bunch of applications for that job and at least one that I know about is outstanding. **Lola Standridge** is an eighth-grade teacher in Crockett. She is an excellent teacher with about twelve years' experience teaching basically the same curriculum we have. She lives within two miles of Hooker and she is tired of that seventy-mile round trip each day. If she were African-American you would never have been contacted."

"Well, he did tell me he was chair of the minority recruitment committee, so I assumed that the fact that I was African-American was a factor. Are you saying something else? Are you having race problems here?"

"It depends on how you define race problems," **Rose** replies. "There have been no demonstrations. Nothing shows up in the newspaper. On the surface everything is great. They handle me with kid gloves and I get anything that I want, within reason. But it's all accommodation. They just want me to keep my mouth shut. They're still very much in control and they give just as much as they have to in order to keep the lid on."

She pauses and gets up and walks to the window. She turns to face **Cassie**. "Did **Farley** mention Carver High?" she asks.

"I don't remember that name. Is that the name of the other middle school?"

"No. That's the name of the district storage facility," **Rose** answered bitterly. "We had a good school and there was nothing wrong with the building. It was considerably newer than what is now Hooker Middle School. But it's in the African-American area of town. If you ask them they will tell you how smoothly the integration of our schools went in 1964. Sure it went smoothly! We lost our school, our name, our school colors and mascot, our entire identity. The same thing happened to the elementary school. I am the only teacher remaining in the district who taught at Carver. No, we don't have problems. At least not yet. They do everything right. We have an African-American on the city council. **Joshua Grant** is seventy-two years old and has just a high school education. He has owned and operated the shoe repair shop on the square for nearly fifty years, so you know he has learned to go along to get along. He's a good man and he's very intelligent, but he's not about to rock the boat. We even have an African-American on the school board. **Shirley Evans** is a professor at the university. She lives on Idiot's Hill. Nobody pushes **Shirley** around, but she is not really a voice for the minorities or the poor."

"What poor?" **Cassie** asks. "When **Mr. Brownell** was driving me around I was surprised at how well off everyone in the town appeared to be."

"Tell you what," **Ms. Ragsdale** suggests. "You don't have to leave real early tomorrow and since tomorrow is Saturday I don't have to work. Let me pick you up in the morning and show you the rest of the town."

After dinner in a small cafe that features Mexican food, **Cassie** and **Margie** talk about the pros and cons of Edge City.

"I had very mixed feelings about coming here myself," **Margie** says. "But the move was a really big promotion with considerably more money and I have never regretted it. I have friends from work and from church, and there's always something going on somewhere in the metroplex."

"What about race relations?" **Cassie** asks. "I got the definite feeling from **Rose Ragsdale** that there was a lot of tension and that things were really not anything like they appear to be."

"I haven't seen any problems. I don't know **Ms. Ragsdale** but her name keeps showing up in the local newspaper and sometimes in the Bowie or Crockett papers. She's part of a group made up primarily of African-Americans and Hispanics, with several liberal college professors. They're pushing hard for more minorities in the schools and in all city and county offices. The big thing right now that is stirring up a lot of problems is their insistence that the Edge City school district and the Edge City council go to single-member districts for school board and council elections. The town paper is pretty conservative and it has been campaigning hard against the movement. I don't understand why **Ragsdale** is discouraging you from taking this job unless she wants something else to hold over the administration's head. It all gets real complicated, but you know me. I never have been very political."

"But you haven't felt discriminated against because you are African-American since you have been here?"

"Never. I guess most of my friends are Anglo, but some are African-American and Hispanic. I go where I want to and do what I want to. I know that the African-Americans living in southeast Edge City and the Hispanics in the southeast don't have much, but then neither do the rednecks in that big trailer park east of town. Talk about a dangerous, deprived area, that's it. I really believe that it's a matter of money, not race," **Margie** explains.

The conversation gradually switches to boyfriends and hometown. It's after one o'clock before they finally go to bed.

Rose and **Cassie** are having doughnuts and coffee in a small wooden building in southeast Edge City. There are people at each of the six chrome-legged formica-topped tables. Nearly all of them are men. All of them are African-American.

"I can see what you mean about the poverty. I can't believe the contrast between what I was shown yesterday and what I've seen this morning," **Cassie** is saying.

"Wait until you see the mobile home parks," **Rose** replies.

For the next two hours they drive through the African-American and Hispanic residential areas, the industrial area, and the mobile home parks. Neither woman says anything for several minutes as they drive around the loop toward **Margie**'s apartment. Finally **Cassie** speaks. "I can't believe that children are living in some of those places. I'm glad that you took me to them but I wonder why you did. I have the feeling that you don't want me to take this job."

"That's not it at all," **Rose** disagrees. "I would like very much to have you with me at Hooker. I just want you to make your decision with your eyes open. We have problems here, and the present administration has so far failed to address them. Some of us are going to keep pushing, and you will be forced to take sides sooner or later."

"Speaking of taking sides. When I was introduced to your principal," **Cassie** pauses—"what was his name?"

"**Martin Quincy**," **Rose** replies.

"Oh, yes. **Quincy**. When **Brownell** introduced us I had the definite feeling that he was not happy with the situation. He tried to hide it but he looked angry or upset."

"I can assure you that he was both angry and upset," **Rose** laughs. "He expected to be named principal at Edge City High but the board chose **Farley Brownell** instead. He resents the living hell out of it. He also doesn't like **Brownell** hiring teachers for his school, but there isn't anything that he can do about it. **Brownell** is only thirty-two years old and has less than ten years' total experience. **Martin** has been a principal much longer than that. He has been in education all of his life and he's in his mid-fifties. You would have no problems with **Martin**, though. He's easy to work with and he doesn't make waves. He isn't aggressive but he is fair."

They have arrived back at the apartment. **Rose** stops the car and they sit there for a moment.

"I'm really confused now," **Cassie** says. "It's almost like I have seen two different places. Yesterday everything was peaches and cream. Today it seems that the district has insurmountable problems. I don't know what to do."

"That's life," **Rose** sighs. "If you do come to work here you will find many things about the school, the city, and the people that you like and things that you don't like, but I suspect that will be true wherever you go."

Questions for Reflection and Discussion

1. What are major arguments that might be made in favor of affirmative action in hiring in a public school setting? Against affirmative action?

2. Describe the demographics of your school district in terms of socioeconomic status of residential areas, racial and ethnic divisions, and religious affiliations. How do you perceive that these factors here impacted the school lives of the students?

3. What are some ways in which you would have conducted the interview with **Cassie** differently from **Farley Brownell**?

4. In what ways are race relations in your home town similar to race relations in Edge City as described by **Rose Ragsdale**? In what ways are they different? What are some of the reasons for these differences?

5. Try to find out the history of minority education in your area. How did the desegregation process work in your school district?

6. What are arguments for and against single-member district elections as opposed to at-large elections? Should the size of the community or of the school district impact the decision as to which procedure to use? Why or why not?

Class and Individual Projects

Job Hunting

Pretend that you are **Cassie** and make a list of the advantages and disadvantages of taking the position at Hooker Junior High.

PROS

CONS

_____   _____

_____   _____

_____   _____

_____   _____

_____   _____

_____   _____

What additional information would you want before you made your decision?

_____

_____

_____

_____

_____

_____

Should **Cassie** take the job? What reasons support your position?

_____

_____

_____

_____

_____

_____

_____

School Board Elections

Following is a map of the Edge City School District showing the locations of some of the sites discussed in this chapter. It also shows the racial and/or ethnic makeup of the various sections of the town. One of the issues facing the school district and the town is whether elections to the school board and to the town council are to remain as they are, with members being elected at-large, or whether the community is going to move to some sort of a single-member district plan for elections.

Assume that the decision has been made to go to a five-member school board with four members elected from single-member districts and the school board president elected at-large. Further assume that the population density is relatively constant in all sections of the city. Using a solid line, divide the district into four single-member districts as you think **Rose Ragsdale** would draw them. Using a dotted line, draw the lines as you think conservative members of the school board might draw them. Before completing this assignment you may want to reread the narrative in Chapter One.

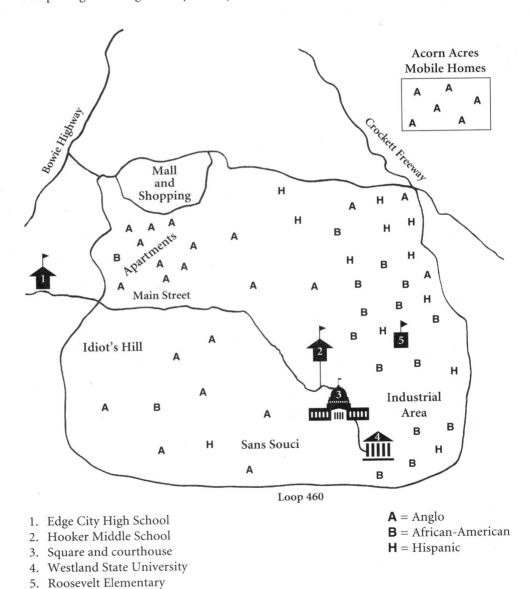

1. Edge City High School
2. Hooker Middle School
3. Square and courthouse
4. Westland State University
5. Roosevelt Elementary

A = Anglo
B = African-American
H = Hispanic

EDGE CITY SCHOOL DISTRICT

In the space below, describe why you drew the lines as you did.

_____

_____

_____

_____

_____

_____

_____

_____

_____

_____

_____

_____

_____

_____

_____

_____

_____

_____

_____

_____

_____

_____

_____

_____

_____

■ *Affirmative Action*

Pretend you are **Lola Standridge** and you hear that a first-year teacher from out of state has been hired for the position for which you have applied. You request and get an appointment with **Farley Brownell**. In dialogue form, write the major questions you would ask and/or the major statements you would make. Write in summary form how you anticipate he would respond.

Your comments and/or questions

_____

_____

_____

_____

_____

_____

_____

Brownell's response

_____

_____

_____

_____

_____

_____

_____

_____

Locate and briefly annotate court cases or legislation that would be applicable to any appeal that **Ms. Standridge** might want to make to the school board.

Case _____ Decision _____

_____

Case _____ Decision _____

_____

Questions Based on Activities

1. What are the most important factors to you in determining whether you would take a particular teaching position?

2. Schooling in America is in many ways a continuing political activity. The school board is composed of members of the community. Discuss the pros and cons of having each member of the board represent an identifiable section of the district.

3. Many aspects of school life today are being determined by court actions. These include school finance, treatment of different groups, affirmative action, student and teacher rights, and many others. Discuss the reasons for this phenomenon.

Additional Teaching and Learning Suggestions

1. Secure application blanks for teaching positions from a number of school districts. Compare the information asked for on the various forms. Discuss the reasons for the kinds of information requested.

2. Obtain brochures and other recruitment materials from school districts both locally and nationally. What aspects of the schools and community do these materials emphasize? Discuss the reasons for this emphasis.

3. Role-play an interview between the personnel director for the Edge City School District and several candidates with differing qualifications applying for a position as a teacher.

4. Research and summarize major court cases dealing with affirmative action hiring practices in public school settings.

5. Role-play a conference between **Farley Brownell** and **Lola Standridge** in which **Lola** is demanding that she be told why she was not hired for the English teaching position at Hooker Middle School.

6. Interview personnel directors or other officials responsible for hiring teachers to determine what they look for in a candidate and how they make decisions about hiring.

FOR FURTHER READING

Adams, D., and Hamm, M. (1991). "Diversity gives schools infinite learning possibilities." *School Administrator* 48: 20–22.

Bishop, G. R. (1986). "The identification of multicultural materials for the middle school library: Annotations and sources." *American Middle School Education* 9: 23–27.

Connell, J. (1986). "The work of finding a job." *The Exceptional Parent* 16: 46–50.

Crosby, F., and Clayton, S. (1990). "Affirmative action and the issue of expectancies." *Journal of Social Issues* 46: 61–79.

Dunn, C. A. (1985). "Actions speak louder than words in job interviews." *Business Education Forum* 40: 15.

Edelfelt, R. (1986). "Managing teacher supply and demand." *Action in Teacher Education*,8: 31–36.

Graham, P. A. (1987). "Black teachers: A drastically scarce resource." *Phi Delta Kappan* 68: 598–605.

Haberman, M. (1989). "More minority teachers." *Phi Delta Kappan* 70: 771–776.

Henson, K. (1987). *Methods and strategies for teaching in secondary and middle schools.* White Plains, NY: Longman.

Magner, D. K. (1991). "Wisconsin struggles in effort to recruit minority students." *Chronicle of Higher Education* 37: 27–28.

Merino, B. J., and Quintanar, R. (1988). *The recruitment of minority students into teaching careers: A status report of effective approaches.* Boulder, CO: Far West Regional Holmes Group, University of Colorado.

Pettus, T. (1981). *One on one: Win the interview, win the job.* New York: Random House.

Rabinove, S. (1990). "Major U. S. Supreme Court civil rights/affirmative action decisions." *Journal of Intergroup Relations* 17: 44–60.

Smith, E., and Witt, S. (1990). "Black faculty and affirmative action at predominantly white institutions." *Western Journal of Black Studies* 14: 9–16.

Stewart, L. P. (1990). "Quotas or goals: Fulfilling the affirmative action mandate." *ACA Bulletin* 71: 89–91.

Task Force on Teaching as a Profession. (1986). *A nation prepared: Teachers for the 21st century.* New York: Carnegie Forum of Education and the Economy.

Wieseman, R. (1986). "Multicultural beginnings and early learning." *Journal of Instructional Psychology* 13: 172–176.

Chapter 13

Who's In Charge Here?

■

ORGANIZATION AND CONTROL OF SCHOOLS

There is little doubt about who controls the professions of medicine and law. The American Medical Association and the National Bar Association set the standards for admission to their ranks, and discipline committees are responsible for setting ethical standards and for policing the conduct of the members of their associations. While there are, of course, state and federal regulations that they must abide by, the professions are relatively autonomous.

Who controls the profession of teaching is much less clear. Two major national professional organizations and their state affiliates, the National Education Association and the American Federation of Teachers, compete for membership from the same pool. There are also numerous small state or local organizations of teachers disenchanted with both of the major groups. Unlike lawyers and doctors, many teachers do not belong to any of these organizations.

Teachers do not control admission to their profession, nor do they play a crucial role in the disciplining of its members. The legislatures of the various states set standards for licensure for teachers, administrators, and other members of the profession. They also determine the process whereby these licenses may be revoked.

Even though these general guidelines are usually set at the state level, there is a long history of local control of public schools in the United States, and many of the most important functions in the administration of schools are carried out by locally elected school boards. Added to this confusing picture is the increasingly important role that state and federal courts play in what happens in public schools. Many school districts in the South have been practically run by the courts as a result of the decision to desegregate the schools, and the question of what constitutes equitable financing of schools is being tested in courts all over the United States today. There is little wonder that given the complex nature of the interrelationships among state, federal, and local governments, professional organizations, parent groups, and other special interest groups that there is an almost constant struggle for control of the educational establishment.

From their perspectives, it is probable that all of the competing groups—school boards, PTAs, professional organizations, business, the courts, interest groups, and so on—are concerned about the child's best interest. It is almost certain that their definition of what constitutes that best interest varies greatly, and teachers often have to grapple with what constitutes their proper place in this mosaic. What stance should a teacher take toward the child whose parents reject the theory of evolution; a school board discriminating against a particular group of students; a professional organization advocating practices rejected by a majority of the members of the community; the banning of a book from the school library?

As in all of the other scenarios in this book, the case presented here has no clear answers. The problem and its solution look different to the various individuals and groups involved. The superintendent, **Mr. Moseley**; the school board president, **Alecia Baggett**; the president of the local professional organization, **Georgia Kessler**; businessman **Marion Zettler**; and teachers **Cassie Hudgkins** and **Rose Ragsdale** all have different views of what is happening. You are asked to involve yourself in the controversy in order to gain insight into how your profession is really governed and controlled.

"I just don't give a damn anymore! I am sick and tired of playing their little games. If you look at their propaganda you would think that Edge City was the most progressive school district in the entire nation. They butter me up—and the few other African-American teachers—just to keep us quiet and satisfied. Whether they will admit it or not, this whole system is shot through with racism and elitism, and I going to do something about it if it costs me my job."

Deborah Mason has never seen **Rose** so agitated. **Rose** is often cynical and sarcastic, but today it is obvious that she is really angry. **Deborah** has invited **Rose Ragsdale** and **Charlie Redfearn** to her house to discuss a proposed bond issue that has just been made public. **Charlie**, in addition to teaching chemistry at the high school, is president of the local chapter of the NAACP, and **Rose** serves on its executive committee.

The provision in the bond package that has so agitated these teachers has to do with one of the elementary schools in the district. Roosevelt Elementary is one of the oldest schools in the district and is located in the heart of the African-American community in the southeast area of Edge City. Even though the secondary schools are integrated and there are some African-American and Hispanic students in all of the elementary schools, Roosevelt is almost totally African-American and Hispanic, with fewer than twenty Anglo students. Nearly 80 percent of the students are African-Americans of low socioeconomic status. The bond package calls for extensive renovations at two of the district's elementary schools and the addition of new playground equipment and a gymnasium in one school. It also calls for the construction of a new elementary school in the Sans Souci–Idiot's Hill area. Roosevelt is not mentioned in the bond package.

"Calm down, **Rose**," **Charlie** says, smiling. "This isn't the first time that they have ignored us and you can bet it won't be the last. We'll show up at the board meetings like we always do and voice our complaints; they will listen politely and tell us that they will certainly take our objections into consideration. Then they will come back with some little piddling concession and go on and do just what they damn well please. That's the way it's always worked and I don't see any reason to expect it to change."

"Maybe we ought to do more than just raise our objections at the board meeting," **Deborah** suggests. "I am also fed up to here with this hypocrisy. Some of the discrimination is so well disguised that you can't really fight it. But this time they have put it right out on the table for everyone to look at."

"And just what the hell do you propose to do, **Deborah**?" asks **Rose**. "We both know that you don't have any more clout than we do. Your ACLU membership and activities put you right in the same boat with us. They tolerate you because it's the line of least resistance. Their whole policy has always been to avoid confrontation and to accommodate just to the extent that they have to. If we raise enough hell we'll get some little token concession, but that's as far as it will go."

"Maybe so," **Deborah** responds. "If the NAACP and the ACLU show them that they aren't going to let them avoid confrontation, it may scare them enough to really listen to us. One other thing I have been thinking about is trying to use the American Federation of Teachers to help us out. As far as I know, I am the only dues-paying member the AFT has in Edge City, but I bet if I could talk them into sending down an organizer it would shake some people up."

"You'd really be asking for it, **Deborah**," **Charlie** says, frowning. "You know how the superintendent and the board—for that matter, the whole state of Westland—feel about unions. You don't have the chance of a snowball in hell of getting an active chapter of AFT in this town, and I'm not sure what the administration might try to do to you if you make that kind of threat."

"You're probably right, **Charlie**. I'm not going to get many recruits from among our faculties. Many of the teachers are also afraid for their jobs. I do know that a school down in the valley actually got a majority of their teachers signed up, and not only did they get better working conditions, but school districts all around them started doing things to strengthen the professional organization in the schools."

"It's a real shame that the professional organization in Edge City is so completely dominated by the power structure that we can't count on them for any support at all," **Rose** says.

The talk continues and it is nearly midnight when **Rose** summarizes their plan.

"OK, we may live to regret this, but as I see it, this is what we have decided to do. **Charlie** is going to get the executive committee of the NAACP together and we are going to plan a continuing demonstration in front of Roosevelt. **Deborah** is going to try to get members of the ACLU to join in. She will also talk to legal counsel there to see if it might be feasible to try to get an injunction to stop the bond election until we get a hearing. **Charlie** is going to contact someone to leak the word to the members of the administration that a representative of the AFT is being invited to come and talk about the possibility of a drive to organize the teachers for his organization. Each of us will talk to people who might help and try to gather as wide a support base as we can before the first public hearing three weeks from now."

"That's where we are," **Deborah** agrees. "Now check me and be sure that, pending feedback from the others as they get involved, what we are asking for is that the new school be built in the African-American section of the city somewhere south of Roosevelt. We also want all of the renovations that are to be done at the other schools to be done at Roosevelt. We don't agree among ourselves on whether we should insist on cross-busing between the new school and the predominantly white schools. Is that basically it?"

The others nod in agreement, and **Rose** and **Charlie** rise and head for the door.

"I think we probably should plan to meet at least twice a week for the next three weeks. Unless the crowd gets too large, why don't we just continue meeting here?" **Deborah** suggests.

Alex Moseley grew up in Edge City. He has made education his career from the very beginning. After graduating from Westland State University with a certificate to teach biology and physical education, he took a position in a high school in Springfield. After three years he had his master's degree in educational administration. He left Springfield for a vice-principal's job in a small district in the hill country near Columbia, where he enrolled in the University of Westland doctoral program. The next year he became the principal of a high school just outside of Columbia. Within four years he had graduated with a doctorate in educational administration with a superintendent's certificate, and had advanced to be the assistant superintendent for personnel. With help from family and friends, he successfully campaigned for the superintendency in Edge City. He is now in his eighteenth year and is looking forward to retirement within the next five or six years.

In his office are **Farley Brownell**, principal of the high school and the one person within the district on whom he most relies; **Alecia Baggett**, president of the school board; and **Marion Zettler**, CEO of Trans-Westland Motor Freight and a very active school board member.

Alecia, dean of the school of music at Westland State, is in her second term on the board and her first term as board president.

"Let me see if I have this straight, Marion," she is saying. "You were told that **Rose Ragsdale**, **Deborah Mason**, and some others are planning demonstrations at the school board office, that they are going to urge a boycott of the schools, and that they are bringing in union organizers to recruit our teachers."

"I don't know whether they said the district offices or at one of the schools. I do know that a bunch of those rabble-rousers are out to make trouble for us. I'm just not sure why they are doing it just now. I have been warning all of you for years about **Deborah Mason**. If that woman isn't a communist I don't know who is. She's ruining my kid right now. I would take him out of her class, but he really gets upset when I say anything about her. You get her together with some of those people from southeast Edge City and there's bound to be trouble."

"Calm down, **Marion**," **Moseley** says. "I certainly know how you feel about **Deborah**. I don't know how much, if any, of this is true and until we get more information I'm not about to do anything that will stir things up. I have handled **Deborah** and **Rose Ragsdale** for years and I think I can continue to do so."

"I think I may know what precipitated this," **Farley Brownell** offers. "**Darlene Doyle** told me that **Deborah** was livid about the bond package proposal. I'm not sure exactly what has her nose out of joint but I understand it has something to do with the proposal for the new elementary school. It doesn't make any sense to me."

"Now come on, **Farley**," **Alecia** says. "I warned all of you that something like this could happen. There's a lot of dissatisfaction in the minority community and it's just a matter of time before we get carried to court. Bowie has been forced to go to single-member districts and Crockett will in the next two or three years. Our time is coming, and we ought to be preparing for it. We shouldn't kid ourselves. If Roosevelt were in our part of town it would have been included in the package."

"And I've told you that it would be a waste of money to fix that old school up," the superintendent retorts. "We're going to close it in the next four or five years. I don't like to go over to that area of town myself and that certainly is no place to have a school. We have more crime there than any place else in the district."

"That's really not true," **Alecia** argues. "The southeast is much safer than Acorn Acres or several of the other mobile home parks on the outskirts of Edge City. Besides, if we close Roosevelt there will not be a school left in a minority community. All of the children from those areas will be being bused outside of their neighborhoods."

"I still say just let me handle it," **Moseley** insists. "If we don't overreact it can be worked out without a lot of fuss. We have to keep in mind that what we are doing is for the good of the students involved."

Cassie Hudgkins and her roommate **Margie Brower** have just finished eating their evening meal and are still sitting at the table sipping coffee.

"OK, who licked the molasses off of your bread today?" **Margie** asks. "I've never seen such a long face in my entire life."

"It's not funny," **Cassie** retorts. "I'm in a mess and I really don't know what to do. It's one of those lose–lose situations. **Rose Ragsdale** caught me at lunch today and told me that the NAACP and the ACLU are going to start boycotting over at Roosevelt Elementary School tomorrow. I really don't understand what it's all about. Something about playground equipment or a new school that's being built or something. She didn't really ask me if I wanted to do it or not. She just acted like she expected me to go there right after school and start carrying a sign. **Rose** has been good to me and helped me a lot, but she's really not a very popular person among many of the teachers. Besides, except for when she drove me around when I was thinking about coming to Edge City, I haven't even been to that section of town. None of the teachers live there and certainly none of our friends do. I don't want to make **Rose** mad but I really like my job at Hooker and if I get mixed up in this thing I could lose it. I don't have tenure. The other teachers like me and I get along well with the parents. I'm not a rabble-rouser and I don't see why I have to get involved just because I'm black."

"If **Rose Ragsdale** is serious about starting a membership drive for AFT, we have to do something," **Georgia Kessler**, president of the local chapter of the state affiliate of the National Educational Association, says to two of her board members, **Clyde Simpson** and **Royce Goodwin**. "Personally, I think she has a good case. There's no doubt in my mind that if I were poor and black I would be joining in her crusade, but our membership has always tended to go along to get along. Maybe it's time for us to take a stand."

"Don't say 'us,' Georgia," **Clyde** retorts. "I've always suspected that you were a closet liberal. Well, this is not the time to come out of the closet. Building a school in southeast Edge City would be a waste of money. There's no way that people from the rest of the town are going to let their children go to school over there. The very best thing we can do for the kids who do live there is to get them out of that environment, at least for part of the day. It's a lot cheaper to bus them to one of the good neighborhoods than to build a new building where we will be back to square one on desegregation. Don't you agree, **Doyle**?"

"I suggest we just sit tight and see what happens. **Moseley** doesn't want the media involved and will do everything he can to downplay it. I wouldn't be surprised if he called **Georgia** to get our help on this one, and if he does he probably will get it. You know that he doesn't like for our organization to do anything except some fund-raising and PR work. If he has to ask our opinion, that more or less implies that our opinions matter, and we all know that they don't. Our membership is changing, but not that fast. Less than half of the teachers belong, and they tend to be the older, more conservative ones. If the new, younger teachers get stirred up we may have a different situation. Let's just wait and see what the superintendent and board do."

Questions for Reflection and Discussion

1. Under what circumstances should teachers as a group participate in a strike or a public protest? What criteria should be used in deciding?

2. Present arguments for and against teachers' being required, like lawyers and doctors, to join professional organizations.

3. Ideally, what role should teachers play in controlling admission to the teaching profession and in disciplining unethical and unprofessional behavior?

4. What are possible strategies that might be used in this situation to alleviate the tension between the school board and the minority community over the proposed school bond?

5. In what ways should teachers and building-level administrators be involved in issues such as hiring of personnel, school budgets, bond issues, and other matters that have traditionally been the prerogative of the school board and the superintendent? What advantages and disadvantages might result from such involvement?

6. How would the teaching profession benefit from mandatory membership in a single professional organization? What are arguments that could be used against such a practice?

Class and Individual Projects

But What Should I Do?

Cassie Hudgkins must make a decision. She will either join the picket line at Roosevelt Elementary or she will not. Indicate possible effects, both positive and negative, of her decision in relationship to each of the following.

1. Her career as a teacher in Edge City.

_____

_____

_____

_____

_____

2. Her relationship with **Rose Ragsdale** and the other teachers at Hooker.

_____

_____

_____

_____

_____

3. Her relationships with the students in her class and with the parents of these students.

_____

_____

_____

_____

_____

Who Controls?

List important ways in which schools are controlled at the federal, state, and local levels.

Federal _____

_____

_____

State _____

_____

_____

Local _____

_____

_____

What are arguments that could be made for increasing the amount of control at the federal level?

_____

_____

_____

What are arguments that could be made for increasing the amount of control at the local level?

_____

_____

_____

Should I Belong?

Investigate the history, organization, and purposes of the American Federation of Teachers and the National Educational Association. List similarities and differences between the two organizations.

Similarities _____

_____

_____

_____

_____

Differences _____

_____

_____

_____

_____

Present an argument for joining either the AFT, the NEA, or neither.

_____

_____

_____

_____

_____

_____

_____

Questions Based on Activities

1. Imagine that **Cassie Hudgkins** were to go to each of the following people and ask what they thought she should do about the picket line. What advice do you think that she would get from each? (1) **Deborah Mason** (2) **Farley Brownell** (3) **Georgia Kessler**.

2. Provide support for the proposition that "The local school district is the purest form of democracy in America." What evidence could you use to refute this statement?

3. Discuss and provide examples of how the courts at all levels have exerted control over the curriculum and operations of schools in the United States.

4. From your investigation of the history, aims, and purposes of the American Federation of Teachers and the National Education Association, critique the picture of these organizations painted in this case.

Additional Teaching and Learning Suggestions

1. Interview officers of professional organizations represented in public schools in your area to obtain information about the percentage of teachers who are members, problems facing the organizations, and short- and long-term goals they are working toward.

2. Interview several teachers about their membership or lack of membership in professional organizations.

3. Search current professional literature for information on the topics of "site-based management" or "school-based management." In small groups, discuss the implications of these concepts for the issue of the teacher's role in the control of schooling in the United States.

4. Interview school board members. What were their motivations in running for this position? What rewards do they get from their service on the board? What are the major problems that they have to deal with? How do they view the role of the teacher in school policy decisions?

5. Role-play a conversation between **Cassie Hudgkins** and **Rose Ragsdale** in which Cassie expresses reservations about taking part in the demonstration at Roosevelt Elementary School.

FOR FURTHER READING

Brandt, R. (1992). "On rethinking leadership: A conversation with Tom Sergiovanni." *Educational Leadership* 49: 46–49.

Campbell, R. F., et al. (1990). *The organization and control of American schools.* Columbus, OH: Merrill.

Danzberger, J. P., et al. (1987). "School boards: The forgotten players on the education team." *Phi Delta Kappan* 69: 53–59.

Dunlap, D. M. and Goldman, P. (1991). "Rethinking power in schools." *Educational Administration Quarterly* 27: 5–29.

Frymeir, J. (1987). "Bureaucracy and the neutering of teachers." *Phi Delta Kappan* 69: 9–14.

Goodlad, J. (1984). *A place called school.* New York: McGraw Hill.

Holzman, M. (1992). "Do we really need leadership?" *Educational Leadership* 49: 36–40.

Ingwerson, D. W. "A superintendent's view: Learning to listen and trust each school faculty—Personal reflections of shared decision-making." *School Administrator* 47: 8–11.

Kessler, R. (1992). "Shared decision making works!" *Educational Leadership* 49: 36–38.

Kretovics, J., et al. (1991). "Reform from the bottom up: Empowering teachers to transform schools." *Phi Delta Kappan* 73: 295–299.

Lieberman, A. (1992). "School/University collaboration: A view from the inside." *Phi Delta Kappan* 74: 147–156.

McDonnell, L. M., and Pascal A. (1988). *Teacher unions and educational reform.* Santa Monica, CA: RAND Corporation.

Meadows, B. J. (1992). "Nurturing cooperation and responsibility in a school community." *Phi Delta Kappan* 73: 480–481.

Meyer, J. W., and Rowan B. (1978). "Institutionalized organizations: Formal structure as myth and ceremony." *American Journal of Sociology* 83: 340–363.

Ornstein, A. C. (1992). "School superintendents and school board members: Who they are." *Contemporary Education*: 157–159.

Tuthill, D. (1990). "Expanding the union contract: One teacher's perspective." *Phi Delta Kappan* 72: 775–780.

Williams, R. B. (1990). "Teacher professional autonomy and collective bargaining: Conflict or compromise?" *Education Canada* 30: 4–7.

Wilucki, B. M. (1990). "Autonomy: The goal for classroom teachers of the 1990s." *Childhood Education* 66: 279–280.

Wise, A. E. (1979). *Legislated learning: The bureaucratization of the American classroom.* Berkeley, CA: University of California Press.

Wise, A. E. (1988). "Legislated learning revisited." *Phi Delta Kappan* 69: 329–333.

Chapter 14

Do You Want to See My Dog and Pony Show?

■

TEACHER EVALUATION

In many states a single salary schedule is used to determine the minimum salary a district may pay a teacher. That means that what a teacher earns is usually a function of tenure, or years of service, and degrees. Under a single salary schedule, all teachers in a district holding the same degree and the same number of years of service would earn the same amount. There are, of course, differences in salary based upon position in the district. Usually counselors, administrators, and coaches earn differential salaries, almost always higher than the salary teachers earn.

For many years, some states and/or individual districts within states have attempted to move from the concept of a single salary schedule to some form of merit pay. The majority of these efforts have ended in failure and the schools have returned to the traditional method of payment of teachers' salaries. That does not mean that the issue is dead, however. Many individuals, especially some parents and members of the business community, have continued to complain that there should be some method of rewarding the outstanding teacher and of not rewarding, or getting rid of, the nonproductive members of the teaching staff. Recently the educational establishment has talked about differential staffing and the idea of a "career ladder" as two ways of achieving the goal of a pay scale that recognizes the contribution of the individual and not just tenure.

Related to this issue of "merit pay" is a concern for accountability. Hundreds of billions of dollars are spent each year on education, and taxpayers are constantly attempting to find some way to determine if they are getting value for the money spent. Recently, many states have mandated new processes for teacher evaluation. In some cases these evaluations are tied to some concept of differential staffing or to a "career ladder" in which movement up the ladder, and hence more prestige and more money, is at least partially dependent upon the quality of teaching as determined by these periodic evaluations.

Edge City School District is struggling with these same issues. The state of Westland has recently passed legislation requiring that any teacher pay raises be based on merit. All future raises will be in terms of "units," with these units representing a dollar value such as $500 or $1,000. Twenty-five percent of the teachers, the lowest quartile, may receive only one unit pay increase; the middle 50 percent will receive two units; and the upper 25 percent will receive four units. The state has further specified that at least 50 percent of the merit score be based on an evaluation of teaching using the state-mandated observational instrument. Twenty-five percent must be based on voluntary participation in school- or university-based in-service activities, including formal courses at a college or university.

As you read the dialogue among the various members of the educational community in Edge City, keep the following questions in mind. Should teachers be paid based on merit? Who should determine what constitutes quality and therefore what should be evaluated? If evaluations are to be conducted, who should do the evaluation? Does a plan of evaluation such as the one described here take away from the image of teaching as a profession? What effect might the implementation of this plan have on teachers? On principals? On parents? On students?

■ *Teacher Evaluation*

"I can't help how you feel, **Quincy**," **Alex Moseley**, Superintendent of Schools in Edge City, is saying. "It's not a question of whether or when we start this process—it's simply a question of how. We will begin this evaluation process this fall if we expect to get any state money for salary increases."

Moseley, **Quincy**, **Alecia Baggett**, and **Farley Brownell** have been meeting in the superintendent's office for more than an hour now, and the discussion about the upcoming change in the method of evaluating teachers has generated considerable heat. **Martin Quincy**, the principal of Hooker Middle School, is adamantly opposed to having to observe all of his teachers using the new observation instrument that has been devised by the Westland Education Agency to meet the legislative mandate for evaluation of teachers and of teaching interns.

"OK," he says, shaking his head in resignation. "I've said my piece. Just be prepared for trouble when we start this. I get along great with my faculty, and most of them get along with each other. This is bound to tear them apart. All of a sudden we're going to have the bluebirds and the buzzards. And you know who is going to get the blame. It's not you, it's me. There's no way that I can get around to each of my teachers for a full period three times each semester, so I'm going to have to delegate some of this to the assistant principals, and they already have more than they can say grace over. All they do down at the legislature is to cause trouble. If they're going to do something like this, the least they could do would be to provide funds to pay for full-time evaluators."

"You're just borrowing trouble, **Martin**," **Alecia** says. "There is no segment of our economy that isn't evaluated. Teachers have been exempt from this for far too long. The public is demanding, and rightly so, that we be held accountable for what we do. I really don't mean this as a threat, but if you really feel that you can't do it then we will have to get someone who will. How about you, **Farley**, do you think that it's an impossible task?"

"Oh, we can do it, all right," **Farley** replies. "It's going to be an even bigger burden on me than on **Quincy** but I've got more staff and I'm just going to have to get more people involved in the process. This isn't going to make some people happy. Philosophically, I think I disagree with **Quincy**. I really think we need a more systematic way of determining who is doing a good job and rewarding them for their efforts. And this new instrument is really good. It focuses in on specific aspects of teaching and isn't just a 'good old boy' form. The teacher has to really be doing these things or they won't get the points. Then when we have everyone evaluated you can just add up the points and decide who gets what."

"All right, let's wind this up," the superintendent says. "**Farley**, get two or three people from research, counselors, or the central office and work out some kind of plan for training all of the people who are going to be evaluators. We have to have some kind of reliability or we might be facing lawsuits before this is over. **Quincy**, since you don't like the observation process, you get a committee together to come up with recommendations for what kinds of in-service are going to count toward merit, what kind of college course work, and what point value is going to be assigned to each of them. I suppose we ought to involve the teachers in this in some way, so I am going to call **Georgia Kessler** in and ask her to select a committee to recommend what else besides the principal's evaluation and the continuing education should count towards the merit rating. We will meet again in two weeks. I will ask **Georgia** to join us at that meeting and we will try to finalize things then and devise a strategy for selling it to the teachers and to the community. In the meantime I don't think I need to remind you that the less said about this the better. I'm sure **Quincy** is right about one thing—this isn't going to be the most popular thing that we have ever done, and it won't help any for rumors to get started."

"I know that all of you are busy, but it was either meet during our planning period or sometime after school."

Georgia Kessler is addressing the three teachers she has asked to assist her with the report that the superintendent has asked her to prepare. **Lisa Rodriguez**, **Deborah Mason**, and **Charlie Redfern** all have a fifth-period planning period, and this is one of the reasons they have been asked to serve. All have readily agreed. The word is out that a new evaluation procedure is being put in place, and they are anxious to at least find out what it is going to be like. Maybe they may even be able to have some influence on the direction it is to take.

"Is what we are doing going to have any effect this time?" asks **Charlie**. "I have been on so many committees that wrote reports that were never looked at that I don't want to waste my time unless we're going to have some say."

"The superintendent assured me that what we recommended would be given very serious consideration by the board. He can't guarantee that they will accept it, but I really think that this is such a hot potato that they will want to be able to say that the teachers were involved in deciding what the system would be like. Even that is deceptive," she adds. "Under pressure, he told me that no more than 25 percent of the total rating would come from what we recommend. Principal evaluations and in-service or course work will account for the other 75 percent.

"So exactly what is it that we are supposed to do?" asks **Lisa**. "I don't want to spend hours on this. I've got other things to do."

"What he told me," **Georgia** replies, "was that we were to decide what kinds of things other than the principal evaluations and in-service stuff should count toward our merit rating. The bottom line is that, if this thing goes through, some of us are going to be getting bigger raises than others in the coming years, and we are being asked to decide what should count toward who's a good one and who's a bad one."

"I'm not sure that I am completely comfortable with this," **Deborah** interjects. "I know that both the NEA and the AFT have taken positions against merit pay in the past. Are we being unprofessional by being willing participants in this process?"

"The same thoughts have crossed my mind," **Georgia** admits. "Here I am, president of the NEA local, making decisions that will determine someone else's salary increment as well as possibly having negative impact on egos, morale, and collegiality. I rationalized it by saying to myself that since it was going to be done I could do a better job than a lot of people I know. We can philosophize later; right now let's just brainstorm some ideas about some things that might be professionally important activities that could count toward a good evaluation and more money."

"Have you seen this yet?"

Paul McKinney hands **Royce Goodwin** a form that he has pulled from the pocket of his jacket that was lying on the bench beside him. They are sitting in the boys' locker room in the gymnasium, having just completed ten laps around the track. **Royce** gives the paper a cursory glance and hands it back.

"I haven't seen it, and I don't want to see it," he replies. "Everybody in the district is getting all hot and bothered about this evaluation stuff. Why? It's just another fad that we're going through, and they will spend hundreds of hours and thousand of dollars and things are going to go on just like they always have. I'm going to teach like I've always taught, and you are too. Just relax. This too shall pass."

"I'm not at all sure that you're right, **Doyle**," McKinney argues. "This isn't something that **Moseley** or **Brownell** dreamed up. They don't have a choice either. They're going to have to do evaluations, and these evaluations have to be based on classroom visits, and they must use some rating form to quantify their observations. This is the one that they have just about decided on. The state department of education put this together as a guide for the districts to use. **Moseley** and the board have decided to adopt it just as it is. As far as I know they have not asked the teachers about it one way or the other. I can't believe that you don't care. Man, this is going to affect whether you get a raise or not, or what size raise it's going to be. Look at this!"

He hands the paper back to **Royce** who looks at it more closely. "This is the same form that the university has been using for us to rate the student teachers," **Royce** says.

"That's what somebody else said," **Paul** agrees. "Look at the items. Nearly every one of them has to do with how you teach your class. They are going to use this same form for first grade and for my eleventh grade American History and for a PE class and for a chemistry lab. Does that make any sense?"

"What makes even less sense," Royce responds, "is to suppose that **Farley Brownell** or **Martin Quincy** over at the middle school know enough about teaching to rate anybody. Plus the fact that even if they try to be objective they probably can't. That's what I was saying. Like so many of the things that we do around here, this makes no sense whatsoever and therefore it will come and go. And it could be worse. At least this form does have some specificity like 'provides feedback' and 'communicates expectations.' I've seen some that just say 'has pleasant personality' or 'teaches effectively.' "

"I think you're dead wrong, **Royce**," **Paul** says somberly. "This isn't just a passing fad, and I'm going to try to get some people together. We ought to make our feelings known to the administration and to the board."

"You do what you feel you have to, **Paul**," **Royce** grins. "I'm going to get me a copy of this form, and when they come to evaluate me I'll have my little dog and pony show all ready for them. I'll make them think that I'm the greatest thing that's happened since sliced bread. Just relax and play the game."

Questions for Reflection and Discussion

1. What are the pros and cons of the question "Should there be merit pay for teachers"?

2. What are the advantages of having the quality of teaching determined by observers who know the teacher, such as colleagues or administrators from within their building, as opposed to independent outside evaluators who do not know the teacher and therefore cannot have preconceived biases? Defend your answer.

3. In what way is the concept of evaluation for purposes of differential pay detrimental to the acceptance of the idea of teaching as a profession? In what ways is it consistent with the idea of professionalism?

4. Critique the process whereby Edge City School District implemented the merit pay process mandated by the state.

5. What are alternative ways in which this mandate might have been met?

6. What are possible effects of the new system on the way in which teachers teach?

7. Do you think that **Royce Goodwin** can put on a "dog and pony show" for the evaluator? In other words, can he do a superior job of teaching for just one day? Give reasons for your answer.

Class and Individual Projects

Does This Count?

Pretend that you are a member **Georgia Kessler**'s committee. List activities that you think should be counted toward merit evaluation. Indicate who should evaluate it and how much weight should be assigned to the activity.

ACTIVITY	EVALUATOR	WEIGHT 1–5

In the space below, provide justification for each of the items listed above.

Do I Really Rate?

Using the teacher observation instrument on the following page, rate **Ms. Mason**'s teaching (Chapter Two). In the space below, indicate your reaction to the observation instrument. What are its strengths and weaknesses? What should be deleted, what added?

STRENGTHS?

_____

_____

_____

_____

_____

WEAKNESSES?

_____

_____

_____

_____

_____

WHAT SHOULD BE ADDED TO THE INSTRUMENT?

_____

_____

_____

_____

_____

WHAT SHOULD BE DELETED FROM THE INSTRUMENT?

_____

_____

_____

_____

_____

STATE OF WESTLAND
TEACHER OBSERVATION INSTRUMENT

Teacher_____Date_____

Evaluator_____ Subject_____ Grade_____

1=Unsatisfactory 2= Needs improvement 3=Satisfactory performance 4=Above average performance

5=Clearly outstanding performance   **Comments**

1. Begins on time   1 2 3 4 5_____

2. Gets students' attention   1 2 3 4 5_____

3. Gives clear instructions   1 2 3 4 5_____

4. Has material and equipment
    ready   1 2 3 4 5_____

5. Communicates expectations   1 2 3 4 5_____

5. Monitors student classroom
    performance   1 2 3 4 5_____

6. Provides feedback   1 2 3 4 5_____

7. Varies activities   1 2 3 4 5_____

8. Obtains student
    participation   1 2 3 4 5_____

9. Allows for appropriate
    student response time   1 2 3 4 5_____

10. Extends student responses   1 2 3 4 5_____

11. Reinforces correct
    responses   1 2 3 4 5_____

12. Maintains focus on
    instructional objectives   1 2 3 4 5_____

13. Paces material
    appropriately   1 2 3 4 5_____

14. Presents information in
    correct sequence   1 2 3 4 5_____

15. Relates content to
    prior learning   1 2 3 4 5_____

16. Describes and defines
    concepts   1 2 3 4 5_____

17. Explains clearly   1 2 3 4 5_____

18. Uses correct grammar   1 2 3 4 5_____

19. Relates material
    to student interests   1 2 3 4 5_____

20. Encourages and assists
    slow students   1 2 3 4 5_____

General Comments

_____

Questions Based on Activities

1. Coaches, counselors, and administrators usually are paid more than teachers. What are the pros and cons of this practice?

2. **Georgia Kessler** argues that high school English teachers have an inordinate amount of paper grading and spend many hours after school and on weekends doing this chore. She contends that this should result in a pay increment. How would you respond to her? How do you think the members of her committee would respond?

3. Pretend that you are having a conference with **Ms. Mason** after your observation of her teaching. What would you say to her? How do you think that she might respond?

4. If a system of teacher evaluation is to be used, who should do the evaluation? What training should they have? How should the issue of reliability of the ratings be addressed?

5. What are dangers in the use of subjective judgments in the evaluation of teachers? What are possible advantages?

Additional Teaching and Learning Suggestions

1. Using the Westland Observation Instrument, rate a colleague who is teaching a unit and then have a conference to compare perceptions about the process.

2. As a total class, rate a videotaped teaching episode using this instrument. What appear to be areas of agreement among raters? Areas of disagreement?

3. After completing one or both of the above activities, write a brief paper outlining possibilities and pitfalls in using an observation instrument for purposes of rating teachers for differential pay.

4. Write a brief paper in which you outline the advantages and disadvantages of using this instrument strictly for the purpose of improvement of instruction, to give teachers feedback on the teaching processes that they are using in their classrooms.

5. Interview a diverse group of people—businesspersons, teachers, professionals, white collar workers, and others—to determine their feelings about merit pay for teachers. Be sure to couch your questions in a way that will ensure that each group is responding to the same question.

6. Interview teachers and/or administrators to elicit their opinions about in-service education. What are the characteristics of in-service sessions that they feel are effective? What are characteristics of in-service sessions that they feel are ineffective?

7. Gather information about the method of evaluation of teachers used in several different school districts. Try to get examples from small towns, metropolitan areas, suburban and rural districts. Compare and contrast the methods used. What appear to be commonalities? Differences? What could account for the differences?

For Further Reading

Brandt, R. (1992). "On research on teaching: A conversation with Lee Shulman." *Educational Leadership* 49: 14–19.

Cuban, L. (1984). *How teachers taught: Constancy and change in American classrooms: 1890–1980.* New York: Longman.

Darling-Hammond, L. (1986). "Teacher evaluation: A proposal." *Education Digest* 52: 30–33.

Farnsworth, B., et al. (1991). "Designing and implementing a successful merit pay program for teachers." *Phi Delta Kappan* 73: 320–325.

Gray, G. R., and Brown, D. R. (1989). "Pay for performance in academia: A viable concept?" *Educational Research Quarterly* 13: 47–52.

Johnson, H. C., ed. (1985). *Merit, money, and teachers' careers: Studies on merit pay and career ladders for teachers.* Washington, D.C.: University Press of America.

Kauchak, S. (1985). "An interview study of teachers' attitudes toward teacher evaluation practices." *Journal of Research and Development in Education* 19: 32–37.

Koehler, M. (1990). "Self-assessment in the evaluation process." *NASSP Bulletin* 74: 40–44.

Laing, S. (1986). "The principal and evaluation." *NASSP Bulletin* 70: 91–93.

Langlois, D. E., and Zales, C. R. (1991). "Anatomy of a top teacher." *American School Board Journal* 178: 44–46.

Manatt, R. P. (1987). "Lessons from a comprehensive performance appraisal project." *Educational Leadership* 44: 8–14.

Medley, D. M., and Coker, H. (1987). "How valid are principals' judgments of teacher effectiveness?" *Phi Delta Kappan* 69: 138–140.

Milner, J. O. (1991). "Suppositional style and teacher evaluation." *Phi Delta Kappan* 73: 464–467.

Ornstein, A. C. (1990). "A look at teacher effectiveness research—theory and practice." *NASSP Bulletin* 74: 78–88.

Parker, J. C. (1985) *Career ladder/master teacher programs.* Reston, VA: National Association of Secondary School Principals.

Peterson, P. L., and Comeaux, M. A. (1990). "Evaluating the systems: Teachers' perspectives on teacher evaluation." *Educational Evaluation and Policy Analysis* 12: 3–24.

Porter, A. C., and Brophy, J. E. (1988). "Synthesis of research on good teaching: Insights from the work of the Institute for Research on Teaching." *Educational Leadership* 45: 74–85.

Reynolds, A. (1992). "What is competent beginning teaching? A review of the literature," *Review of Educational Research* 62: 1–36.

Root, D., and Overly, D. (1990). "Successful teacher evaluation—key elements for success." *NASSP Bulletin* 74: 34–38.

Sportman, M. A. (1986). "Evaluating teacher's performance fairly." *Curriculum Review* 25: 8–10.

Turner, R. R. (1986). "What teachers think about their evaluations." *Education Digest* 52: 40–43.

Weber, L., and McBee, J. (1990). "Teacher evaluation instruments for merit pay decisions: Is their use justifiable?" *Evaluation Review* 14: 11–26.

Wise, A. E., et al. (1984). *Teacher evaluation: A study of effective practices.* Santa Monica, CA: RAND Corporation.

Chapter 15

What Have I Gotten Myself Into?

■

CONFLICTS IN STUDENT TEACHING

Surveys consistently reveal that teachers as a group consider their student teaching to have been the most valuable part of their teacher education program. This is not a surprising finding since doctors say the same thing about their residency and lawyers about their first cases. We learn by doing and by reflecting on our experiences. That is not to say that all students have an enjoyable and productive student teaching experience.

Before presenting the dilemma facing **Connie Munos,** we should point out that many teacher education institutions have moved beyond the kind of student teaching arrangements in place at Westland State University. Professional development centers—schools devoted to exemplary education for their pupils and to an improved model for teacher education—are being established all over the country. In these schools, the concept is of a "community of learners" where everyone works together to improve the amount and the quality of learning for everyone: students, teachers, student teachers, administrators, and community members. Even in these centers, questions of responsibility and power arise.

Westland State University is in the planning stages for such a professional development school, but most of their program would be described as "traditional." One of the characteristics of a "traditional" student teaching experience is a frequently ill-defined set of power relationships. At least three people are usually involved: the student teacher, a public school teacher/cooperating teacher, and a university professor/college supervisor. A common practice at colleges of education is for the student teacher to apply at the college for student teaching in a particular area. The college then forwards the application to a designated administrator in the public school system who actually does the placement. The college then assigns a faculty member or teaching fellow to supervise the student during this student teaching experience. Since student teaching occurs in a public school classroom and since the public school teacher is legally responsible for what goes on in the classroom, that teacher has ultimate authority over what the student teacher may or may not do. The college supervisor must work with the cooperating teacher in the establishment of a climate beneficial to the students in the classroom and to the teacher in training. To further complicate the situation, the grade and/or decision to pass or fail the student teacher ultimately rests with the college supervisor. This traditional and complex arrangement is portrayed as being successful, but on occasion it is beset with serious problems.

This case describes such a problem. **Connie Munos,** a computer science major, has been placed with **Mr. Greg Simpson.** She will be teaching computer literacy and keyboarding classes. Like most students, **Connie** has mixed feelings about the coming semester. **Mr. Simpson** also has his anxieties and expectations about what this experience may hold.

■ *Conflicts in Student Teaching*

A week before student teaching begins, **Connie Munos** talks about the upcoming experience with her friend, **Cindy**.

"I'm both excited and scared. I mean, I've got all these great things to do with the kids—lots of activities that should be fun and yet help them learn. I've saved everything from my education classes and I've got this file with everything organized. So I feel like I'm ready. And then I start to wonder what my cooperating teacher will be like—if he'll be somebody that the kids like, somebody who has the class under control, somebody good."

"I know what you mean, **Connie**. I've heard horror stories about student teaching. I'm sure glad that you're doing it first so that I can get the real story of what it's going to be like. Remember that one girl from the content area reading class? She had so many bad things happen to her, all because her cooperating teacher was so terrible and couldn't get her class under control. I sure hope something like that doesn't happen to us!"

"Yeah, but that teacher was pretty new, and remember she told us later that they ended up getting a permanent sub in the class because the teacher just said she wasn't coming back. At least my teacher, **Mr. Simpson**, has been there a while, so I should be in pretty good shape. At least he should have things under control. I just hope that we get along!"

In their first meeting, **Mr. Simpson** lets **Connie** know that he has things under control.

"I remember my student teaching days, **Ms. Munos**. I had no idea what I should be doing and I was so grateful for a teacher who knew just what to do. We're going to get along just fine because I can tell you exactly what to do. I've got the classes arranged for the whole year. All you have to do is step in and teach what I've got written down. Now that's not too hard, is it? It should make this student teaching a snap for you. Besides, you'll probably have your hands full worrying about how to keep these hooligans under control. Power, that's what you use—lots and lots of power. Don't worry, I'll show you the ropes. You'll do fine. Just do what I tell you. Well, do you have any questions?"

"Uh, just a few, **Mr. Simpson**. My university supervisor wants me to write lesson plans for each period that I teach. Will you let me know the material so that I can write out the plans the way he wants them done?"

"Well, I have things written in my plan book. It's kind of old, but you can still read what we're going to be doing. Just copy these things down. That should be enough, shouldn't it?"

"Well, I guess I can just fill in between the lines, because the lesson plans need to be very detailed. **Dr. Leems** says that we should get comfortable with planning in detail before we move to a shorter form. He did say that most teachers don't use this long form, but that we still need the practice in organizing our thoughts. Sure, your plan book will be fine. Oh, I'm also supposed to create a unit to teach this semester. If you could give me some idea of what you'd like me to teach or suggest some topics, I'll get started putting the unit together."

"Hey, I already told you. We're set. I've got everything that you need to teach. We'll just go through the plan book and find a unit, then you use that for your unit plan. OK. Listen—I've got to tell you about one of our students. This girl, **Sarah Tompkins**, is quite a problem. She's in a wheelchair and has some learning disability, but don't you worry about her. She probably can't do too much anyway. I plan to keep my eye on her so that she doesn't cause any trouble. In fact, I've placed a table and chair right by her station so that I can keep an eye on her. OK. Any other questions?"

"Oh, I guess not, **Mr. Simpson**. But I'll probably have some later. Thanks for talking with me."

"No problem. I'm here to guide you. Stick with me and you'll get through this ordeal. Uh oh, here come the urchins. Let's get them before they get us. Busy, busy, busy. It's the only way to go."

Student Teaching Seminar Assignment—JOURNAL ENTRY # 1:

I've made it through my first three days (or week) of student teaching and I've got some mixed feelings. I was so worried about my teacher not being able to control the class and leaving me with a bunch of discipline problems. Well, I sure don't have to worry about that. CONTROL is his motto. The kids move around in his class like robots. They come in, sit down at a work station, turn on the computer, and begin typing. All they ever do is type things off a piece of paper. So far I haven't seen much direct instruction. And I had hoped to do some different activities to make the direct instruction more fun.

Student Teaching Seminar Assignment—JOURNAL ENTRY #2:

I think that I might have some problems with **Mr. Simpson**. He doesn't seem to want to let me come up with any of my own material to use in teaching. He told me that he would give me everything that I needed. I know that's not what you want us to do, so after you read this I'd sure appreciate some help in trying to convince him to let me do what I'm supposed to do. Oh, one other thing . . . he let me teach a couple of classes this week, and while I was teaching he kept yelling at kids for misbehaving. There were a couple of times when I had already disciplined the students and I felt that they were responding to me, but he jumped in and said, "That's two detentions for not obeying Ms. Munos!" What am I supposed to do about that? I really am concerned that he won't ever let me really teach on my own. Isn't that what we're supposed to do? At least for part of the time? I'll try to be more positive next time.

Student Teaching Seminar Assignment—JOURNAL ENTRY #3:

I've been reading my journal and noticed that all I do is talk about the bad things. So this entry is going to be all positive! I love my students! They're neat kids. I even have a learning-disabled student. I've talked to her a bit and she seems to really like computers. Mr. Simpson seems to think that she's a problem, but so far she has been fine. In fact, she told me that she has her own computer at home and wants to learn how to write programs for it. She asked if I would teach her how to do that. Isn't that great!!!!

Six weeks into student teaching, **Cindy** and **Connie** finally connect in a telephone conversation.

"Gee, **Connie**, it seems like months since we've had a chance to talk. So how's it going? Have you been *that* busy?"

"You will never believe what these six weeks have been like. If it weren't for the kids in class, I'd . . . Do you remember when we talked about people having their worst nightmares during student teaching? Well, I'm having somebody's nightmare. Let me tell you what happened today.

"I've been teaching the kids how to do some simple programming—you know, write a program to do a Mad Lib. It's more or less a reward for them surviving the boring lessons that we do every day. Anyway, there are five kids who speak better Spanish than English, and they were having trouble understanding what I was telling them to do. So I translated the directions into Spanish and told them to continue working. I've done that before, but I guess that **Mr. Simpson** didn't know. Well, he stopped class and asked me what I had said to these five kids. I told him that I had translated the directions into Spanish so that they could finish the assignment in time. He was furious, and started raving about how this school is an American school and the language spoken here is English. Anyone who can't understand English well enough to complete an assignment, has no business here. And as a *student* teacher—he said that like I was some kind of alien—I was under his guidance; he had never told me to translate anything for these students and until he did, I was to speak only proper English. Then he assigned each of the five kids a detention for not completing the assigned classwork.

"I was mortified and furious. I didn't know what to do. I mean, he has to give me an evaluation for my placement folder so I really can't make him too mad. I sure didn't think that I had done anything wrong. What a day! I feel like an idiot going into Seminar tomorrow with another horror story. It seems like I'm the only one who is having so much trouble. I just wonder if it's me?"

"Wow. So a lot of other stuff has happened?"

"Are you kidding? It took almost a month for both **Dr. Leems** and me to convince **Mr. Simpson** to let me create a unit of my own material. He really didn't want to relinquish any of the control over his class. **Dr. Leems** was really good though. He sorta made it sound like I was using **Mr. Simpson**'s ideas and doing more work to leave extra material for him to use. Anyway, **Simpson** bought it—at least some of it—I created this unit on programming and he's let me teach it, but he watches me like a hawk.

"Oh, and he also interrupts my classes to discipline students. He said something about me not giving enough detentions. So he sits in class and watches for students to breathe wrong, then he gives them a detention. It's amazing, though—none of the kids ever complains about him."

"Would you have complained about a teacher in high school, especially before that teacher gave you your grade for the year? He sounds like a case. But do you think that you're going to pass? I mean, he's not the only one who says if you pass or not, is he?"

"No, **Dr. Leems** really gives me my grade and I guess I'm doing all right. Although a couple of my observations have not been what I would call great. Mainly because of stuff that he's really caused. Oh well, yeah, I'm gonna pass because I won't let him get the better of me. I just wish it would be more fun, you know?"

"Listen, don't wait so long to call next time. I can't wait to hear what happens next."

"Right! You like horror stories!"

Two weeks later, **Connie Munos** has her mid-semester evaluation conference with **Dr. Leems**, her university supervisor.

"Well, **Connie**, how do you think things are going so far?"

"I guess OK. I mean, I wish my evaluations were all fives. I don't like not getting perfect scores. I mean, I've always had good grades and I just assumed that I'd get good grades in student teaching."

"I wouldn't call your evaluations bad, by any means. Remember that student teaching is supposed to be a learning experience. You're not supposed to be perfect in student teaching; you're supposed to be learning in student teaching. I've seen you do a lot of really good teaching. Especially considering the circumstances that you're working under. Let's talk about your strengths. What do you feel are the strongest elements of your teaching?"

"Well, I guess that I really have three areas. I feel really good about how I know a lot of innovative things to do with the kids. I mean, the book is strictly a textbook, and a lot of what the kids have to do is follow directions, type something in, print it and turn it in for a grade. They really don't do much thinking when we work with the text. Lately I've been trying some different kinds of assignments—you know, having the kids compose something or giving them some kind of choice or decision to make. They seem a bit more receptive to these kinds of activities, and surprisingly their grades are better on these tasks. So I like the kinds of assignments that I'm using for my students. I feel like I'm helping them to learn to think.

"I also feel good about my planning. I try to be really prepared for class. I've been writing these lesson plans out, and before I create each one I have a layout of what my class is going to be like for that day. It may seem like a lot of work, and I guess it really is, but I feel good that I'm sure about what I intend to teach.

"And the last thing that I think is a strength for me is that I really like and care about these kids. It's easy for me to talk with them and to try and help them. They really seem to respond to me, too. You would not believe how different they act when **Mr. Simpson** is out of the room. Usually you would expect them to really act up, but they just keep on working, and when we're having a discussion, they even ask more questions once he's left the room. You know, one of them came up to me after you left the other day and said, 'So did you do all right today?'"

"I know," says **Dr. Leems**, "one of them always seems to come up to me and ask if you're getting a 'good grade.' I agree with what you describe as your strengths; you are always quite prepared and your rapport with the students is evident. But now let's talk about some areas that you'd like to work on during the last half of the semester. You wrote on your self-evaluation that you'd like to improve (1) your classroom management, (2) your note taking, and (3) your tiredness. Let's talk about these, where do you want to begin?"

"OK. Really, classroom management and note taking sort of go together. You remember you graded me down for the students continually asking me to repeat things when I was trying to lecture. You suggested that I use an overhead or the board. I talked with **Mr. Simpson** about that and he came up with excuses why I shouldn't do either of those things. We don't use an overhead because there aren't enough plugs in the room with all of the computers connected. And anyway, there isn't a screen to show the picture on. Then he said we can't use the board because he doesn't want chalk dust in the room with the computers. We have a board that uses those wipe-off markers, but it's very small and I can't get much information on there. So when I do a lecture or mini-lesson before turning the kids loose on their computers, I still have the constant questions and noise. What else can I do?"

"All right, have you tried using a handout—maybe an incomplete outline or a fill-in-the-blank worksheet. You know, you might try giving them directions and even notes on the computer. Can you create a program or something to do that?"

"You know, that computer direction activity might work. Let me think about it. That way they'd be solving problems while they're practicing their keyboarding skills too."

"What about the tiredness, **Connie**? This really concerns me. Are you staying up too late or working or doing something where you can't get enough rest? What exactly do you mean by 'tiredness'?"

"I'm always tired, **Dr. Leems**. Exhausted is more like it. By the time seventh period gets here, I can hardly think. When I get home, I always have to take a nap before I start preparing things for tomorrow's lessons. **Mr. Simpson** says that I try to do too much; that I should have just stuck to his plan and I wouldn't be tired. Part of the reason I think I'm tired is because of the way the room is arranged. I spend every forty-five-minute period running from one end of the room to the other because the computers are not arranged so that I can see all of the students. I remember in my classes at the university, we talked about arranging the room so that you could see the kids from one place in the room. It's just that **Mr. Simpson**'s room is impossible to rearrange. And what's more, he likes it that way. I'm just worried that the kids won't keep working on their assignment if I sit at the desk like he does. Besides, some of them need help, and that's what I'm there for, isn't it? So what do I do?"

"Why can't you rearrange the room?"

"Because of the outlets, and because **Mr. Simpson** likes it the way it is."

"All right, should we talk to **Mr. Simpson** about why you seem to be wearing yourself out in the classroom? I want this to be a good experience for you, but I want you to be realistic, too. Do you think that you're trying to do *too much* in the classroom? I wonder if you care too much and that's what's wearing you out. What I'd like you to do is to log in your journal some reflections on days when you're not as tired and days when you're really tired. Write about what you did that day. Then next time, let's take a look at those entries and see if we can come up with something. OK?"

At least twice a semester the university supervisor conducts a three-way conference with the student teacher and the cooperating teacher. The following conference occurs about three-quarters of the way through the semester.

"**Mr. Simpson**, I appreciate your joining **Ms. Munos** and myself this afternoon. You've been a great help to her and we both are interested to hear your assessment of her progress. If you would, please begin by telling us how you think things are going."

"**Ms. Munos** is a hard worker, **Dr. Leems**—probably too hard for her own good. She's a bit too ambitious and that leaves her stuck sometimes. If she would just do less in the classroom, she would save herself a lot of heartache and have more spare time as well."

"I'm not quite sure what you mean by being too ambitious. Could you clarify that for us, please?"

"I think she's trying to reach every student in every class. That's not possible. I know she tries to give them information that she thinks will help them—information that's important. The problem is that these kids don't care about that information. What's more, they don't need to know the information. A computer literacy class is supposed to make the students literate on computers; that means they can read what a computer says and they can put some words into a computer so someone else can read it. That's all. So she doesn't have to work so hard. It hurts me to see her working herself to death."

"**Ms. Munos**, how would you respond to that?"

"I really don't feel like I'm working myself to death. I'm trying to do things that are fun; trying to engage all of the students in classroom learning. At the university, we were told to do these kinds of things; we were also told that students need certain kinds of information for . . ."

"That's the problem—the university courses teach you stuff that doesn't work in the real classroom; stuff that you don't need to know; stuff the kids don't need to know either. If you would spend more time in a real classroom and less time in a university classroom you'd be better off. I'm sure **Dr. Leems** sees the value of more real-life experience."

"So **Connie**, I'm calling for my update on student teaching. How are things going this week?"

"Oh, **Cindy**, I guess I'm surviving. You know I've tried to look at this experience from different angles, and my latest survival tactic is to view my time at Edge City High, or at least my time with **Mr. Simpson**, as an experience in what not to do. By watching him I am really coming to grips with all of the things that I know I don't want to do. It's sure been hard, though. I just wonder if real teaching is this hard. Sometimes I almost wish that we students taught for a whole year, or at least with two people, so that I could see things from another perspective."

"That bad, huh?"

"Well, sometimes it's depressing. I mean, I was *so* excited at the beginning of the semester and I've not been able to do half of the neat things that I wanted to do. **Dr. Leems** keeps reminding us that we are guests in this teacher's classroom and that when we get our own classroom we will be able to do more of what we want to do. I sure hope that's true. It just seems so long before I'll have my own classroom . . ."

Questions for Reflection and Discussion

1. Think back to the three-way conversation that **Dr. Leems, Mr. Simpson,** and **Connie Munos** had. If you were in **Dr. Leems**'s position, how would you have responded during the conversation? If you were the student teacher, what would you have said?

2. What kinds of options does **Connie** have for dealing with **Mr. Simpson**?

3. How realistic are **Connie**'s perceptions of **Mr. Simpson**'s expectations?

4. Based on all of the information provided in this case, speculate on **Connie**'s potential for being a successful teacher.

5. How would you feel about having **Mr. Simpson** as a cooperating teacher?

6. Brainstorm the qualifications that a cooperating teacher should have in order to work with student teachers.

7. Think about the instance in which **Connie** modified her instruction for the ESL students in the classroom. Was her adaptation appropriate? What else could she have done?

8. Discuss **Mr. Simpson**'s response to **Connie**'s adaptation for the ESL students. How do you feel about his response? Why do you think he would feel or react in this way? How should **Connie** react to his response?

9. Which is more important for a teacher, classroom management or motivating the students? Speculate on how **Mr. Simpson** and **Connie** would answer this question.

Class and Individual Projects

You Be the Judge

Following this page are several completed student teaching evaluation forms on **Connie Munos**. Analyze these forms and then formulate a final letter of evaluation for **Connie**. This letter should be addressed to the Director of Student Teaching at Westland State University.

WESTLAND STATE UNIVERSITY
STUDENT TEACHER OBSERVATION INSTRUMENT

Teacher _Connie Munos_ Date _1st observation_

Evaluator _Leens_ Subject _Keyboarding_ Grade _10_

1=Unsatisfactory 2= Needs improvement 3=Satisfactory performance 4=Above average performance
5=Clearly outstanding performance

Comments

1. Begins on time — 1 ②3 4 5 _took a long time to get started – attendance_

2. Gets students' attention — 1 2 ③4 5 _____

3. Gives clear instructions — 1 2 3 ④5 _used foreign language to help ESL students_

4. Has material and equipment ready — 1 2 ③4 5 _____

5. Communicates expectations — 1 ②3 4 5 _Vague_

5. Monitors student classroom performance — 1 2 ③4 5 _circulates well_

6. Provides feedback — 1 ②3 4 5 _____

7. Varies activities — 1 2 ③4 5 _____

8. Obtains student participation — 1 2 ③4 5 _many students participated_

9. Allows for appropriate student response time — 1 2 ③4 5 _____

10. Extends student responses — 1 ②3 4 5 _could do more_

11. Reinforces correct responses — 1 2 ③4 5 _____

12. Maintains focus on instructional objectives — 1 2 ③4 5 _____

13. Paces material appropriately — 1 ②3 4 5 _spent too much time on certain tasks_

14. Presents information in correct sequence — 1 2 ③4 5 _____

15. Relates content to prior learning — 1 2 3 ④5 _____

16. Describes and defines concepts — 1 ②3 4 5 _could use overhead, etc._

17. Explains clearly — 1 2 ③4 5 _____

18. Uses correct grammar — 1 2 ③4 5 _____

19. Relates material to student interests — 1 2 3 ④5 _____

20. Encourages and assists slow students — 1 2 3 ④5 _Encouraging to these_

General Comments

While there are several areas to work on, the basic lesson + performance was sound. Excellent rapport with students! Not bad for a first observation!

WESTLAND STATE UNIVERSITY
STUDENT TEACHER OBSERVATION INSTRUMENT

Teacher _Connie Munos_ Date _2nd observation_

Evaluator _Lums_ Subject _Computer Literacy_ Grade _10-11_

1=Unsatisfactory 2= Needs improvement 3=Satisfactory performance 4=Above average performance
5=Clearly outstanding performance

Comments

1. Begins on time   1 (2) 3 4 5 _slow start – attendance + interruptions_

2. Gets students' attention   1 2 (3) 4 5 _____

3. Gives clear instructions •   1 2 (3) 4 5 _some students did look confused_

4. Has material and equipment ready   1 (2) 3 4 5 _it would help to use the overhead + not "spell out"_

5. Communicates expectations   1 2 (3) 4 5 _____

5. Monitors student classroom performance   1 2 (3) 4 5 _circulated_

6. Provides feedback   1 2 (3) 4 5 _____

7. Varies activities   1 2 (3) 4 5 _____

8. Obtains student participation   1 2 3 (4) 5 _many students; what about the one in row 3?_

9. Allows for appropriate student response time   1 2 (3) 4 5 _____

10. Extends student responses   1 2 (3) 4 5 _____

11. Reinforces correct responses   1 2 (3) 4 5 _____

12. Maintains focus on instructional objectives   1 2 (3) 4 5 _____

13. Paces material appropriately   1 2 (3) 4 5 _____

14. Presents information in correct sequence   1 2 (3) 4 5 _____

15. Relates content to prior learning   1 2 3 (4) 5 _good job of referring to "last week's homework"_

16. Describes and defines concepts   1 (2) 3 4 5 _why not use the overhead?_

17. Explains clearly   1 2 (3) 4 5 _tries to clarify_

18. Uses correct grammar   1 2 (3) 4 5 _____

19. Relates material to student interests   1 2 3 (4) 5 _exceptional motivation for students_

20. Encourages and assists slow students   1 2 3 (4) 5 _encouraging_

General Comments

Interesting class – many students participated! Need to work on starting on time + making sure all students understood you. Why did you let kid in row 3 sleep?

WESTLAND STATE UNIVERSITY
STUDENT TEACHER OBSERVATION INSTRUMENT

Teacher _Connie Munos_   Date _3rd observation_

Evaluator _Lums_   Subject _Keyboarding_   Grade _10_

1=Unsatisfactory   2= Needs improvement   3=Satisfactory performance   4=Above average performance
5=Clearly outstanding performance   **Comments**

1. Begins on time   1 ②3 4 5 _Better - but 5 minutes was still wasted_

2. Gets students' attention   1 ②3 4 5 _several students were never with you today_

3. Gives clear instructions   1 ②3 4 5 _pretty vague - that may have been the problem_

4. Has material and equipment ready   1 2 ③4 5 _____

5. Communicates expectations   1 ②3 4 5 _again - students were confused_

5. Monitors student classroom performance   1 2 ③4 5 _____

6. Provides feedback   1 ②3 4 5 _need to respond to all questions_

7. Varies activities   ①2 3 4 5 _this time the activities were monotonous to several students_

8. Obtains student participation   1 ②3 4 5 _students off task_

9. Allows for appropriate student response time   1 ②3 4 5 _you rushed a bit today_

10. Extends student responses   1 ②3 4 5 _cut students off_

11. Reinforces correct responses   1 2 ③4 5 _____

12. Maintains focus on instructional objectives   1 2 ③4 5 _____

13. Paces material appropriately   1 ②3 4 5 _either you waited or rushed_

14. Presents information in correct sequence   1 2 ③4 5 _____

15. Relates content to prior learning   1 ②3 4 5 _I didn't notice this today; haven't they done something like this before?_

16. Describes and defines concepts   1 ②3 4 5 _Overhead ??_

17. Explains clearly   1 2 ③4 5 _____

18. Uses correct grammar   1 2 ③4 5 _____

19. Relates material to student interests   1 2 3 4 5 _N/A = hard topic to relate_

20. Encourages and assists slow students   1 2 ③4 5 _you seemed rushed today_

General Comments

I get the feeling that today isn't one of your best. Is there something we need to talk about? Let's talk about today!

WESTLAND STATE UNIVERSITY
STUDENT TEACHER OBSERVATION INSTRUMENT

Teacher _Connie Munos_ Date _4th observation_

Evaluator _Lums_ Subject _Computer Lit_ Grade _10-11_

1=Unsatisfactory 2= Needs improvement 3=Satisfactory performance 4=Above average performance
5=Clearly outstanding performance   **Comments**

1. **Begins on time** 1 2 ③ 4 5 _much better start! I like your choice to let student help!_

2. **Gets students' attention** 1 2 3 ④ 5 _great attention getter_

3. **Gives clear instructions** 1 2 ③ 4 5 _liked the instruction "block" on computer screen_

4. **Has material and equipment ready** 1 2 ③ 4 5

5. **Communicates expectations** 1 2 ③ 4 5

5. **Monitors student classroom performance** 1 2 3 ④ 5 _good circulation_

6. **Provides feedback** 1 2 ③ 4 5

7. **Varies activities** 1 2 3 ④ 5

8. **Obtains student participation** 1 2 3 4 ⑤ _excellent_

9. **Allows for appropriate student response time** 1 2 ③ 4 5

10. **Extends student responses** 1 2 ③ 4 5

11. **Reinforces correct responses** 1 2 3 ④ 5

12. **Maintains focus on instructional objectives** 1 2 3 ④ 5

13. **Paces material appropriately** 1 2 3 ④ 5 _well paced lesson; all elements included_

14. **Presents information in correct sequence** 1 2 3 ④ 5

15. **Relates content to prior learning** 1 2 3 ④ 5

16. **Describes and defines concepts** 1 2 3 ④ 5 _your handout was a good way to do this!_

17. **Explains clearly** 1 2 3 ④ 5

18. **Uses correct grammar** 1 2 3 ④ 5

19. **Relates material to student interests** 1 2 3 ④ 5

20. **Encourages and assists slow students** 1 2 3 ④ 5 _as usual! ☺_

General Comments

A good lesson, Connie. You've made a lot of additions to strengthen your teaching! Good for you.

WESTLAND STATE UNIVERSITY
STUDENT TEACHER OBSERVATION INSTRUMENT

Teacher _Connie Munny_ Date _1st observation_
Evaluator _Thompson_ Subject _Key. B._ Grade _10_

1=Unsatisfactory 2= Needs improvement 3=Satisfactory performance 4=Above average performance
5=Clearly outstanding performance

Comments

1. **Begins on time** 1 2 ③ 4 5 _____

2. **Gets students' attention** 1 ② 3 4 5 _class not paying attention_

3. **Gives clear instructions** 1 ② 3 4 5 _not sure the kids understand_

4. **Has material and equipment ready** 1 ② 3 4 5 _____

5. **Communicates expectations** 1 ② 3 4 5 _they need to do just one thing at a time_

5. **Monitors student classroom performance** 1 2 3 4 5 _____

6. **Provides feedback** 1 2 3 4 5 _____

7. **Varies activities** 1 ② 3 4 5 _too much jumping around_

8. **Obtains student participation** 1 2 3 4 5 _____

9. **Allows for appropriate student response time** 1 2 3 4 5 _____

10. **Extends student responses** 1 2 3 4 5 _____

11. **Reinforces correct responses** 1 ② 3 4 5 _stay on task_

12. **Maintains focus on instructional objectives** 1 2 3 4 5 _____

13. **Paces material appropriately** 1 2 3 4 5 _____

14. **Presents information in correct sequence** 1 ② 3 4 5 _Ask me about an easy way to do this assignment._

15. **Relates content to prior learning** 1 2 3 4 5 _____

16. **Describes and defines concepts** 1 2 3 4 5 _____

17. **Explains clearly** 1 2 ③ 4 5 _____

18. **Uses correct grammar** 1 2 3 4 ⑤ _____

19. **Relates material to student interests** 1 2 3 4 5 _____

20. **Encourages and assists slow students** 1 2 3 ④ 5 _____

General Comments

You spend a lot of time on stuff that you don't need to. You can make things easier for yourself.

WESTLAND STATE UNIVERSITY
STUDENT TEACHER OBSERVATION INSTRUMENT

Teacher _Connie Munoz_ Date _2nd observation_
Evaluator _Simpson_ Subject _Key 3_ Grade _10_

1=Unsatisfactory 2= Needs improvement 3=Satisfactory performance 4=Above average performance
5=Clearly outstanding performance   **Comments**

1. Begins on time   1 2 ③ 4 5 _____

2. Gets students' attention   1 2 ③ 4 5 _____

3. Gives clear instructions   1 ② 3 4 5 _simple is better_____

4. Has material and equipment
   ready   1 2 3 ④ 5 _____

5. Communicates expectations   1 2 ③ 4 5 _____

5. Monitors student classroom
   performance   1 2 3 4 5 _____

6. Provides feedback   1 2 ③ 4 5 _Told correct answers____

7. Varies activities   1 2 3 4 5 _____

8. Obtains student
   participation   1 2 3 ④ 5 _a lot participated_____

9. Allows for appropriate
   student response time   1 2 3 4 5 _____

10. Extends student responses   1 2 3 4 5 _____

11. Reinforces correct
    responses   1 2 3 4 5 _____

12. Maintains focus on
    instructional objectives   1 2 ③ 4 5 _____

13. Paces material
    appropriately   1 ② 3 4 5 _slow down_____

14. Presents information in
    correct sequence   1 2 3 4 5 _____

15. Relates content to
    prior learning   1 2 3 4 5 _____

16. Describes and defines
    concepts   1 2 3 4 5 _____

17. Explains clearly   1 2 3 4 5 _____

18. Uses correct grammar   1 2 3 ④ 5 _____

19. Relates material
    to student interests   1 2 3 4 5 _____

20. Encourages and assists
    slow students   1 2 3 4 5 _____

General Comments

You can simplify lessons to focus on one thing. It will make things easier.

Finding the Good and the Bad

Use any information in this case to identify **Connie**'s strengths and weaknesses as a teacher. Once you have finished listing these, then make some recommendations to guide her teaching.

STRENGTHS

WEAKNESSES

RECOMMENDATIONS

■ *Talk to Me*

Select a partner and together create a series of dialogue journal entries between **Connie Munos** and **Dr. Leems**. The basis for these entries can be anything described in this case. Compare your entries with those of the rest of the class.

CONNIE _____   DR. LEEMS _____

_____   _____

_____   _____

_____   _____

_____   _____

_____   _____

_____   _____

CONNIE _____   DR. LEEMS _____

_____   _____

_____   _____

_____   _____

_____   _____

_____   _____

_____   _____

CONNIE _____   DR. LEEMS _____

_____   _____

_____   _____

_____   _____

_____   _____

_____   _____

_____   _____

Questions Based on Activities

1. Obtain some student teaching evaluation forms that are used at other universities. Discuss how these forms compare to the ones used at Westland State University. Make sure that you know what all of the categories of information on each form refer to.

2. Make a list of things you feel are important to indicate in a letter of reference for a student teacher. Find some individuals who write letters of reference for student teachers on a regular basis and ask what items they typically refer to. Compare the two lists.

3. Discuss the value of using dialogue journals during a student teaching experience. Find some people who have used these kinds of journals and ask their opinions of the activity. Compare their statements with your own.

Additional Teaching and Learning Suggestions

1. Examine the literature on professional development schools. How will these kinds of schools change the nature of student teaching?

2. Invite the director of student teaching to speak to your class. Find out what expectations are held for student teachers at your university.

3. Invite a panel of student teachers, cooperating teachers, and university supervisors to class. Encourage them to share information about the student teaching experience. You may also want to interview each of them in small groups.

4. Explore the literature on the subject of student teaching. Share your findings with the rest of the class.

For Further Reading

Clifford, G. J., and Guthrie, J. W. (1988). *Ed School: A brief for professional education.* Chicago: University of Chicago Press.

Davidman, P. T. (1990). "Multicultural teacher education and supervision: A new approach to professional development." *Teacher Education Quarterly* 17: 37–52.

Giroux, H. A. (1988). *Teachers as intellectuals: Toward a critical pedagogy of learning.* Granby, MA: Bergin and Garvey.

Hoy, W. K., and Woolfolk, A. E. (1990). "Socialization of student teachers." *American Educational Research Journal* 27: 279–300.

Lortie, D. (1975). *Schoolteacher.* Chicago: University of Chicago Press.

Maehr, M. L. 1976. "Continuing motivation: An analysis of a seldom considered educational outcome." *Review of Educational Research* 46: 443–462.

Marshall, H. H. (1990). "Metaphor as an instructional tool in encouraging student teacher reflection." *Theory into Practice* 29: 128–132.

Meade, E. J. (1991). "Reshaping the clinical phase of teacher preparation." *Phi Delta Kappan* 72: 666–669.

Natriello, G., and Dornbusch, S. M. (1984). *Teacher evaluative standards and student effort.* New York: Longman.

Olson, P. M., and Carter, K. (1989). "The capabilities of cooperating teachers in USA schools for communicating knowledge about teaching." *Journal of Education for Teaching* 15: 113–131.

Veenman, S. (1984). "Perceived problems of beginning teachers." *Review of Educational Research* 54: 143–178.

Warren, D. (1989). *American teachers: Histories of a profession at work.* New York: Macmillan.

Weinstein, C. S. (1989). "Teacher education students' preconceptions of teaching." *Journal of Teacher Education* 40: 53–60.

Appendix I

Biographies and Cumulative Folders

■

Derrick Abbott | The counselor and several teachers at Edge City High School are convinced that **Derrick Abbott** needs psychological counseling. Teachers have referred him to the school counselors in the past and they have tried to work with him with little or no success. One of the counselors has had conferences with the **Abbotts** and has recommended that they take **Derrick** to see a local psychiatrist to try to find out just what his problem is. **Mr. Abbott**, a pharmacist, and **Mrs. Abbott**, an elementary school teacher, were both indignant and offended that this suggestion was made. It is their contention that **Derrick** is completely normal and is just going through a "phase," and that if he were getting more help and support from the school he wouldn't be having any problems at all. They point out that their two younger children are both outstanding students and that **Derrick** could be also.

The case could certainly be made that his parents are right. On intelligence tests he is high normal, and during his elementary school career he showed that he could do the academic work required by the school. It has now been a long time since he has displayed this ability, and he is in danger of failing everything he is taking.

Deborah Mason, **Derrick**'s political science teacher, is convinced that his problem is social, not academic. She almost never sees **Derrick** with other students. He comes into her class alone and he leaves alone. He eats by himself in the school cafeteria. He appears to have no energy, and spends much of his time in her class with his head on the desk. He is usually not sleeping but he is certainly not participating in the class activities. She has even called **Mrs. Abbott** and suggested that she have him checked by a physician. **Mrs. Abbott** thanked her but assured her that he had plenty of energy and spent a great deal of time playing with their dog.

Cumulative Record
Edge City School District

Name: Abbott, Derrick　　　　　　　　　**Birthdate:** May 4, 1976
Address: 132 Elm Street

Parents: Father: Ralph Abbott　　**Mother:** Elsie Abbott

Occupation: Father: Pharmacist　　**Mother:** Teacher

Number of Siblings: Two　　**Ages:** 10 and 12

Test Data: I.Q.: 109　　**Math:** 9.6　　**Reading:** 10.4　　**Writing:** 9.6
(Achievement test data in grade level)

Extracurricular Activities:

None

Discipline Record
- Referred to counselor and principal for inappropriate classroom behavior
- Tardiness (averages 2–3 times/grade period)

Teachers' Comments
- Derrick is a loner, he doesn't seem well-adjusted to high school
- Derrick appears very listless and tired; I am worried about his frame of mind and health
- I feel that Derrick may have some type of family problem

Raphael Aquilar

Raphael lives with his mother and three sisters in the northeast section of Edge City. This area is known by the townspeople as "Little Mexico." Home is a small, wood frame, two-bedroom house, very similar to the other houses in the area. His mother knows little English, and therefore much of the conversation between **Raphael**, his mother, and his older sister is conducted in Spanish. Several of **Raphael**'s friends have dropped out of school, and there is pressure both from them and from his mother for him to quit. His mother's reason for wanting him to leave school is so that he can get a job to supplement the money she and her older daughter earn to support the family.

Raphael has difficulty in school, but he almost intuitively realizes that if he is ever to accomplish the things that he wants to accomplish he must not only finish high school but go on to college as well. He also believes that he is just as smart as the other kids in his classes. He blames his low achievement on his lack of proficiency in the English language, and also on the fact that he doesn't have other advantages like new clothes, a car, and the other things that his classmates seem to take for granted.

Raphael is quiet and almost withdrawn in his classes at school, but this is primarily because of his insecurity with English. Although he recognizes the odds against him, his dream is to someday become a lawyer like the character Jimmy Smits played on "L.A. Law." He would like to be a good student, but lack of encouragement at school, at home, and especially among his out-of-school friends makes the task doubly difficult.

His older sister, **Maria**, is his only confidante. She has been telling him that if he will just keep trying and finish high school, even if his grades leave something to be desired, scholarships for Hispanic students are available and he will be able to afford college.

Cumulative Record
Edge City School District

Name: Aquilar, Raphael   **Birthdate:** Nov. 23, 1977
Address: 3429 Mendoza Court

Parents: Father: **Mother:** Conchita Aquilar

Occupation: Father: **Mother:** Nurses' aide, Edge City Hospital

Number of Siblings: Three   **Ages:** 11, 13, 20 (all girls)

Test Data: I.Q.:   **Math:** 10.3   **Reading:** 8.4   **Writing:** 7.9
(Achievement test data in grade level)

Extracurricular Activities:
None

Discipline Record
- no infractions recorded.

Teachers' Comments
- Raphael is an eager student who appears to be overcoming his English deficiencies.
- I am aware that Raphael is receiving pressure to quit school and work. He really wants to finish school. Perhaps someone from the school should make a home visit and reinforce this?
- We are trying to find Raphael an after-school job at a grocery store; this way he can work and still finish school; we need parental permission, which, in his case, is difficult to come by.

Wilma Booker

Daniel Booker joined the United States Air Force when he finished high school. After basic training in Wichita Falls, Texas, he was sent to mechanics' school. He found that he was good at, and enjoyed, working on powerful jet planes. He met Doris Schmidt at a church in Fort Worth where he was assigned after completing mechanics' school. They were married shortly after. Eleven years later their only child, **Wilma**, was born.

Doris Booker is an artist. She has established several outlets throughout the world for her watercolors and charcoal drawings. The constant moving that was a part of the first twenty years of her marriage furnished her with an ever-changing environment in which to practice her craft. She is also a highly intelligent, curious person who is an avid reader.

Daniel, who had reached the rank of master sergeant, resigned from the service after completing twenty years and becoming eligible for retirement benefits. Still a young man, he moved his family to Edge City and he got a position as a mail carrier for the United States Postal Service. He and his family have lived in Edge City ever since.

For the first ten years of her life **Wilma** never lived in one place for more than three years. She started school in Germany, and lived and went to school in Japan and New Zealand before returning to the United States when she was eleven years old. Her home, wherever it was, was full of books, art work, and music. Her parents talked to each other and to her. Even though her father had joined the Air Force after high school and her mother had married after just two years of college, the home climate would have to be characterized as intellectual.

She entered the sixth grade at Travis Elementary School when her family moved to Edge City, and has been in the Edge City schools—Hooker Junior High and Edge City High—ever since. She has never made a grade lower than A. Even though the level of work in many of her classes does not challenge her, she never complains. She participates in the class, does the work that is required, and knocks the top out of whatever tests are administered. She is pleasant and friendly but is not one of the social leaders of the school.

Cumulative Record
Edge City School District

Name: Booker, Wilma   **Birthdate:** Sept. 9, 1976
Address: 1222 Horace Terrace

Parents: Father: Daniel Booker   **Mother:** Doris Booker

Occupation: Father: U.S. Postal Service   **Mother:** Artist, housewife

Number of Siblings: None   **Ages:**

Test Data: I.Q.: 127   **Math:** 13.4   **Reading:** 13.9   **Writing:** 13.9
(Achievement test data in grade level)

Extracurricular Activities:

Honor Society
Latin Club
Band

Discipline Record

- no infractions recorded

Teachers' Comments

- Wilma is a delight to have in class. With students like her I would reconsider my decision to quit teaching.
- An outstanding student, but I sometimes think she is *too* cooperative and *too* submissive.
- She is not only a good student but she is very bright. A really first-class mind.

Nanci Drake

Being black in America has never bothered **Nanci Drake**. She grew up in a family that affords a maximum of love and security. Her father is a sociology professor at Westland State University. The family moved to Edge City when **Nanci** was five years old. She has spent all of her school years in the Edge City school district. An excellent student, she is not only accepted but looked up to and admired by many of her classmates.

She lives in a large brick home in one of the more affluent areas of town with her father and mother and an older sister, **Deidra**. Her brother is a sophomore at Georgetown University. The family regularly takes vacations together; last summer they spent a month in France. **Nanci** is certain that she wants to be a pediatrician and is already reading college catalogs and talking with her parents about where she should go to college.

The good grades that she consistently brings home on her report card are achieved with little effort. She developed good study habits early in her life and has maintained them throughout her school years. **Nanci** is attractive and always impeccably groomed. Socially she is well accepted by nearly everyone, but she is basically quiet and not very outgoing. Academic achievement is what she wants out of school, and most of her social needs are met by her immediate family.

Cumulative Record
Edge City School District

Name: Drake, Nanci   **Birthdate:** Feb. 14, 1978
Address: 1114 Robinwood Terrace

Parents: Father: Adam Drake   **Mother:** Hilda Drake

Occupation: Father: Professor   **Mother:** Housewife

Number of Siblings: Two   **Ages:** 18 (female) 20 (male)

Test Data: I.Q.: 108   **Math:** 9.2   **Reading:** 10.7   **Writing:** 10.4
(Achievement test data in grade level)

Extracurricular Activities:
Odyssey of the Mind

Discipline Record
- no infractions recorded

Teachers' Comments
- Nanci is an excellent student.
- Nanci studies quite hard for a high school student; perhaps she should ease up just a bit and enjoy life.
- Nanci is highly motivated and serves as a good model for others

Gladys Farrish | Many of **Gladys Farrish**'s teachers refer to her as sullen. She seldom smiles, and if she feels that anyone is making an unflattering or disparaging remark about her she is quick to take exception, and this may include physical retaliation. An African-American, **Gladys** lives with an aunt and the aunt's four children in the public housing project in Edge City. For most of her younger life **Gladys** lived with her mother in Atlanta, but when her mother remarried for the third time, **Gladys** could not get along with her new stepfather and she repeatedly ran away from home. She came to visit her aunt nearly two years ago and has been here ever since. There is little room in the small apartment, and **Gladys** has to share a bed with the oldest daughter, but the four girls love her and her aunt is delighted to have her there to look after the girls after school. She also often cooks the meals and is a big help in keeping the apartment clean. Around her aunt and her cousins she is much more outgoing than she is at school.

Her inability to relate to many of the students at Edge City High School is due to her resentment of the fact that she does not have the things that many of them have. She and her aunt have learned when the "good" things come in at the Goodwill store and so she is always dressed in clean and presentable clothes, but she would like to dress like **Nanci Drake**. Her attitude and her unwillingness to put forth much effort results in her having a report card filled with C's and with an occasional B. She is academically able and with sufficient effort could be making straight A's.

Cumulative Record
Edge City School District

Name: Farrish, Gladys   **Birthdate:** Aug. 25, 1978
Address: John R. Dunbar Apts., Apt. #303

Parents: Father: **Mother:** Celia White (aunt—guardian)

Occupation: Father: **Mother:** (Guardian) Cleaning Service Employee

Number of Siblings: None   **Ages:**

Test Data: I.Q.: 110   **Math:** 8.8   **Reading:** 11.4   **Writing:** 10.0
(Achievement test data in grade level)

Extracurricular Activities:

None

Discipline Record
- Referred for "smart-aleck" remarks to various teachers
- Tardiness (frequent; averages 2–3 times/week—unexcused)

Teachers' Comments
- Gladys seems to have a problem with her female teachers; she is always referred by the female teachers (counselor)
- Gladys could try harder; she could be a better student
- Gladys, in my opinion, is an underachiever; she simply doesn't care about school

Clarise Gerrard

Clarise has the reputation of being one of the "loose" girls at Edge City High School. If the number of sexual experiences and the variety of partners in those encounters is used as the criterion, the reputation is well deserved. She is basically very insecure and desperately seeking acceptance and reassurance of her worth as an individual, and has found this acceptance and reassurance from the boys who are more than willing to say the things she needs to hear. She lives with her mother, father, and younger brother on a small dairy farm twelve miles west of the city. Her father does not own the farm but is hired by the owner, a professor in the history department of the university, to milk the herd and to manage the farm. They have been living here for over three years, the longest time **Clarise** has ever lived in one house.

Clarise is not happy at home. Her parents are both very devout fundamentalist Christians. They are opposed to dancing, card playing, any music other than religious music, television, and radio. They demand immediate and unquestioned obedience to any requests that they make of their children. Failure to meet the parents' expectations almost inevitably leads to severe whippings with a belt. **Clarise** is counting the days until she can move out of the house, get herself a job, and lead her own kind of life.

At school, **Clarise** is bubbly and vivacious around the junior and senior boys. She has learned to live with the fact that she is not accepted by the vast majority of the girls. This does not prevent her from trying to mimic the behavior, dress, and grooming of the most popular girls in school. The severe lack of money in the **Gerrard** household, and the attitudes of her parents, make this attempt to conform pathetically futile.

Cumulative Record
Edge City School District

Name: Gerrard, Clarise   **Birthdate:** Nov. 2, 1978
Address: Rt. 1 Box 334

Parents: Father: Buster Gerrard   **Mother:** Clara Gerrard

Occupation: Father: Dairy Worker   **Mother:** Housewife

Number of Siblings: One   **Ages:** 14

Test Data: I.Q.: 93   **Math:** 8.4   **Reading:** 8.8   **Writing:** 8.9
(Achievement test data in grade level)

Extracurricular Activities:

Pep Club

Discipline Record

- Referred for wearing inappropriate attire to school function
- Referred for tardiness due to inappropriate activity in the hall
- Referred for public display of affection in cafeteria

Teachers' Comments

- Clarise is not a happy girl!
- Clarise has trouble relating to the other girls in the class
- Clarise should concentrate more on her classwork than on the boys in the class
- I think Clarise desperately wants to fit in, but can't somehow

Clifford Handley

Some people would call **Clifford Handley** a disadvantaged rich boy. Although he lives in an opulent house surrounded by other new, large, and ostentatious homes, he does not enjoy going home. His only sibling, an older brother who is an aspiring songwriter, has left home, and the family does not know where he is. They think he may be in Los Angeles, New York, or Nashville, but they have made few attempts to get in touch with him.

Clifford's mother and father own and operate their own real estate business. Although they employ eight full-time agents and maintain a large office in what was once a department store on the square in Edge City, they find that it is not unusual for them to work twelve to fourteen hours a day. When not working they maintain a whirlwind of social activities that are centered in the Edge City Country Club. They both play golf and try to get in at least one or two rounds a week. They made **Clifford** take golf lessons when he was in junior high school but he was never interested and has resisted all of their attempts to get him involved in the country club's events for high school age students.

Clifford is very intelligent and keeps up with what is going on in the world. He also spends much time reading, usually biography, history, and science fiction. Basically very insecure, he is sarcastic and condescending to nearly everyone. He envies his brother, who, he feels, has escaped from a boring prison. He does not know what he wants to do with his life but he can hardly wait until graduation so that he can leave for college and get away from home.

Cumulative Record
Edge City School District

Name: Handley, Clifford   **Birthdate:** January 19, 1976
Address: 1228 Bustamonte

Parents: Father: Arthur Handley   **Mother:** Gracie Handley

Occupation: Father: Owns real estate agency   **Mother:** Real estate

Number of Siblings: One   **Ages:** 22 (male)

Test Data: I.Q.: 139   **Math:** 14.4   **Reading:** 12.9   **Writing:** 13.2
(Achievement test data in grade level)

Extracurricular Activities:

Editor of school newspaper
Young Democrats
Debate Team

Discipline Record

- Referred for inappropriate language use with a teacher
- Referred for parking in the teachers' parking lot
- Referred for inappropriately confronting a teacher during homeroom

Teachers' Comments

- Cliff is extremely bright, but quite egotistical
- Clifford is an able student, but could certainly try harder
- We really need to challenge Clifford; he tends to loaf in school
- Cliff's parents are dfficult to locate for parent/teacher conferences (counselor)

Eduardo Hinijosa

Eduardo was born in Monterrey, Mexico, and moved with his family to the United States when he was twelve. He attended several different schools in southern California over a two-year period before his family moved to Edge City three years ago. His father and mother both work for a custodial service and they live in a small rented house in northeast Edge City. **Eduardo** is the oldest of four children. His ten-year-old brother and eight-year-old twin sisters are all more fluent in spoken English than he is.

Eduardo is soft-spoken and shy around other people but is happy and outgoing with his family. He has an afternoon job at a small, home-owned grocery store, where he bags groceries, stocks shelves, and cleans up. He has experienced little success in school, either academically or socially. He would probably have dropped out of school had it not been for his father's determination that he graduate, and for the influence of his friend, **Raphael Aquilar**. **Eduardo** and **Raphael** are inseparable at school and spend most of their time together on weekends when one or the other is not working. At least partially because of the academic requirements for participation in interscholastic sports, **Eduardo** is not involved in any organized activity at school.

Cumulative Record
Edge City School District

Name: Hinijosa, Eduardo   **Birthdate:** May 29, 1977
Address: 2330 Hickory Street

Parents: Father: Juan Hinijosa   **Mother:** Marie Hinijosa

Occupation: Father: Custodial service employee   **Mother:** Custodial service employee

Number of Siblings: Three   **Ages:** 10 (male) and 8 (twin girls)

Test Data: I.Q.:   **Math:** 7.9   **Reading:** 6.8   **Writing:** 7.1
(Achievement test data in grade level)

Extracurricular Activities:
None

Discipline Record
- Tardiness (not excessive)

Teachers' Comments
- Eduardo is a quiet student who works to his ability
- Eduardo seems to be very concerned about finishing school; for some reason he feels that he won't be able to
- Eduardo and Raphael Aquilar are close friends; I am concerned that if Raphael quits school then Eduardo will feel that he has to (counselor)

Mark Jackson

Mark Jackson has a measured IQ of 113. His early elementary report cards show grades of primarily A's and B's. Beginning in junior high school, the quality of his school work began to tumble. In the seventh and eighth grades he had mostly B's and C's but since entering Edge City High School there have been several D's and a few F's. He should have graduated last year, but failures in biology, senior English, and political science prevented him from graduating. He turned eighteen in September and most of the teachers thought he would drop out, but so far he is still enrolled and attends fairly regularly.

Mark lives with his mother and two younger sisters at the Acorn Acres Mobile Home Park just outside of Edge City. The park is not well maintained and there is a constant turnover of tenants. A group of four high school students who also live at Acorn Acres are constant companions, and they are frequently in trouble with teachers and administrators. One of the group has been charged with shoplifting and is awaiting trial. So far, **Mark** has escaped being associated with this gang of boys. In order to get the kind of clothes he wants to wear and to earn money to buy a used car, **Mark** works after school and on weekends at a convenience store. When asked what he wants to do after high school he mentions joining the Army or going to a trade school. He is aware, however, that his mother cannot afford to pay the tuition.

Cumulative Record
Edge City School District

Name: Jackson, Mark   **Birthdate:** Sept. 9, 1975
Address: Lot 26, Carrie Rd., Acorn Acres Park

Parents: Father: Gerald Jackson   **Mother:** Bonnie Jackson
Parents divorced. Lives with his mother.

Occupation: Father: Carpenter   **Mother:** Seamstress, Griswold Lingerie
Waitress, Tri-State Truck Stop

Number of Siblings: 2 girls   **Ages:** 12 and 14

Test Data: I.Q.: 113   **Math:** 9.6   **Reading:** 9.2   **Writing:** 8.8
(Achievement test data in grade level)

Extracurricular Activities:

Varsity Football Team

Discipline Record
- 1992—6 office referrals by teachers, 4 in-house suspensions
  Three sessions with counselor
  Mother called in twice
- 1993—Office referrals by teachers, 2 in-house suspensions
  Involved in serious fight before school, police called but no charges
  were made.

Teachers' Comments
- Don't sell Mark Jackson short. He is extremely difficult to motivate but he does have the ability if you can just get him to work.
- Rude and impertinent. Lazy.
- Could do the work if he just would.

Lissa James

All of the teachers at Edge City High School like **Lissa James**. She is a good student and is always willing to help with school activities or projects. She is often, however, forced to refrain from participating because of family obligations.

Lissa's mother died four years ago in a car accident, and since then **Lissa** has had to assume a large part of the responsibility for taking care of her two younger brothers, **Matt** and **Joey**. Her father works the late shift at the large city newspaper and often tries to pick up some overtime pay by leaving early for work. As a result, **Lissa** must care for her brothers from the time they get home from school until they leave for school the next morning. She never seems to complain about this, but some counselors have revealed that she is often upset about missing out on some school activities.

Lissa appears socially well adjusted. She has many friends, and attends social functions when she can get a sitter or her father is off for the evening. She is an eager participant in classes and is viewed as a good student who typically has the "right" answers. One of her best friends is **Sarah Tompkins**, a student confined to a wheelchair. They are frequently seen together in the cafeteria and at school functions. On many occasions, **Lissa** has come to **Sarah**'s defense when other students were "making fun" of her.

Cumulative Record
Edge City School District

Name: James, Lissa   **Birthdate:** March 30, 1978
Address: 447 Primrose

Parents: Father: Charles James   **Mother:** Deceased

Occupation: Father: Copy Editor, Newspaper   **Mother:**

Number of Siblings: Two   **Ages:** 9 (male) 6 (male)

Test Data: I.Q.: 112   **Math:** 11.1   **Reading:** 10.9   **Writing:** 11.6
                                (Achievement test data in grade level)

Extracurricular Activities:
Reporter for school newspaper

Discipline Record
- no infractions recorded

Teachers' Comments
- Lissa is a delightful student
- Lissa is a good friend of Sarah Tompkins; she willingly defends Sarah to the other students; she is a good friend to have
- Lissa seems distressed about having to watch her younger brothers every day after school; could not arrange a meeting with the father (counselor)
- Lissa is a good writer and should pursue a career in writing

Karl Latham ▎With a very unhappy home life, **Karl Latham** finds it difficult to get much enjoyment out of life. He has only two close friends and he spends many hours daydreaming about what he is going to do as soon as he get out of school.

His home has not always been unhappy. He can remember when he was young how he and his older sister and mother and father had spent many happy hours together at home. He also remembers the vacations they had gone on together. But those memories are fading and getting more difficult to call up to consciousness. His sister was killed in an automobile wreck. His father started drinking and became more and more withdrawn from **Karl** and his mother. Gradually he became violent. Now the home is a battleground when his father is around. **Karl** has become very close to his mother, and often makes plans about how he can rescue her from his father.

Karl is not an outstanding student but is capable of doing the work if he is motivated. Unsure of what he wants to do after school, he finds little incentive to excel.

Cumulative Record
Edge City School District

_____

Name: Latham, Karl   **Birthdate:** June 12, 1978
Address: 3394 Old Town Highway

Parents: Father: Daryl Latham   **Mother:** Patricia Latham

Occupation: Father: Mechanic, Troy's Auto Repair   **Mother:** Unemployed

Number of Siblings: None   **Ages:**

Test Data: I.Q.: 98   **Math:** 9.4   **Reading:** 9.6   **Writing:** 8.7
(Achievement test data in grade level)

Extracurricular Activities:
None

Discipline Record
• Referred for refusing to work in classroom
• Referred for not attending parent/teacher conference
• Referred by his father for being incorrigible

Teachers' Comments
• Karl cannot keep his mind on his classwork; I am concerned about his frame of mind
• Karl needs to work harder; he could make much better grades
• Karl seems to have quite a problem with his father; efforts to bring family together at a parent/teacher/counselor conference have failed (counselor)

Margie Laurence | Unlike many of her classmates, **Margie Laurence** thoroughly enjoys almost every aspect of school life. She even enjoys the work and study that she finds necessary to meet the high standards that she has set for herself. She also enjoys out-of-class activities such as the honor society and the student council. She is well-liked by her teachers and by her classmates.

When she first arrived in Edge City two years ago, she was apprehensive at moving into a new situation. She had been very comfortable with her situation in Florida and didn't know what to expect in this new setting. She found that the teachers made her feel welcome, and she quickly formed a circle of friends. **Margie**'s father is an executive with Mayflower Insurance Company, and the transfer to Edge City was a big step forward in his career. Her parents were divorced when she was ten. Her stepmother had never worked outside of the home, but she recently enrolled in the Master's of Business Administration program at Westland State. **Margie** gets along with her stepmother without major conflict, but she also tries to maintain a relationship with her mother, who has remarried and is once again involved in divorce proceedings.

Cumulative Record
Edge City School District

Name: Laurence, Margie   **Birthdate:** October 23, 1976
Address: 3444 Meandering Way Circle

Parents: Father: Horace Laurence   **Mother:** Elizabeth Laurence

Occupation: Father: Vice-President, Mayflower Ins.   **Mother:** Student

Number of Siblings: None   **Ages:**

Test Data: I.Q.: 113   **Math:** 11.7   **Reading:** 12.1   **Writing:** 11.8
(Achievement test data in grade level)

Extracurricular Activities:

Honor Society
Student Council
Swim Team

Discipline Record
- no infractions recorded at this time

Teachers' Comments
- Margie is a delightful student
- Margie is a fine worker; excellent student
- Margie appears upset about her mother again; her grades are suffering; can we arrange for a conference with the parents? (swim team coach)
- Margie is well-liked by all the students; her adjustment to Edge City has been smooth

Bryan Limb | Bryan Limb is one of the best students at Edge City High; the teachers love him. He may not always have the best grades, but he is eager to participate, pleasant, and usually has grades near the top of the class. He is active in school organizations, but is not a member of the ROTC. He is good in PE classes, but he has never participated on the interscholastic sports teams, despite the urging of the various coaches.

Bryan's parents are not active in the school PTA, but they are members. They do visit the school on open house nights to come to visit with Bryan's teachers. These teachers describe his parents as pleasant and very interested in their son. The counselor and principal, on the other hand, have had several confrontations with Bryan's father, Joshua. It seems that the Limbs belong to a religious group that has rigid regulations about the kinds of activities that its members are allowed to be involved in. The group has pacifist views, and any violent or war-like activities are forbidden. The confrontations have usually been over the fact that Bryan or his sister, Ellen, have been forced to participate in school-related activities that involve them in these kinds of forbidden areas. Mr. Limb has been quite persistent in taking care that his children do not violate any of the religious order's regulations, even when they come into direct conflict with the school's curriculum. Both Ellen and Bryan seem rather embarrassed by their father's persistent adherence to the order's rules, but they have been raised to "suffer in silence."

Cumulative Record
Edge City School District

Name: Limb, Bryan   **Birthdate:** July 4, 1977
Address: 884 Maid Marion

Parents: Father: Joshua Limb   **Mother:** Ethel Limb

Occupation: Father: Attorney   **Mother:** Accountant

Number of Siblings: Two   **Ages:** 14 (female) 11 (male)

Test Data: I.Q.: 131   **Math:** 13.6   **Reading:** 12.5   **Writing:** 13.2
(Achievement test data in grade level)

Extracurricular Activities:

Newspaper Staff
Student Council
Prom Committee
Spanish Club

Discipline Record
• Referred for unexcused absences from class

Teachers' Comments
• Bryan is a wonderful student
• It's a delight to have such a hard-working student in class
• Bryan is a good thinker
• Bryan is a good writer; I would encourage him to pursue journalism in college (newspaper sponsor)

Art Scott

Although he has been in Edge City for only a year, **Art Scott** has found a place for himself and is actively involved both in and out of school. An above-average student, he has little difficulty maintaining grades that are acceptable to his parents. He has the ability to do much better, but would rather devote his time to social and extracurricular activities.

His father is a neurologist in the local health maintenance organization and his mother does not have an outside job. Even though she is new in town, she is already very active in the Catholic Church and in the League of Women Voters. She is considering running for a place on the City Council when the next election is held. While they have high expectations for both of their children, **Art** and his younger sister **Cynthia**, they do not exert much pressure for them to excel in the academic area.

Art is on the staff of the school newspaper, is a member of the debate team and plays shortstop on the baseball team. He is outgoing and popular with both teachers and students. He plans on running for the student body president in the elections at the end of the year. Although his father would really like him to pursue a career in medicine, **Art** plans on eventually going to law school, with an eye down the road to a career in politics.

Cumulative Record
Edge City School District

Name: Scott, Art   **Birthdate:** February 17, 1977
Address: 654 Poinsettia Parkway

Parents: Father: Reginald Scott   **Mother:** Beverly Scott

Occupation: Father: Neurologist   **Mother:** Housewife

Number of Siblings: One   **Ages:** 13 (female)

Test Data: I.Q.: 109   **Math:** 11.7   **Reading:** 10.6   **Writing:** 10.2
(Achievement test data in grade level)

Extracurricular Activities:

Newspaper Staff
Debate Team
Baseball Team
Student Council

Discipline Record

- No infractions recorded at this time

Teachers' Comments

- Art is a fine student; he could do better on his grades if he spent more time studying and less time in school activities
- Art is a creative thinker and problem solver
- Art seems to be adjusting to Edge City just fine; no problems are noted (counselor)

Sarah Tompkins

Sarah is the only child of **Michael** and **Diana Tompkins**. The family moved here almost ten years ago and lives in what is known as the high-class part of town. Their home is equipped with an in-ground swimming pool, which Sarah's parents are quick to identify as a necessity due to her "condition."

Sarah's education has taken place in special education classes ever since the accident that left her paralyzed from the waist down. At seven, while learning to dive at a local swimming pool, she ran and plunged into the shallow end, striking her head and neck on the bottom of the pool. Since then she has been confined to a wheelchair.

Her special education teachers describe her as bright and well-adjusted. They view her parents as somewhat less well-adjusted, and as overprotective. These teachers have repeatedly tried to work with the parents in an attempt to change their thinking about **Sarah**'s condition. Much of their effort has simply been wasted; her parents are still too overprotective and are probably stifling **Sarah**'s progress.

Two years ago one of **Sarah**'s teachers noticed the trouble that she was having when reading novels and longer passages of text. After careful observation and some testing, it was determined that **Sarah** did have a learning disability that affected her comprehension and reading of long passages. Her IQ is normal and the disability is confined to her processing of printed language.

In terms of social relations, **Sarah** seems relatively normal. She has friends, but she has confided in various counselors that she has never had a boyfriend. She wants very badly to fit in with the other kids.

Cumulative Record
Edge City School District

Name: Tompkins, Sarah   **Birthdate:** March 29, 1978
Address: 145 Hickory Court

Parents: Father: Michael Tompkins   **Mother:** Diane Tompkins

Occupation: Father: Manager, Montgomery Ward   **Mother:** Professor

Number of Siblings: None   **Ages:**

Test Data: I.Q.: 101   **Math:** 9.5   **Reading:** 9.0   **Writing:** 8.9
(Achievement test data in grade level)

Extracurricular Activities:
Reporter for newspaper

Discipline Record
- No infractions recorded

Teachers' Comments
- Sarah complains about having trouble reaching the desks in some classes; we have examined the room and made the necessary adjustments (counselor)
- Sarah is a bright girl and a good student (special education supervisor)
- Sarah is definitely trying to overcome the handicaps that she must deal with; she reports to me (weekly) on her relations with the other students and teachers (counselor)
- Sarah's English teachers have routinely requested her disability identification number to obtain books on tape for their classes

Bobby Utter

Bobby Utter does not enjoy the academic requirements of school. He doesn't hate them, but he feels that they get in the way of the real purpose of school, which he perceives to be to get together with his friends and have a good time. Since teachers and administrators have a different view of why they are there, **Bobby** quite frequently finds himself in conflict with the adults in the school setting. It is never anything serious, and **Bobby** is usually very adept at convincing teachers that he is going to be doing much better in the very near future.

Bobby lives down the street from **Nanci Drake** in the Idiot's Hill section of Edge City. Both of his parents grew up in Edge City. His father is a deputy sheriff of Edge County and his mother is a nurse. He has a younger sister and an older brother. They are a very close family and make a point of taking vacations together, and **Bobby** and his father share a love for fishing and can quite frequently be found together on local lakes. His parents would like for him to be doing better in school but he is quite happy with his "average" grades.

Cumulative Record
Edge City School District

Name: Utter, Bobby   **Birthdate:** December 12, 1977
Address: 1101 Robinwood Terrace

Parents: Father: Troy Utter   **Mother:** Angie Utter

Occupation: Father: Deputy Sheriff **Mother:** Nurse

Number of Siblings: Two   **Ages:** 13 (female) 19 (male)

Test Data: I.Q.: 98   **Math:** 8.6   **Reading:** 9.3   **Writing:** 8.4
                    (Achievement test data in grade level)

Extracurricular Activities:

None

Discipline Record
- Referred for inappropriate classroom behavior
- Referred for arguing with cafeteria monitor
- Unexcused absences (excessive—parents contacted)

Teachers' Comments
- Bobby is an underachiever
- Bobby needs to try harder to make good grades
- Bobby is a likeable fellow; I wish he cared more about school

Maurice Yeatts | Maurice is small for an eighth grader. His voice is just beginning to change and he has started to grow, but his parents know that he will probably never be very large, for both his father and his mother are relatively short and slim. The fact that he has always been one of the smaller students in his class may account partially for the fact that he has always been the class cutup and clown.

What **Maurice** may lack in size he makes up in intelligence. Not only does he score well on standardized ability and achievement tests, he is also extremely creative. He has a good sense of humor and does not hesitate to use it on other students and on those teachers who he perceives will be receptive.

Maurice's father is a partner in an accounting firm and his mother gives private piano lessons in their home. He has an older sister who is a tenth grader at Edge City High and a younger sister who is in the sixth grade at Hooker. There is not a lot of money in the family, but with careful budgeting the family travels, goes to concerts and the opera, and visits art galleries on a regular basis.

Well liked by the majority of his classmates, **Maurice** is often elected to committees and class offices and can be depended on to fulfill the responsibilities of these committees and offices. Possessed of lots of energy, he is constantly flirting with discipline problems but so far he has managed to talk himself out of any serious consequences.

Cumulative Record
Edge City School District

Name: Yeatts, Maurice   **Birthdate:** Sept. 19, 1980
Address: 175 Oak Street

Parents: Father: Jacob Yeatts   **Mother:** Marilyn Yeatts

Occupation: Father: Accountant   **Mother:** Piano instructor and housewife

Number of Siblings: Two   **Ages:** 11 and 15

Test Data: I.Q.: 119   **Math:** 9.8   **Reading:** 10.0   **Writing:** 9.75
(Achievement test data in grade level)

Extracurricular Activities:

Drama Club
Student Council
Spirit Club
Jr. Band

Discipline Record
- Referred for disturbing class
- Referred for disrupting assembly

Teachers' Comments
- Maurice is a pleasant individual, but he could be a bit more serious about class
- Maurice needs to concentrate more on his schoolwork and leave the entertaining outside of the classroom
- I am concerned that we may not be challenging enough for Maurice; I am recommending that his name be placed into candidacy for the Gifted and Talented Programs (counselor)

Edwin Zettler

Like **Clifford Handley**, **Edwin Zettler** comes from a family with means. Also like **Clifford**, he is not particularly happy in his home environment. His unhappiness is not from lack of attention, however. An only child, he was loved and cared for by his mother until she was injured in an automobile accident six years ago. Since then she has been confined to a wheelchair and has gradually withdrawn from life outside of their home. During his childhood his father also showered him with attention and made sure that he had what he needed and pretty much what he wanted. Beginning in early adolescence, **Edwin** rebelled against what he saw as his father's attempt to totally dominate him. This rebellion at first took the form of verbal battles, which **Edwin** usually won.

Their relationship deteriorated. They are civil and polite to each other at meals but they seldom talk. When they do, it usually ends in one or the other storming out of the room. **Edwin** is solicitous of his mother and spends time with her in her room nearly every day. He is an avid reader, and he and his mother sometimes discuss the books that they are reading. He is not at all sure what he wants to do with his life. He assumes, as do his parents, that he will be attending university, but it has not been decided which one and he does not have an idea as to what he wants to major in.

Edwin is popular at school, both with teachers and with most of the students. He is not active in extracurricular activities but can be depended on to pull his fair share of any task he is assigned.

Cumulative Record
Edge City School District

Name: Zettler, Edwin   **Birthdate:** May 29, 1976
Address: 2456 Pennsylvania Drive

Parents: Father: Marion Zettler   **Mother:** Carrie Zettler

Occupation: Father: CEO, Trans-Westland Motor Freight   **Mother:** unemployed

Number of Siblings: None   **Ages:**

Test Data: I.Q.: 115   **Math:** 11.9   **Reading:** 13.9   **Writing:** 13.9
(Achievement test data in grade level)

Extracurricular Activities:
None

Discipline Record
- Referred for unexcused absence
- Referred for unexcused tardiness

Teachers' Comments
- Edwin is a good thinker and an excellent reader; I'd like to encourage him to do something with his abilities in English
- Edwin is a dependable student
- I believe that Edwin needs some direction in his life; he seems unaware of what he should strive for and what he intends to do with his life; counseling is recommended (counselor)

Appendix

II

United
States
Constitution

■

We the People of the United States, in Order to form a more perfect Union, establish Justice, insure domestic Tranquility, provide for the common defence, promote the general Welfare, and secure the Blessings of Liberty to ourselves and our Posterity, do ordain and establish this Constitution for the United States of America.

Article I

Section 1   All legislative Powers herein granted shall be vested in a Congress of the United States, which shall consist of a Senate and House of Representatives.

Section 2   The House of Representatives shall be composed of Members chosen every second Year by the people of the several States, and the Electors in each State shall have the Qualifications requisite for Electors of the most numerous Branch of the State Legislature.

No Person shall be a Representative who shall not have attained to the Age of twenty-five Years, and been seven years a Citizen of the United States, and who shall not, when elected, be an inhabitant of that State in which he shall be chosen.

Representatives and direct Taxes shall be apportioned among the several States which may be included within this Union, according to their respective Numbers. The actual Enumeration shall be made within three Years after the first Meeting of the Congress of the United States, and within every subsequent Term of ten Years, in such Manner as they shall by Law direct. The Number of Representatives shall not exceed one for every thirty Thousand, but each State shall have at Least one Representative.

When Vacancies happen in the Representation from any State, the Executive Authority thereof shall issue Writs of Election to fill such Vacancies.

The House of Representatives shall choose their Speaker and other Officers; and shall have the sole Power of Impeachment.

Section 3   The Senate of the United States shall be composed of two Senators from each State, chosen for six Years; and each Senator shall have one Vote.

No Person shall be a Senator who shall not have attained to the Age of thirty Years, and been nine Years a Citizen of the United States, and who shall not, when elected, be an Inhabitant of that State in which he shall be chosen.

The Vice President of the United States shall be President of the Senate, but shall have no Vote, unless they be equally divided.

The Senate shall choose their other Officers, and also a President pro tempore, in the Absence of the Vice President, or when he shall exercise the Office of the President of the United States.

The Senate shall have the sole Power to try all Impeachments. When sitting for that Purpose, they shall be on Oath or Affirmation. When the President of the United States is tried, the Chief Justice shall preside: And no person shall be convicted without the Concurrence of two thirds of the Members present.

Judgment in Cases of Impeachment shall not extend further than to removal from Office, and disqualification to hold and enjoy any Office of Honor, Trust, or Profit under the United States: but the Party convicted shall nevertheless be liable and subject to Indictment, Trial, Judgment, and Punishment, according to Law.

Section 4   The Times, Places and Manner of holding Elections for Senators and Representatives, shall be prescribed in each State by the Legislature thereof: but the Congress may at any time by Law make or alter such Regulations, except as to the Places of choosing Senators.

The Congress shall assemble at least once in every Year.

Section 5   Each House shall be the Judge of the Elections, Returns, and Qualifications of its own Members, and a Majority of each shall constitute a Quorum to do Business; but a smaller Number may adjourn from day to day, and may be authorized to compel the Attendance of absent Members, in such Manner, and under such Penalties, as each House may provide.

Each House may determine the Rules of its Proceedings, punish its Members for disorderly Behavior, and, with the Concurrence of two thirds, expel a Member.

Each House shall keep a Journal of its Proceedings, and from time to time publish the same, excepting such Parts as may in their Judgment require Secrecy; and the Yeas and Nays of the Members of either House on any question shall, at the Desire of one fifth of those Present, be entered on the Journal.

Neither House, during the Session of Congress, shall, without the Consent of the other, adjourn for more than three days, nor to any other Place than that in which the two Houses shall be sitting.

Section 6   The Senators and Representatives shall receive a Compensation for their Services, to be ascertained by Law, and paid out of the Treasury of the United States. They shall in all Cases, except Treason, Felony, and Breach of the Peace, be privileged from Arrest during their attendance at the Session of their respective Houses, and in going to and returning from the same; and for any Speech or Debate in either House, they shall not be questioned in any other Place.

No Senator or Representative shall, during the Time for which he was elected, be appointed to any civil Office under the Authority of the United States, which shall have been created, or the Emoluments whereof shall have been increased, during such time; and no Person holding any Office under the United States shall be a Member of either House during his continuance in Office.

Section 7   All Bills for raising Revenue shall originate in the House of Representatives; but the Senate may propose or concur with Amendments as on other bills.

Every Bill which shall have passed the House of Representatives and the Senate, shall, before it become a Law, be presented to the President of the United States; If he approve he shall sign it, but if not he shall return it, with his Objections, to that House in which it shall have originated, who shall enter the Objections at large on their Journal, and proceed to reconsider it. If after such Reconsideration two thirds of that House shall agree to pass the bill, it shall be sent, together with the objections, to the other House, by which it shall likewise be reconsidered, and if approved by two thirds of that House, it shall become a Law. But in all such Cases the Votes of both Houses shall be determined by Yeas and Nays, and the Names of the Persons voting for and against the Bill shall be entered on the Journal of each House respectively. If any Bill shall not be returned by the President within ten Days (Sunday excepted) after it shall have been presented to him, the Same shall be a Law, in like Manner as if he had signed it, unless the Congress by their Adjournment prevent its Return, in which Case it shall not be a Law.

Every Order, Resolution, or Vote to which the Concurrence of the Senate and House of Representatives may be necessary (except on a question of Adjournment) shall be presented to the President of the United States; and before the Same shall take Effect, shall be approved by him, or being disapproved by him, shall be repassed by two thirds of the Senate and House of Representatives, according to the Rules and Limitations prescribed in the Case of a Bill.

Section 8   The Congress shall have Power To lay and collect Taxes, Duties, Imposts and Excises, to pay the Debts and provide for the common Defence and general Welfare of the United States; but all Duties, Imposts and Excises shall be uniform throughout the United States;

To borrow Money on the credit of the United States;

To regulate Commerce with foreign Nations, and among the several States, and with the Indian Tribes;

To establish an uniform Rule of Naturalization, and uniform Laws on the subject of Bankruptcies throughout the United States;

To coin Money, regulate the Value thereof, and of foreign Coin, and fix the Standard of Weights and Measures;

To provide for the Punishment of counterfeiting the Securities and current Coin of the United States;

To establish Post Offices and post Roads;

To promote the Progress of Science and useful Arts, by securing for limited Times to Authors and Inventors the exclusive Rights to their respective Writings and Discoveries;

To constitute Tribunals inferior to the Supreme Court;

To define and punish Piracies and Felonies committed on the high Seas, and Offenses against the Law of Nations;

To declare War, grant Letters of Marque and Reprisal, and make Rules concerning Captures on Land and Water;

To raise and support Armies, but no Appropriation of Money to that Use shall be for a longer Term than two Years;

To provide for calling forth the Militia to execute the Laws of the Union, suppress Insurrections and repel Invasions;

To provide for organizing, arming and disciplining, the Militia, and for governing such Part of them as may be employed in the Service of the United States, reserving to the States respectively, the Appointment of the Officer, and the Authority of training the Militia according to the discipline prescribed by Congress.

To exercise exclusive Legislation in all Cases whatsoever, over such District (not exceeding ten miles square) as may, by Cession of particular States, and the Acceptance of Congress, become the Seat of the Government of the United States, and to exercise like Authority over all Places purchased by the Consent of the Legislature of the State in which the Same shall be, for the Erection of Forts, Magazines, Arsenals, dock-yards, and other needful Buildings; And

To make all laws which shall be necessary and proper for carrying into Execution the foregoing Powers, and all other Powers vested by this Constitution in the Government of the United States, or in any Department or Officer thereof.

Section 9 The privilege of the Writ of Habeas Corpus shall not be suspended, unless when in Cases of Rebellion or Invasion the public Safety may require it.

No Bill of Attainder or ex post factor Law shall be passed.

No Capitation, or other direct, Tax shall be laid, unless in Proportion to the Census or Enumeration herein before directed to be taken.

No Tax or Duty shall be laid on Articles exported from any state.

No Preference shall be given by any Regulation of Commerce or Revenue to the Ports of one State over those of another: nor shall Vessels bound to, or from one State, be obliged to enter, clear, or pay Duties in another.

No Money shall be drawn from the Treasury, but in Consequence of Appropriations made by Law; and a regular Statement and Account of the Receipts and Expenditures of all public Money shall be published from time to time.

No Title of Nobility shall be granted by the United States: and no Person holding any Office of Profit or Trust under them, shall, without the Consent of the Congress, accept of any present, Emolument, Office, or Title, or any kind whatever, from any King, Prince, or foreign State.

Section 10 No state shall enter into any Treaty, Alliance, or Confederation; grant Letters of Marque and Reprisal; coin Money; emit Bills of Credit; make any Thing but gold and silver Coin a Tender in Payment of Debts; pass any Bill of Attainder, ex post facto Law, or law impairing the Obligation of Contracts, or grant any Title of Nobility.

No State shall, without the Consent of the Congress, lay any Imposts or Duties on Imports or Exports, except what may be absolutely necessary for executing its inspection Laws: and the net Produce of all Duties and Imposts, laid by any Senate on Imports or Exports, shall be for the Use of the Treasury of the United States; and all such Laws shall be subject to the Revision and Control of the Congress.

No State shall, without the Consent of Congress, lay any Duty of Tonnage, keep Troops, or Ships of War in time of Peace, enter into any Agreement of Compact with another State, or with a foreign Power, or engage in War, unless actually invaded, or in such imminent Danger as will not admit of delay.

Article II

Section 1

The executive Power shall be vested in a President of the United States of America. He shall hold his Office during the Term of four years, and, together with the Vice President, chosen for the same Term, be elected as follows.

Each State shall appoint, in such Manner as the Legislature thereof may direct, a Number of Electors, equal to the whole Number of Senators and Representatives to which the State may be entitled in the Congress: but no Senator or Representative, or Person holding an Office of Trust or Profit under the United States, shall be appointed an Elector.

The Congress may determine the Time of Choosing, the Electors, and the Day on which they shall give their Votes; which Day shall be the same throughout the United States.

No person except a natural born Citizen shall be eligible to the Office of President; neither shall any Person be eligible to that office who shall not have attained to the Age of thirty-five Years, and been fourteen Years a Resident within the United States.

In Case of the Removal of the President from Office, or of his Death, Resignation, or Inability to discharge the Powers and Duties of the said Office, the Same shall devolve on the Vice President, and the Congress may by Law provide for the Case of Removal, Death, Resignation or Inability; both of the President and Vice President, declaring what Officer shall then act as President, and such Officer shall act accordingly, until the Disability be removed, or a President shall be elected.

The President shall, at stated Times, receive for his Services, a Compensation, which shall neither be increased nor diminished during the Period for which he shall have been elected, and he shall not receive within that Period any other Emolument from the United States, or any of them.

Before he enter on the Execution of his Office, he shall take the following Oath or Affirmation:

"I do solemnly swear (or affirm) that I will faithfully execute the Office of President of the United States, and will to the best of my Ability, preserve, protect and defend the Constitution of the United States."

Section 2

The President shall be Commander in Chief of the Army and Navy of the United States, and of the Militia of the several States when called into the actual Service of the United States; he may require the Opinion, in writing, of the principal Office in each of the executive Departments, upon any Subject relating to the Duties of their respective offices, and he shall have Power to grant Reprieves and Pardons for Offenses against the United States, except in Cases of Impeachment.

He shall have Power, by and with the Advice and Consent of the Senate, to make Treaties, provided two thirds of the Senators present concur; and he shall nominate, and by and with the Advice and Consent of the Senate, shall appoint Ambassadors, other public Ministers and Consuls, Judges of the supreme Court, and all other Officers of the United States, whose Appointments are not herein otherwise provided for, and which shall be established by Law: but the Congress may by Law vest the Appointment of such inferior Officers, as they think proper, in the President alone, in the Courts of Law, or in the Heads of Departments.

The President shall have Power to fill up all Vacancies that may happen during the Recess of the Senate, by granting Commissions which shall expire at the End of their next Session.

Section 3 He shall from time to time give to the Congress Information of the State of the Union, and recommend to their Consideration such Measures as he shall judge necessary and expedient; he may, on extraordinary Occasions, convene both Houses, or either of them, and in Case of Disagreement between them, with Respect to the Time of Adjournment, he may adjourn them to such Time as he shall think proper; he shall receive Ambassadors and other public Ministers; he shall take Care that the Laws be faithfully executed, and shall Commission all the Officers of the United States.

Section 4 The President, Vice President and all civil Officers of the United States, shall be removed from Office on Impeachment for, and Conviction of, Treason, Bribery, or other high Crimes and Misdemeanors.

Article III

Section 1 The judicial Power of the United States, shall be vested in one supreme Court, and in such inferior Courts as the Congress may from time to time ordain and establish. The Judges, both of the supreme and inferior Courts, shall hold their Offices during good Behavior, and shall, at stated Times, receive for their Services, a Compensation, which shall not be diminished during their Continuance in Office.

Section 2 The judicial Power shall extend to all Cases, in Law and Equity, arising under this Constitution, the Laws of the United States, and Treaties made, or which shall be made, under their Authority;-to all Cases affecting Ambassadors, other public Ministers and Consuls;-to all Cases of admiralty and maritime Jurisdiction;-to Controversies to which the United States shall be a Party;-to Controversies between two or more States;-between Citizens of different states;-between Citizens of the same State claiming Lands under Grants of different States.

In all Cases affecting Ambassadors, other public Ministers and Consuls, and those in which a State shall be Party, the supreme Court shall have original Jurisdiction. In all the other Cases before mentioned, the supreme Court shall have appellate Jurisdiction, both as to Law and fact, with such Exceptions, and under such Regulations as the Congress shall make.

The trial of all Crimes, except in Cases of Impeachment, shall be by Jury and such Trial shall be held in the State where the said Crimes shall have been committed; but when not committed within any State, the Trial shall be at such Place or Places as the Congress may by Law have directed.

Section 3 Treason against the United States, shall consist only in levying War against them, or in adhering to their Enemies, giving them Aid and Comfort. No Person shall be convicted of Treason unless on the Testimony of two Witnesses to the same overt Act, or on Confession in open court.

The Congress shall have Power to declare the Punishment of Treason, but no Attainder of Treason shall work Corruption of Blood, or Forfeiture except during the Life of the Person attainted.

Article IV

Section 1 Full Faith and Credit shall be given in each State to the public Acts, Records, and judicial Proceedings of every other State. And the Congress may by general Laws prescribe the Manner in which such Acts, Records and Proceedings shall be proved, and the Effect thereof.

Section 2 The Citizens of each State shall be entitled to all Privileges and Immunities of Citizens in the several States.

A Person charged in any State with Treason, Felony, or other Crimes, who shall flee from Justice, and be found in another State, shall on Demand of the Executive Authority of the State from which he fled, be delivered up, to be removed to the State having Jurisdiction of the Crime.

Section 3 New States may be admitted by the Congress into this Union; but no new State shall be formed or erected within the Jurisdiction of any other State; nor any State be formed by the Union of two or more States, or Parts of States, without the Consent of the Legislatures of the States concerned as well as of the Congress.

The Congress shall have the Power to dispose of and make all needful Rules and Regulations respecting the Territory or other Property belonging to the United States; and nothing in this Constitution shall be so construed as to Prejudice any Claims of the United States, or any particular state.

Section 4 The United States shall guarantee to every State in this Union a Republican Form of Government, and shall protect each of them against Invasion, and on Application of the Legislature, or of the Executive (when the Legislature cannot be convened) against domestic Violence.

Article V

The Congress, whenever two thirds of both houses shall deem it necessary, shall propose Amendments to this Constitution, or, on the Application of the Legislatures of two thirds of the several States, shall call a Convention for proposing Amendments, which, in either Case, shall be valid to all Intents and Purposes, as Part of this Constitution, when ratified by the Legislatures of three fourths of the several States, or by Conventions in three fourths thereof, as the one or the other Mode of Ratification may be proposed by the Congress; Provided that no State, without its Consent, shall be deprived of its equal Suffrage in the Senate.

Article VI

All Debts contracted and Engagements entered into, before the Adoption of this Constitution, shall be as valid against the United States under this Constitution, as under the Confederation.

This Constitution and the Laws of the United States which shall be made in Pursuance thereof; and all Treaties made, or which shall be made, under the Authority of the United States, shall be the supreme Law of the Land; and the Judges in every State shall be bound thereby, any Thing in the Constitution or Laws of any State to the Contrary notwithstanding.

The Senators and Representatives before mentioned, and the Members of the several State Legislatures, and all executive and judicial Officers both of the United States and of the several States, shall be bound by Oath or Affirmation, to support this Constitution; but no religious Test shall ever be required as a Qualification to any Office or public trust under the United States.

Article VII

The Ratification of the Conventions of nine States, shall be sufficient for the Establishment of this Constitution between the States so ratifying the Same.

DONE in Convention by the Unanimous Consent of the States present, the Seventeenth Day of September in the Year of our Lord one thousand seven hundred and eighty seven and of the Independence of the United States of America the Twelfth. IN WITNESS whereof we have hereunto subscribed our names.

Character Index

Note to the reader: This index is provided to assist your efforts at exploring the various "players" in the Edge City Schools. The references we have given are those that we feel will provide further insight into each character's persona.

Students

Teachers and Administrators